Kill Me Once...
Kill Me Twice

Murder on the Queen's Playground

Carol Shuman

authorHOUSE®

AuthorHouse™
1663 Liberty Drive
Bloomington, IN 47403
www.authorhouse.com
Phone: 1-800-839-8640

© 2010 Carol Shuman Ph.D., LLC. All rights reserved

No part of this book may be reproduced, stored in a retrieval system, or transmitted by any means without the written permission of the author.

First published by AuthorHouse   12/28/2010

ISBN: 978-1-4520-3596-3 (sc)
ISBN: 978-1-4520-3598-7 (e)
ISBN: 978-1-4520-3597-0 (hc)

Library of Congress Control Number: 2010909004

Printed in the United States of America

This book is printed on acid-free paper.

Book Designer Adalee Cooney
Cover by Kathleen McClain
Production coordinated by Jennifer Slaybaugh

CONTENTS

PART ONE: Beneath the Casuarinas
Chapter One: Detour to Murder 3
Chapter Two: Lures of Paradise 7
Chapter Three: View from the Top 23
Chapter Four: Nothing Like This 29
Chapter Five: 'That Child Won't Sleep' 35

PART TWO: Masquerade
Chapter Six: Glamour and Politics 47
Chapter Seven: The 'Isle of Unsolved Murder' 53

PART THREE: The Queen -v- Kirk Orlando Mundy
Chapter Eight: 'Safe…' 67
Chapter Nine: Another Nail on Becky's Coffin 75

PART FOUR: The 'Most Curious' of Events
Chapter Ten: Bad News, Worse News 83
Chapter Eleven: 'Operation Cleansweep' 89

PART FIVE: The Queen -v- Justis Raham Smith
Chapter Twelve: The Trial of Justis Smith 103
Chapter Thirteen: Recorder to the Rescue 111
Chapter Fourteen: Facts, Law and Ad Hominems 121
Chapter Fifteen: 'A Gigantic You-Know-What' 135
Chapter Sixteen: Repercussions 145

PART SIX: A Not so Independent Inquiry

Chapter Seventeen: Past Chances upon Present..................159
Chapter Eighteen: Sex, Lies and a Tape Recorder..................165
Chapter Nineteen: Changes in Tune..................171
Chapter Twenty: 'The Only Evidence'..................177
Chapter Twenty One: Clashing Recollections..................185
Chapter Twenty Two: Human Wrongs..................201

PART SEVEN: Truths, Consequences, or Neither of These?

Chapter Twenty Three: Mundy's Tale..................213
Chapter Twenty Four: A Shocking Allegation..................225
Chapter Twenty Five: Retribution..................229
Chapter Twenty Six: Another Attack...Another Deal?..................235
Chapter Twenty Seven: A Wake Up Call?..................239
Chapter Twenty Eight: Sinister Seas..................245
Chapter Twenty Nine: 'Like Nailing Jelly to a Tree'..................261
Chapter Thirty: Strong Support, Silent Support..................269

Epilogue   277
Addendum   296
Appendix A   298
Appendix B   303

For Becky

"Without this testimony, my life as a writer—or my life, period—would not have become what it is: that of a witness who believes he has a moral obligation to try to prevent the enemy from enjoying one last victory by allowing his crimes to be erased from human memory…To forget would be not only dangerous but offensive; to forget the dead would be akin to killing them a second time."

Night by Elie Wiesel
(1958) New York: Hill & Wang

Some cry 'lat's study history to see how our fold ver treated,

"But forgat dat history's verth is makin' sure it's not repeated,

And black treats white as vhite treats black, keeps spinnin' like a top.

Oh Gawd I vish dis Ig'rance vud stop!

                    The Uniquely Bermudian Poetry of Jeremy Frith

                                (1996) Inna Myce Publishing

Acknowledgements

INFORMATION IN THE BOOK comes from more than one hundred and eighty people who were directly involved in the events, including U.S. forensic scientists, U.K. officials, Bermuda cabinet members (the existing Bermuda and U.K. governments and previous), Bermuda police, both current and former members of the attorney general's offices, Britain's Foreign and Commonwealth Office (FCO), the Canadian government, and Rebecca Middleton's family and friends. Many of the direct quotations of dialogue, dates, times, and other details come from documents, official and unofficial records, tapes, transcripts, and personal notes. Where statements are attributed, I have obtained these from the person directly or from written records. Researching and interviewing, while Rebecca's case continued on, took more than six years.

I would like to thank, foremost, human rights lawyer Cherie Booth, QC, of Matrix Chambers, who listened to Becky's story and stood up for her when others failed. Also, U.S. forensic scientists Drs. Michael Baden and Henry Lee, both of whose expertise made clear the horror of Becky's death and both of whom continued to advocate for justice.

My greatest respect for victims' advocate LeYoni Junos, who courageously shared with me her valuable research, not to be taken lightly in Bermuda, with no freedom of information in place. Also, particularly, to former Police Commissioner Colin Coxall, who continues to stand with the Middletons. Former Senior Crown Counsel Brian Calhoun, former Solicitor General William Pearce, former Government Analyst Kevin Leask, former head of Serious Crimes Howard Cutts, the late Richard Hector, and retired Bermuda police investigator William A. Black, all of whom helped in efforts for justice.

I would like to express my appreciation to author T.C. Sobey, whose own books *Bermuda Shorts* and *Courting Disaster* exposed sometimes amusing truths about both Bermuda and the court of Queen Elizabeth II, and who helped me separate the forest from those trees of evidence. Also, to author

Beverly Swerling and literary agent Doris Booth, whose editorial contributions were integral to this work.

To representatives of Bermuda government who, despite having no obligation to do so on an island where transparency is not the law, I express my thanks for, while still in office, opening records and holding frank discussions with me, Becky's dad, Dave Middleton, and Becky's caregiver when she was murdered, Rick Meens. These include former Bermuda Attorney Generals Larry Mussendon and Philip Perinchief, former Director of Public Prosecutions (DPP) Vinette Graham-Allen, former DPP consultant Kulandra Ratneser, and former Police Commissioner Jonathan Smith. Also, to representatives of Britain's government, particularly FCO Desk Officer Hugo Frost, who advised me of territorial obligations and FCO human rights responsibilities.

My deep regard for *Bermuda Sun* editor Tony McWilliam, the first to recognize that Becky's story was by no means ended when I began my research in 2003. Also former reporters Nigel Regan and Coggie Gibbons; *Royal Gazette* editor William (Bill) Zuill, publisher Keith Jensen, research director Deborah Charles, photograph editor David Skinner, chief reporter Matthew Taylor, reporters Liz Roberts and Sam Strangeways, and former reporter Raymond Hainey, all of whom helped me to tell Becky's true story and provided photographs of the major events that followed Becky's murder.

Deserving particular recognition is Bermudian Dennis Bean, a victim of Bermuda's racial and social injustices, but whose experiences did not blind him, as it did many in Bermuda, to the connection between the handling of the murder of Rebecca Middleton and those events of the 1970s. His story has not been told publicly before now.

My writing associates Linda Kasten and Scott Gray, whose readings and suggestions were essential, along with Rich Van Lue, Peter Perdue, Timothy Reeves, Gregory Eckart, Jennifer Slaybaugh, Jessie Klingler, and designer Kathleen McClain of Authorhouse.

My family's support, including from my son, Denny Atkin, who read and reread, offering creative suggestions over many years since the project began. My dad, Donald Thorburn, who taught me that when the little boys chase you down the street, you can chase them back (carefully). My mom, Eileen Mary Thorburn, who didn't live to see this project reach fruition, but who left me with her sensitivity, so that I would be committed to telling Becky's story. And my husband, Gary, always.

The kindness of Bermudians Walter and Mary Middleton Cook, Marsha Jones, John Gardner, and Dr. Ian Campbell are representative of the best of Bermuda, along with the many others who supported Becky's cause throughout and memorialized Becky in Bermuda; Dave Middleton and Rick Meens, who led the search for truth; Jasmine Meens, who told her story with strength; Becky's mom, Cindy, who continues to speak out for her daughter; and Becky's brothers, Matt and his wife Leanna, and Mark and his wife Patti, who put aside their pain to tell about Becky's life and her tragedy.

Moreover, along with Ms. Booth, appreciation is extended to Allison McDonald and Amanda Illing of Matrix Chambers in London, and John Riihiluoma, Kelvin Hastings-Smith, Jackie Astride-Stirling, and Leanne Jent of Appleby Global, Bermuda, who spoke loudly and clearly for Becky.

This book is dedicated to Becky, but it is written for Emma Margaret Rebecca, Mary Cynthia, and Samantha Jane so that they will remember their Aunt Rebecca with love and knowledge—and with courage, as did her family and friends, to stand up for truth.

Prologue

December 1, 1977

ON THAT EXQUISITE autumn morning sunshine warmed the sapphire sea surrounding the twenty-square mile volcanic mass in the Atlantic Ocean that stands alone and, as some say, "different."

But as night approached, rain clouds escorted a tuxedo-clad hangman, brought for this occasion all the way from England, making his approach by boat to foreboding Casemates Prison, its bleak rocks protruding from the banks of Ireland Island, one of those in the chain comprising the place we know as Bermuda.

The governor's announcement a week before that two black men would hang that night for the political murders four years earlier of five white men had detonated island-wide violence. No doubt, land travel across narrow roads leading to the tiny barbed wire-barricaded bridge guarding the lodging of Bermuda's villains would be far too dangerous. Hence the approach by sea.

Agitated crowds swarmed over Hamilton, while attorney Lois Browne Evans, the first black female to have the audacity to lawyer on the tiny island controlled by rich white men, made her final desperate appeal inside Supreme Court, carrying a petition pleading that the men be spared the gallows. Outside, mobs stoned the courthouse, breaking windows, causing frightened judges to hurry their refusal and rush from the courthouse to safety. About 10 p.m., Browne Evans' dynamic young black colleague Julian Hall emerged from the building and gave the crowd the thumbs down signal. All hell broke loose. Baton wielding police fought rioters. Buildings set ablaze, the sting of pepper spray everywhere, and an all-night prayer vigil at the African Methodist Episcopal Church on violence-charged Court Street.

Distraught, Browne-Evans told gatherers she would go to Casemates and be with the men as they died. Four hours after midnight, despite anguished pleas for mercy, in hastily-constructed gallows, the two men swung to their deaths. That night would mark Browne Evans' darkest hour.

On the opposite end of the twenty-square-mile island, another young black woman, sixteen-year-old LeYoni Junos, shuddered as the skies turned into a crimson inferno. She and her Salvation Army family huddled in their house while rioters demolished vehicles, smashed windows and set fires, tossing homemade bombs at police firing tear gas into the crowds. Sirens screamed as fire trucks rushed to one blaze after another. At the majestic Southampton Princess Hotel, where some thought the hangman stayed, arsonists killed two tourists and an employee.

The next morning, Junos crept behind a wooded area next to her house to a nearby grocery store, now burned to ashes. She stroked the charred remains of a guard dog, its bones still chained to the ground. Carefully, she moved its brittle skeleton to a spot between two casuarinas, their magnificence protecting her tiny consecration. She wondered how humans could care so little for those who are helpless, no matter what their kind.

That night of violence, its deep-rooted repercussions long whispering beneath the cold limestone floor of this tiny speck in the sea, contoured the moral fibers of both women: Lois the lawyer and LeYoni the advocate, born a generation apart.

It would take the murder twenty years later of Rebecca Middleton, a young white Canadian tourist, for their paths to collide on this island, once considered "the Queen's Jewel in the Atlantic," where murder often happens in black and white.

PART ONE
BENEATH THE CASUARINAS

ONE

Blood once more soaks the soul of balmy Bermuda—the isle of unsolved murder. For the close-knit island community clams up when outsiders...call."

The Sun (London)--March 12, 1973

Detour to Murder
July 3, 1996

DANA RAWLINS CHECKED his watch. Three thirty a.m., a time when very little good happens in Bermuda to those who aren't safely nestled in their beds. Clouds that a few hours earlier dropped dense rain over the island had drifted away, leaving a murky, sinister haze.

Rawlins wanted to get home, but a new guy needed a ride to a tent he'd pitched earlier in the day at Ferry Reach Park. It was well out of Rawlins' way, but he felt sorry for Coy Fox, who was homeless and working odd jobs, typical of more than a few on this wealth-saturated island.

Fox had managed permission to stay a few nights at the Bermuda Regiment barracks, but he had outlived his stay and set up housekeeping at Ferry Reach. This isolated park at the end of Ferry Road clings to Bermuda's airport waterway on one side and lapping ocean waves of Whale Bone Bay on the other. Down to his last few dollars, Fox had returned a rental bike earlier that day, and so needed the ride. Rawlins' friend Angela took the front seat, and Coy Fox piled into the back seat with two others, Sharon and Antonio.

Rawlins' veered his car with its four passengers off the main road and climbed a steep hill along the narrow roadway originally designed for horse and carriage traffic. There were no other cars in sight.

The few twinkling lights from tiny pastel houses would have disappeared by then. Rawlins remembered noticing two enormous hounds, barking and dancing on their leashes, not far from limestone walls that tighten into callous chambers, frightening reminders of the great eruptions that gave birth to the island millenniums ago. That night the rocks' musty odor added to gloom that would seem to welcome the devil, daring all others to pass.

Nonetheless, the five young people in the car were laughing and listening to music as they bumped along.

Suddenly Angela shrieked.

"What the fuck," Coy Fox yelled.

Had a dog had run in front of the car? Or maybe a motorbike accident, a frequent deadly event late at night on Bermuda's isolated roads. Or possibly what some call a "Saturday Night Special," alleged baseball bat slams to the back of a bike rider's neck by another passing rider during gang warfare.

Dana Rawlins slammed on the brakes.

It's not hard to imagine what the four saw. Branches of the casuarinas hanging down, like tentacles of ghostly creatures. Tree frogs would have been screaming like banshees. A scene that can be found in many such locations in Bermuda.

This time there was an added element. A body lay across the road.

"It's a woman," Angela shouted.

All four got out of the car and went to look. They saw an almost naked young woman covered in so much blood that it had pooled on the road beneath her. Her blonde hair streamed across the yellow line. Her neck was covered in slashes. The headlights of Rawlins' car shone on a grass verge directly under the two casuarinas, the location of two more pools of scarlet blood. A ripped skirt, panties, and sandals lay nearby. The girl's blood-soaked bra and shirt still clutched to one of her shoulders. Rawlins knelt next to her, watching her diaphragm move as she struggled for air and to speak, able to produce only wheezing, no words, silent tears.

Rawlins found a strong pulse; she turned her head toward him. "Can you hear me?" he asked.

She blinked. Tears ran down her cheeks. Rawlins took her pulse again. It was now faint.

Coy Fox was too frightened to go near. Someone suggested that one of them stay while the three others went to the nearby park phone booth. But they were worried that an attacker might be lurking, and they left the young woman alone. When the four returned about ten minutes later the dying girl hadn't moved. Rawlins listened for a heartbeat and heard nothing. He checked her pulse again and found it, barely palpable.

"She didn't try to talk anymore," Angela later told police. "Dana held her hand. We were all trying to talk to her to keep her going. Her eyes were dilating, I could see her drifting."

Rawlins kneeled down and kept talking. "Hang on, hang on, you'll make it."

Sharon got a light blue towel from Rawlins' car and covered her nearly naked body.

"We wanted so badly to try and save her life," Coy Fox recalled.

A man on a motorcycle rode up. Sharon asked the stranger to go back and summon police. Before the man left, he gave them a rolled cigarette.

When the first police officer arrived, Angela was screaming, Coy Fox was throwing up.

Rebecca Middleton was dead.

TWO

"...The most damaging foreign import is the peaceable tourist... Governments are only now beginning to realize that tourism is a double-edged weapon. It may revive a stagnant economy, but at the cost of growing political agitation and, perhaps in the long run, revolution."

Birmingham Post—March 13, 1973

Lures of Paradise

June 20, 1996

A TOMBOY WHO LIVED in a world of "cool," sixteen-year-old Rebecca Middleton normally cast aside dresses in favor of pants and sweatshirts. But for this special day, golden-haired Becky wore the new sundress that her mom made her by hand, along with her straw hat with a sunflower, her favorite. She and Jasmine Meens, who Becky fondly called "Jazzy," both beauties, were heading to Bermuda for their vacation of a lifetime.

Becky and Jasmine's quiet home town, Belleville, Ontario, lies a little more than an hour driving time east of bustling Toronto with its five million people, never claiming the grandeur of Britain's wealthiest territory, Bermuda. Nonetheless, the close knit community, with its some 37,000 residents at the time, welcomed tourists to its yacht harbor on the peaceful Bay of Quinte, boasting fishing, boating, and "world famous cheddar." The Middletons had never known of a murder in Belleville—ever.

There Dave and Cindy Middleton, who named their children after Biblical characters, Matthew, Mark and Rebecca, lived quietly in a neighborhood filled with children, laughter, and strict standards. Her two older brothers watched over Becky, roughhoused, and played sports with her. With her dad coaching, her team won the local soft ball league division. Becky's strength and coordination belied her five foot three-inch stature.

Like her mom, Cindy, whose liveliness fills a room, Rebecca Jane was a beauty since birth. Her blonde hair, highlighted by the summer sun, matched blue eyes as sparkling as Bermuda's waters. For Cindy, the angels had gotten together…. "sprinkled gold dust…and starlight," a vision of the Carpenters' song.

When four-year-old Matt first saw pink blankets wrapped around his new sibling, he gasped—he'd requested a brother. But his dad told him that God had looked down and knew who they needed--Becky. Dave took photos of Matt and his year-and-a-half old brother Mark holding their thriving eight-pound baby sister, born in 1979--the International Year of the Child.

Matt, like most first-born children, Becky's dad recalled, "is the most serious of the three. Mark is athletic and good-humored. Becky was the cheerleader for all of us."

Dave and Cindy Middleton had divorced three years before Becky and Jasmine set out for Bermuda, a loss that Dave found difficult to accept. Losing Cindy, he said, was like "losing a limb."

Dave's world focused on his kids and his job as water plant superintendent in Belleville, never believing life could get worse.

All three children, then in their teens, romped between Dave's house overlooking the bay and Cindy's not far away, where she lived with Wayne and worked for the Canadian government. Becky cherished her older brothers, and welcomed Wayne's children, her new step-siblings, John and Debbie. All of the kids, for the most part, accepted family changes, continuing to bring their friends to their parents' houses.

Becky was right at home in the tranquil Thousand Islands of the St. Lawrence, bringing friends to camp and dinghy through the islands, taking sailing lessons with her cousin Michelle. She loved swimming and fishing, and she and Mark slept on the dock down by the water on nice summer evenings at the Bay of Quinte Yacht Club.

She took to the piano quickly, carrying home a first place trophy from the Belleville Rotary Festival, thrilled that this was her first time playing a baby grand.

At twelve, Becky inherited from Mark her first job delivering newspapers. Like her brothers, she worked after school to save money for college. By fourteen, Becky was pumping gas and washing windows at a Belleville service station, her smile a welcome sight for locals who adored her enthusiasm, energy, and high spirits.

Becky treasured Mark's high school girlfriend Patti. Cindy recalled Becky hearing a girl on the school bus saying that she was going to date Mark. "Becky told the girl 'No way!'" Becky, though, wouldn't attend Mark and Patti's wedding a few years later.

Becky loved her overnight sleeps when she and her girlfriends giggled all night. She and her friend Meghan Clarke spent countless hours sitting on Becky's waterbed, writing notes to each other in silence. The two thought this was hilarious, saying things they believed they couldn't say out loud. Meghan still has those notes.

Some years later, Becky's mother wept when she found Becky and Meghan's names etched in the drawer of Becky's chest.

For Cindy, it was "like a gift."

A year before Becky and her long-time friend Jasmine Meens set out for Bermuda, Becky had hoped to travel with her friend on her exclusive vacation, out of reach to most Belleville kids, who didn't have a friend with a dad living on the high-priced island where tourism marketers employed by the island government had long made it no secret they preferred wealthy visitors.

Things didn't work out that year, but the next summer, Becky and Jazzy tried again. The girls knew Becky's parents weren't certain they wanted Becky to go, a reluctance shared by Becky's stepfather, Wayne.

Dave Middleton had known Jasmine's dad Rick Meens and his brothers from their teenage days when both played Belleville sports. Divorced from Jasmine's mother, Rick Meens had moved to Bermuda in the late 1980s and remarried. Rick and his Bermudian wife Lynne had a new baby, Micah. Lynne's son, Reese, joined Rick's children, Jasmine and Jordan, on long stays with Rick and Lynne. For Jasmine and the small town girls she brought with her, the visits reached splendor beyond their imaginations.

Cindy and Wayne, on the other hand, had never met Rick Meens, but they knew Jasmine and her mom, Cheryl. Since the girls were seven years old, Jasmine had been one of Becky's favorite schoolmates. Becky's mom and Jasmine's dad spoke at length about the girls' travel. Eventually, Rebecca Middleton's parents gave their okay for Becky to accompany Jasmine on a Bermuda vacation.

When they did, Becky raced to her dad's to get her birthday present, spending money for her trip. Her family also agreed that since she had been living with Cindy and Wayne for some time, Becky would live with Dave when she returned from Bermuda. This kind of accommodation had long marked Becky's reaction to her parents' divorce.

Becky's eighth grade graduation

Her favorite hat and dress

Watching out for each other

Two nights before their trip, Becky and Jasmine took Woody, a Schnauzer devoted to Becky, for a walk in the park. They chattered about beaches, souvenir shops, and how they'd meet new friends in Bermuda.

They woke up to a beautiful morning the day their adventure would begin. "The sun was shining in the window, and we had smiles on our faces as Becky's mom tickled our feet," Jasmine remembered. They headed to stay overnight with family friends in Whitby, a small town not far from the Toronto airport, so they could be there before dawn the next day.

When they arrived at the airport, Becky jogged up and down corridors. The girls dashed into a photo booth and made comical faces for the camera.

In all the excitement, Jasmine misplaced her purse. They found it without much fuss, and Cindy and Becky told Jasmine not to worry. "Just don't lose anything else," Cindy said.

"I'll miss you, baby." Cindy hugged Becky.

"I'll miss all of you, too. Whenever I look at the moon I'll think of you."

Becky seemed uncharacteristically serious.

Becky scribbled to her dad on an Air Canada postcard as their jet prepared for takeoff. "We're having a great time already. Talk to ya later, alligator."

Airport fun

As they flew over the Atlantic, a fellow passenger took pictures of them with Becky's new camera, an early birthday gift for this special trip. The pilot circled the isolated island in the glistening ocean on a windless, radiant day. Poinciana trees blossomed, and the tiny speck in the sea glowed scarlet. Houses covered small hills like baskets of pastel candy. The sparkling teal water exposed darker reefs, secret graveyards for many shipwrecks and downed planes.

"We're in the Bermuda Triangle." Becky giggled and made scary faces at Jasmine, the more serious of the two.

"We talked about how warm the water was going to feel when we swam," Jasmine remembered.

Jasmine's dad, Rick Meens, met them at the airport and took them on their first tour. "What a difference from Belleville," Jasmine recalled. "The streets were half the size of our Canadian roads, and all around were men cleaning to make it look beautiful. They don't need to try, it is."

Meens showed Jasmine and Becky the island's capital, Hamilton--the waterfront tourist area, with its hotels, yacht club, shops, and billion dollar offshore investment industries. Then the old British section, passing Bermuda's House of Assembly, modeled on the British House of Commons. Afterward visiting a magnificent cathedral, just one of the many Bermuda churches filled to the brim on Sunday mornings.

Past enormous hotels, encircled by lush golf courses and teal seas, Jasmine and Becky shared brochures that Cindy had given them. "Along with the beautiful things, Dad showed us where we never were to go, especially Court Street and 'the back of town,'" Jasmine remembered. This area, where drugs are no secret, was off limits. The girls promised they wouldn't go there, and they didn't.

Moreover, Rick Meens warned them not to rent motor bikes, unsafe on the tiny, winding island roads, and the cause of more than a few tourist deaths. They could take buses, or Jasmine's father would drive them.

At the waterside, they laughed as crabs scurried across the road. That first night they sat on a St. George dock and watched people catch minnows and fish.

Early on Wednesday morning, not long after their arrival, Becky and Jasmine returned to quaint St. George, wandering the twisting alleyways and back streets with names such as Old Maid's Lane, Shinbone, One Gun, and Featherbed alleys.

The girls romped between the whipping post and dunking stool that once kept gossips and scoundrels in their place. Becky popped her head into one of the stockades, while another tourist photographed her grinning at Jasmine.

Becky's family would later find disconcerting the photos of Becky pretending to be locked in place.

On Becky's seventeenth birthday, June twenty seventh, the Meens family surprised her with a cake and gifts. That night, Becky wrote to Cindy and Wayne, "On our way home (from Hamilton) a couple of days ago, I tried to look for the moon, but I couldn't find it. This time on our way home, I found the moon and thought about you guys."

To her dad, Dave, Becky wrote, "The sand here isn't as dark as it is in Canada…and the water is very beautiful." Both she and Jazzy had sunburns, but they went to Hamilton anyway.

Becky wouldn't have the opportunity to mail either letter.

Meanwhile, Cindy had sent a postcard to Becky, joking about the purse incident in the airport, adding a postscript: "Jasmine, don't lose Becky."

The message would reach its destination on a dark day.

Russell McCann and his friend, Ben Turtle, arrived in Bermuda from Britain on Monday the twenty fourth of June, four days after Becky and Jasmine did. Russell and Ben had been in school in Belfast with Jonathan Cassidy, son of a police constable in Bermuda's "Old Town" of St. George. Cassidy's father was among a few remaining white officers from the U.K., a hiring practice now avoided whenever possible. Bermuda now recruits mostly from its neighbors in the Caribbean.

On June twenty fifth, two days before Becky's birthday, the three school friends partied at the White Horse Tavern, a small restaurant and club that attracted mostly tourists in the town square of St. George, a few blocks from Cassidy's house.

Russell McCann went home early, spotting Jasmine and Becky, waiting at a bus stop next to Jonathan Cassidy's house. McCann introduced himself, and the three chatted until the bus came.

The following night, at club in Hamilton, Russell again spotted Jasmine and Becky. Jasmine gave Russell her dad's phone number.

Russell McCann invited Jasmine and Becky to join him, Ben Turtle, and Jonathan Cassidy the following Tuesday night in St. George to celebrate his birthday. They'd take a boat cruise from St. George to tiny Hawkins Island for a buffet and dancing. But an unexpected summer rain halted the boat ride. Instead, they agreed to meet at the White Horse Tavern.

Kill Me Once...

Picture perfect it would seem

Carol Shuman

Fun in St. George

Becky and Jonathan Cassidy

Jasmine and Russell McCann

"We were in such a hurry that Becky didn't even have time to put on her makeup. She looked wonderful anyway," Jasmine recalled.

Rick and Lynne Meens drove them to St. George about seven p.m. Lynne reminded them not to telephone Rick late because he had to get up early for work the next morning.

"When we got there, it really started to rain, so we went into the stores," Jasmine said. "We looked at souvenirs and silly little toys. Becky liked kid things, I loved that about her. When the storm got worse, we headed to meet our friends at the White Horse."

The five met about 7:30 p.m., listened to music, talked, and, despite the girls' ages, drank beer and mixed drinks. Someone threw in a challenge--who could drink beer quickest? "Becky lost by one sip, so she had to buy a round of gold sluggers" (Jasmine's term for Goldschläger, an Swiss liqueur). Jonathan Cassidy later estimated they had about "six to seven" drinks each.

They took photos with Becky's new camera, showing the clothes the girls wore, the light gold chain Jasmine had given Becky, and Becky's tiny ring with three hearts, a gift from her maternal grandparents, Peter and Margaret Lewis. The hearts were meant to represent her grandparents and Becky together.

Jasmine wore a white top, long baggy jeans and sleeveless denim top. She stood about five feet, eight inches and had long blonde hair. Becky wore a soft white, thin-strapped tank top, with a crisp white blouse over it, her panties and bra, a blue denim skirt, and brown sandals.

"She had medium length blonde hair," Jonathan Cassidy would later tell Bermuda police. He described Becky as "...very pretty." At the White Horse, Becky and Jonathan hugged for the camera, recording the jewelry and the tank top beneath her white blouse.

A young tourist couple offered to drop the girls on their way back to Hamilton. Becky and Jasmine declined. It was too early, they were having fun. Plus, Jasmine and Russell were hooked up, as were Becky and Jonathan.

When the White Horse closed, they ran together to Cassidy's house nearby. "It felt good running, like we were birds caged and then set free to experience the world again," Jasmine recalled.

Ben fell asleep in the living room. Jasmine and Russell went into one bedroom, Jonathan and Becky into another. "Russell was a really nice guy.

He told me about what he did, working and studying, and he played rugby. I wanted to get to know him a little better. We ended up kissing."

"While we were in the bedroom we talked and just messed around, but we didn't have sex," Jonathan Cassidy would later tell police. "I don't think Russell had sex either, because every five minutes or so Jasmine was knocking on the bedroom door, asking Becky if she was okay, and if she was ready to leave now."

Around one a.m., Jasmine insisted they had to go. "My dad wouldn't like it that we were out this late. I really wanted to call him." But Jasmine remembered her step mom's warning not to phone late. "So I decided to call a cab." Jasmine told the dispatcher they'd meet the cab in front of the house.

Jasmine made her first call at 1:08 a.m., police would confirm later. The dispatcher promised Jasmine a taxi would pick them up in ten to fifteen minutes.

Immediately after Jasmine's first call for a taxi, she and Russell headed outside. Becky remained inside with Jonathan. Two cabs passed, but neither stopped. Jasmine went back inside to make a second call, telling Becky she needed to come outside. By now, it was 1:45 a.m., and Jasmine knew her father would be angry that they had missed their curfew.

"This time I wasn't nice," Jasmine said. "The dispatcher again promised that a cab would be there." By 2:16 a.m., when Jasmine made her third call, both girls were frantic. Again, a promise, the cab was on its way. "I was really irate, and the lady, the same dispatcher, said she would send one for me. We stayed outside and waited for the taxi at the bottom of the Cassidy's driveway. Yet again, no taxi came."

Jonathan Cassidy waited with Becky and Jasmine until the third call. Tired, he went inside. Ben Turtle and Russell McCann already were asleep in the den.

Cassidy looked at his watch as he glanced out his bedroom window. Nearly two thirty a.m., still no taxi. The last time Jonathan Cassidy saw Becky and Jasmine they were standing alone at the end of his driveway.

Cassidy went to bed.

The rain had stopped. A disturbing aura fell over the dank island as paths intersected, setting into motion unspeakable events.

Some in Bermuda refer to female tourists like Rebecca Middleton and

Jasmine Meens as "long tails." The small mostly white bird, with its distinctive long tail, winters at sea then flies onto the island in spring. Like tourists, long tails go as quickly as they come.

In the early morning hours, after two a.m., Becky and Jasmine perched like prey on the main road leaving St. George, under that full moon, partly hidden by mist and clouds. The few taxis that passed ignored their waves. The Cassidy house was dark. It was forty five minutes after Jasmine's last taxi call.

Jasmine's watch showed three a.m. when a young black man rode up on his motorbike. "Do you have any cigarettes?" he asked. Becky and Jasmine said they didn't. His name was Dean, he said, reaching into his pocket, pulling something rolled. He had traded some cigarettes for a package of tobacco, he told Jasmine and Becky.

Five minutes later, two more black men passed them, together on another cycle. Suddenly the pair made a u-turn.

"Hey, what's up?" The driver "high-fived" Dean. The men seemed to know each other. The passenger got off and stood in front of Becky.

"He couldn't take his eyes off her," Jasmine recalled. "I just believed he thought she was pretty, because she was."

Becky showed him a gold necklace that Jasmine had given her. The driver of the bike that carried the two men offered them a ride home. Becky and Jasmine refused. "I told them it wouldn't be a good idea because we didn't know them, and we didn't have helmets. Plus the bike looked old and beaten up, with a ripped black seat. It was fast and the engine had a bubbling sound." Not safe, Jasmine thought.

One of the men suggested that if police stopped them, they'd say they left helmets at the pub. He repeated the invitation. Now frantic, with no taxis, promised three times they'd be there in a few minutes, bus service halted hours ago, lights off in the Cassidy home, no access to a telephone, and Jasmine knowing that her dad, by now, would be furious, the girls accepted.

"I said I would go with Dean. Rebecca, who was smaller, could go with the two guys on the other bike. I told them not to ride too fast and stay in sight."

Instead, the men sped off with Becky.

Jasmine clutched Dean, who struggled to drive on the slick roads. "I could have run faster," she remembered. When they finally reached the long causeway heading across the harbor toward home, Jasmine stretched around Dean, searching for Becky and the men. Try as she did, she couldn't find them. Perhaps the dark night, or because Dean was going so slowly. Surely, Becky and the two men had to be in front.

"We lost all sight of them. I never saw Rebecca or the two guys again," Jasmine later told police.

As later would become clear, the fact that Becky and the men had veered off the main road came as no surprise to Dean Lottimore.

Driving toward the Meens home in Flatts, located in the center of the island, Dean told Jasmine he was a security guard, although the truth was he didn't yet have the job, and also that he had a little boy. "He said a lot of other things, but I ignored it."

Outside the house, Jasmine got off the bike. "I waited and waited." She chewed her nails, sucked the ends of her hair, paced.

"Relax," Dean said. "Stop doing that." He told Jasmine not to worry.

"I asked him if they would have done something to Rebecca, and he said something to the effect that they might. I asked him, 'Do you think they will rape her?' He just shrugged."

By then, Jasmine estimated, it was 3:45 a.m. "I don't have a good feeling about what's happening. Why aren't they here?"

"I was trying to give you the eye. You shouldn't have let her get on that bike," Dean told her.

"I guess he was trying telepathy," Jasmine suggested. "How am I supposed to know his eye signs? Those men knew each other, and he knew where she was. He told me to get back on the bike, told me he would show me where they were."

Jasmine refused, telling him that she was going inside to get her father. Dean Lottimore rode away. Frantic, Jasmine ran in the house. "Dad, I've been down the hill waiting for Becky, she hasn't shown up."

"Where is she? Who have you been with?" Half asleep, jolted, Meens grabbed his car keys. Jasmine told him that she got a ride home with a friend, "and Becky got a ride with another person." Rick didn't know then that Becky was with two men. Afraid of consequences, Jasmine didn't tell her father until the next day.

On Bermuda's thirty-five kilometer per hour roads, with countless side streets snaking up hills, into dark corners, some leading nowhere, Becky could have been anywhere. "We drove as far as the causeway on both sides of Harrington Sound, the only roads to St. George. We found no sign of Becky."

"We stopped at all those little nooks and crannies along the way, and I really expected to find Becky at home when I got there." When she wasn't, Rick Meens called police. Officers had been summoned to Ferry Reach, but the dispatcher didn't connect Meens' report with the murder. Instead, police advised him to phone back in twenty four hours if Becky hadn't come home.

Unlike Rick and Jasmine Meens who didn't know where to find Becky—Dean Lottimore was heading to Ferry Reach.

THREE

"Class and racial antagonisms are rife, and there are few islands to which it would not be easy to apply the well-known local adage:
"If you're white, you're all right
"If you're brown, hang around
"If you're black stand back."

Birmingham Post—March 13, 1973

View from the Top
July 2, 1996

A DAY BEFORE Rebecca Middleton's murder, Kirk Mundy found life just fine, at least for the moment. The twenty-one-year-old Jamaican spent most of his life in Bermuda, living with his family in cramped quarters, across from the Augustus Funeral Home, in "back of town," just down the hill from the vast grounds of Government House that accommodates Bermuda's representative of Queen Elizabeth II.

A turreted grey and white mansion set back from Black Watch Pass on the outskirts of Hamilton, the site allows the governor a superb view of the ocean, while lush foliage protects him from noticing those tightly packed structures below that often house multiple generations. Moreover, tour guides don't remind ladies who take tea at Government House of the bloody murders that happened there in 1973, a situation so explosive Bermuda had to bring in

British soldiers, Scotland Yard, and the hangman at night when the murderers faced justice years later.

Neither do guides say that the grand manor on its nearly forty acres of lush cedar, casuarinas, rubber trees, and oleanders rubbed some of Mundy's struggling neighbors so raw after those political killings that London's Foreign and Commonwealth Office (FCO) assigned a committee to find a less ostentatious site. The site is still offensive to some, but there is speculation that the committee never met.

Now on this July second, 1996, seven months after Kirk Mundy's arrest for armed robbery, and thanks to Richard Hector of Guyana, a lawyer associated with one of the island's most visible criminal defense firms, Mundy was free on bail, often leaning on the "white walls" of once seething volcanic rock with other "disenfranchised" young black Bermudian men.

By day Mundy hung with his friends or with his pregnant girlfriend, Keasha. At night he partied, crashing at Keasha's when he chose. Typical of more than a few local men, Mundy was familiar with Court Street's night clubs, held no job, and hung aimlessly on the wall, where the men notoriously shared stories, drugs and alcohol.

Mundy's friend, seventeen-year-old Justis Smith, no relation to Keasha, looked up to "my boy, Fly," as he called Mundy. Smith also lived with his parents in the "back of town" and, like all too many young black Bermudian males who attended an admittedly failing public system, said to hell with school. Their interests had little to do with academics.

Sporting viper sunglasses to prop up his image, Mundy enjoyed the adoration of the younger Smith, who hung on as Mundy propelled Keasha's ragged motor bike. Both were small built, so they fit on one seat, with room to spare.

Justis Smith had his own problems. He'd been charged five months before with obstructing police officers, violently resisting arrest, and using offensive words during a drugs search that turned up neither drugs nor weapons. His father, Richard Smith, saw his son fighting with police and joined the fracas. As Justis Smith tried to flee, according to police, he threatened, "I'm going to get you. You're a dead man." Police quoted Smith during his arrest: "Fuck you. I don't care. I will go to prison for all of you."

By the time Smith's hearing relevant to that incident came about, he had more serious matters going on.

About midnight of the same evening on which Becky and Jasmine were partying at the White Horse Tavern with the young Belfast students, Kirk Mundy and Justis Smith were headed to a louder, darker reggae club nearby in St. George. Nuzzled in the narrow pathways, obscured in an alley, the club called Moonglow was hidden from tourists' view, a skeleton in the closet of "the Old Town."

Later, Kirk Mundy would remember dancing with a white girl there. What a beautiful face the girl had, and a stunning body, at least after several beers. She disappeared when he left to get more to drink. He didn't much care, he said later; he just kept dancing. Mundy felt quite good about himself, smoothing his slick yellow and black nylon sweat suit as he danced, proud of his short Rasta braids that his girlfriend Keasha called "twicks."

On the night of Becky's murder, however, Kirk Mundy's mind wasn't on Keasha.

On schedule, exactly three a.m., Shell installation guard Wendall Burchall logged the arrival of his supervisor, Freedom Burrows, who departed fifteen minutes later. Burchall headed to the crew room behind the garage to make hot chocolate. Half way back to the office, Burchall heard a bike coming out of the woods along Ferry Road, which fronts the installation. As the bike approached the well-lit main gate, Burchall saw two men speed by. Odd, he thought. A white rag hung over the back, covering the license plate. It was somewhere "between 3:15 and 3:20 at the latest."

Meanwhile, Dana Rawlins, who disk jockeyed at Arretta's, a quieter St. George club that had closed at one a.m., partied at Moonglow with his friends, Sharon, Angela and Antonio, oblivious to Kirk Mundy and Justis Smith, who by now also were there, but who ran in different social circles. Race—all the men and women were black—often was not a unifier. Mundy was Jamaican, and Bermudians rarely forget one's country of origin on this isolated place once known as "Devil's Island."

Their shift nearly half over, Constables Stephen Symons and Frank Vasquez parked their patrol car in the dark aquarium lot in Flatts, not far from the Meens home. They stopped a man on a red motorcycle for a traffic offense. It was 3:30 a.m.

Symons and Vasquez watched as two men riding together on a black motorcycle hailed the man who police had stopped. The three talked briefly, then headed side by side on the two bikes toward Hamilton. It now was about 3:45 a.m.

A police dispatcher's call jolted Symons and Vasquez: "A naked woman is lying in the middle of Ferry Road." The officers headed for the scene, crossing a small bridge leading to Ferry Reach, passing two men standing next to a broken-down orange Toyota.

Symons knew the driver, Sean Smith. "Are you alright?" Symons asked.

"Ya, everything is okay. A tow truck's on its way."

As Symons and Vasquez neared Ferry Reach, they heard a female police officer, at the scene with an emergency worker, on the radio. "This is a suspected murder. I can't find a pulse."

They sped up, passing a man who yelled, "Down there."

For Rick and Jasmine Meens, searching for Becky everywhere, the passing hours seemed an eternity. "We looked in every corner, on every road. We just hoped Becky had stopped to talk with somebody." That possibility was beginning to seem remote.

A few minutes after four a.m., Jasmine's father pulled over near Swizzle Inn, a tourist spot near the causeway, to allow an ambulance to pass. However, he had no reason, he later told police, to realize that ambulance was heading in that direction for Becky.

About six a.m., they returned to the Meens home in Flatts. Rick Meens believed he had searched every logical spot, given Jasmine's report that she had seen Becky and the men cross the causeway, something she'd tried to convince herself had happened.

At seven a.m., police telephoned the Meens home and instructed Rick to go to the St. George police station. He asked why.

"Just come," an officer said.

He obeyed the summons, taking Jasmine and her brother Jordan with him. As the three sped toward St. George, they heard the first report on the radio. "A young white woman was murdered at Ferry Reach." Meens, who was passing the area at the time, veered down Ferry Road.

Jasmine stared in disbelief at the fire trucks and, worse, at the blood on the road. Their father told Jasmine and Jordan to stay in the car. "All I could hear was my dad's scream," Jasmine said. "That told me enough. He was gagging and throwing up."

Meens vomited in the nearby brush. Then he returned to Becky's body, by now lying in the ambulance, wrapped in a body bag. He vomited again.

Rick Meens would never forget what he saw—every detail.

FOUR

"The atmosphere is a mixture of shame, embarrassment, a desire to shed responsibility ("This is totally out of character for Bermuda")...

London Times-- March 12, 1973

'Nothing Like This....'
July 3, 1996

THE VOICE ON THE TELEPHONE belonged to Peter Lewis, Dave Middleton's former father-in-law. Dave had just gotten to work. "Dave, Becky has been murdered. She's dead."

Dave thought Peter was screwed up, had gotten it wrong. His daughter couldn't be dead. This couldn't possibly be Becky. Nonetheless he told his foreman, "I've got to go home. I'll be back," still convinced it was all a mistake.

"It was absolutely unbelievable. I was numb. If it had not been Peter who called me, I wouldn't have believed it at all."

Cindy, Rebecca's mom, was returning to work after Canada's July first holiday weekend. Wayne dropped her off at the secure Canadian government building. She had been there only about fifteen minutes when she looked out the window and saw Wayne returning. Guards allowed him inside. "You have to come home," he said.

"All I could think of was the fact that Wayne's father had cancer. I thought perhaps something bad had happened."

Cindy asked if that was the case. "No," Wayne said, "you have to come home. Becky's dead." He'd gotten a call at work from Rick Meens in Bermuda.

Right away, without leaving the government building, Cindy telephoned the Bermuda police. "I told them I was the mother of Rebecca Middleton, and someone said, 'Let me see if I can give you to somebody.' I told them I had to talk with someone. They were vague."

"We have to go and tell Dave," Cindy said, hanging onto Wayne's arm as he helped her to his car.

At Dave's house, Cindy found her younger son, Mark, pacing. He kept repeating, "Where's Becky? What's the matter with Becky?" Over and over. Cindy's parents arrived.

Dave held a map, still praying there was a mistake. "I was in disbelief." He took his turn trying to reach the Bermuda police. "They were passing me all around the police station. Kept saying somebody was going to call me back."

John Ferguson, a radio newsman in Belleville, Ontario, who had spent a decade in Bermuda some years before, telephoned to say he'd heard the news. "John Ferguson," Dave said later, "gave me more information than anyone else."

Another friend who had a home in Bermuda gave Dave the telephone number of someone he knew there. When Dave telephoned, a woman who identified herself as "the maid" answered.

"It turned out," Dave reported, "the maid's boyfriend" was among police officers first on the scene. The maid told Dave that a girl had died. But Dave still hoped "perhaps someone had taken Becky's identification."

Finally, Bermuda Detective Superintendent Vic Richmond telephoned. Jasmine was okay; Becky had died. To everyone's outrage, Cindy recalled, "he told us that we didn't need to come, they would just send Becky home."

"No way," said Cindy, and she and Dave agreed they'd both go. But first, all of them went to tell Becky's older brother, Matt, who was at work and broke down.

Early on the fourth of July, Cindy sat next to Dave, gazing out the window of the Air Canada jet headed for Bermuda. It was the same flight Becky had taken exactly two weeks before. By now, only a day after Becky's murder, international media swarmed Belleville, their plane to Bermuda, and the island. An attendant moved Cindy and Dave to first class to avoid curious reporters.

Detective Superintendent Vic Richmond met their plane. He was leading the investigation into the murder of Rebecca Middleton, by now causing international angst. Richmond escorted Becky's parents through the media-filled airport, then to police headquarters for a press conference.

Oppressive heat filled the tiny room. Dave Middleton asked an officer if they could open windows. An officer suggested the conference would end sooner with the windows closed.

Dave told media how the family had heard Bermuda was a safe place to be--one of the reasons they allowed Becky to take the trip. Cindy said she'd talked with Becky several times by phone. "I asked her, 'Is it pretty?' She said, 'Mom, it's just like a dream.'" Cindy called upon Bermudians to help find the killer of their beautiful child. Jasmine, pale and fragile, dissolved in tears.

After the interview, Dave and Cindy met with Detective Richmond. "We had to dig as he appeared to be trying to shield us from the gruesome facts," Dave recalled. "As parents, we can't sit in a vacuum. You do and don't want to know."

Some information needed clearance from the attorney general's office, Richmond told them.

"It seemed so confidential," Dave Middleton said. "Richmond said he'd keep us up to speed. However, we'd already heard what was happening from the newspapers, reporters, or from Rick Meens. But we never cut Vic Richmond off. We hoped he would come up with something.

"Even when we got back to Belleville, it was hard to get information, just statements that already had been given to news reporters," Dave recalled. "Even then I didn't feel police were forthcoming, but Richmond assured me the killers would be caught and that no one could get off the island."

Richmond did advise Dave and Cindy that a second autopsy might be necessary. "That would mean we'd have to stay another day," Dave said. "But we very firmly told police to do whatever was necessary. There was going to be no second chance." Becky was to be cremated as was the family's custom.

Police claimed to be satisfied with results. They saw no need for an overseas forensic pathologist, no second autopsy. Certainly no need to call in Scotland Yard.

Secrecy, the Middletons would learn, remains Bermuda's style. "They said nothing like this had ever happened in Bermuda," Cindy recalled. In truth, only four years before, police found German tourist Antjie Herkommer's body hidden in caverns at Dockyard, on the opposite end of the island from St. George. A man on work release from Casemate's, the old prison at Dockyard's gates, had raped and killed Herkommer. Although Bermuda has no legal provision for "deals," prosecutors, with the nod of the court, agreed to drop the murder charge in exchange for his guilty plea to manslaughter. The Herkommers quietly took their daughter's body home to Germany.

On the day they arrived in Bermuda, Tourism Minister David Dodwell met with Dave and Cindy and told media, "I am concerned, and all Bermudians should be concerned." A minister from a local church called on them. Bermuda Premier Dr. David Saul sent a letter of condolence, terming Becky's death "absolutely shocking and tragic."

The Department of Tourism had leaped into damage control mode. Becky's murder came during a period when visitor satisfaction with Bermuda was on a downslide. Sixteen years had passed since tourism peaked in 1980. Now competition loomed, with easy access to destinations worldwide. Complaints focused on the quality of Bermudian restaurants, transportation, and the island's high costs.

While Dave and Cindy waited to board the Air Canada flight back to Toronto with Becky's body, they met Brian Calhoun, a seasoned Canadian criminal lawyer, now Bermuda's senior Crown counsel, leaving for a month's vacation off the island. "He assured us that they would see that the killers were caught, and that they would do anything they could to help us," Dave recalled.

Calhoun's words still haunt the Middletons. They would come to trouble Brian Calhoun as well.

Within hours of Becky's murder, Bermuda police sought the two men who Jasmine Meens and Dean Lottimore told officers had ridden off with Becky. The *Royal Gazette* reported, "A killer on the loose has turned peaceful St. George into a town of terror... The brutal murder of teenager Rebecca Middleton near the town has cast a shadow over visitors' summer holidays." Police warned teens to avoid dangerous situations, saying women should carry "some sort of warning device, like an air horn."

"Heinous," among the most vicious murders he'd ever seen, Lead Detective Vic Richmond told media. Attorney General Elliott Mottley met with Dave Middleton and Rick Meens, promising that he would personally prosecute the case. Officials reminded Becky's parents, murder was a hanging offense in Bermuda.

The day before they left Bermuda, her mother and father saw Becky for the first time since her death. Cindy held her child, the lights of her eyes gone and her skin slashed, bruises, swelling, distorting her face, her body bitterly cold. A shower cap sat atop her shaved head, a failed attempt to hide those appalling injuries and autopsy marks.

"It was a numbing experience," Dave recalled. "The worst part of this nightmare has been confirmed. You've lost the game, and it's time to go home."

Dave never would have imagined supporting capital punishment, but now he did. His daughter was dead, murdered in the most intentional, violent and gruesome of crimes.

For now, however, Dave and Cindy wished only to return to Belleville with Becky, while police and the attorney general found and prosecuted Becky's killers.

"We had no idea the investigation had been so botched," Dave said later as the story of Becky's murder and its handling emerged.

The violations of customary procedure were many. Becky's hands had not been bagged. Her body was hosed before the authorities collected all the trace evidence that may have been available. Condom wrappers as well as other evidence were thrown away, and the crime scene was not fully searched.

The Middletons' child was unrecognizable. Her body was blood-soaked, her face battered and slashed, bloody, swollen, black and blue. She was covered in deep slashes and apparent torture wounds, even cutting into the bone on top of her head. Her neck had been slashed repeatedly one side to the other, then back again. There were gashes between her legs, on her rectum, her jugular, her heart, abdomen and lungs; all had been sliced. The skin all over her body was bruised and torn, evidence of not only rape but what experts would later call sodomy and frenzy.

But there were only one, or at the most two, tiny defense wounds reported. Some thirty cuts and stabs were documented. Becky clearly hadn't managed to hold up her hands, an automatic defensive response. Moreover, the autopsy showed bruises at the top of both arms where experts would confirm she'd no doubt been held down during the attacks.

However, while officials consoled Becky's parents, someone was drawing conclusions that more than a few would find horrendous.

FIVE

…A further incident last night. Five shots were fired at buildings at police headquarters, including the murder room… almost certainly fired from a revolver by someone riding on the back of a motor bike.

Acting Governor Ian Kinnear to Washington and the FCO
--March 12, 1973

'That Child Won't Sleep'
July 3, 1996

FROM THE START, police had no doubt they were dealing with a tourist murder. Little else would explain finding a body in such an isolated spot. Police knew their priority was to waste no time solving the case.

Only moments after Becky died, Deputy Police Commissioner Michael Mylod joined Scenes of Crime Lead Inspector Howard Cutts and the island's police photographer at Ferry Reach as officials memorialized the bloody scene. Other inspectors, not assigned to the murder, came out of curiosity. In fact, far too many officers trampled over the scene, police admitted later.

Mylod telephoned Bermuda's Police Commissioner Colin Coxall, who was at a conference in England. A no-nonsense former Scotland Yard officer, seconded to Bermuda by the FCO one year before Becky's murder, his brief was to clean up crime, halt the drug flow, and reorganize the police service. Coxall ordered that Becky's murder take police priority, and that police entrust the case to the island's top officers, Assistant Commissioner Harold Moniz and Detective Superintendent Vic Richmond.

That's not surprising. Very little worries Bermuda more than threats to its two main sources of wealth – tourism and off-shore industry. For the island to prosper, its reputation as a safe destination is essential.

Back at Ferry Reach, with Becky's body already transported to the morgue, Chief of Training Inspector Jonathan Smith arrived with sixteen recruits. Smith, who would later become police commissioner, split his inexperienced men into two groups. Each was charged with searching beneath the two casuarinas, marking objects and climbing into bushes. Smith documented that police found an under wire from Becky's bra, a small white button, "several different lengths of thread – blue, green and white – and a torn portion of a condom wrapper." Scenes of Crime Officer Howard Cutts retrieved her bloodied clothes, the bra cut from her shoulder, and her skirt, sliced all the way down its front. Viper style sunglasses turned up some time later; Cutts wasn't sure where.

Later Smith defended his search tactics, insisting the trainees were well supervised, arguing that he and his men were sent to search for a sharp weapon. When he and his men arrived, the scene already had been released by Serious Crimes, Smith said, and he had complained to his superiors that it shouldn't have been. Thus, how could it ever be known whether the scene had been compromised, and if semen, blood and saliva, hair fibers, or other microscopic evidence were lost? An unanswerable question.

Police completed sketches, normally an immediate task, more than a year later. At the scene, not only did police fail to bag Becky's hands to preserve trace evidence, no one took fingernail scrapings for analysis of blood, skin, hair, or anything else. At the morgue a technician hosed Becky's body before experts could gather foreign materials. Trace evidence from the killers, which photographs suggested were on Becky's body, may have floated down the drain.

What happened to the soft blue towel Dana Rawlins and his friends – the people who found Becky lying almost naked in the middle of the road – had with the best intentions placed across her body? Trace evidence from Becky's attackers could have transferred from Becky's body to the towel.

Neither did police find Becky's under garment, the white tank top she'd worn beneath the white blouse, or her jewelry, the ring with three hearts from her grandparents, and the thin gold chain necklace from Jasmine. They didn't report publicly that Becky's jewelry or the tank top was missing, possibly making a transfer or sale of the items less difficult. The jewelry, one could understand--killers take souvenirs. But a soft white undergarment?

Police later would have little doubt about what happened to that—a security guard and the two men whose car had broken down on the bridge both reported a white cloth dangling over the license plate of the motor bike on which Mundy and Smith rode.

There were additional problems with physical evidence. While guarding the scene shortly after police transferred Becky's body for autopsy, an officer spotted a torn condom wrapper on foliage. The next day, he revisited the murder scene, finding the condom wrapper still in the same place. He carried it to Scenes of Crime Inspector Howards Cutts, breaking the chain of custody and reminding of a less than perfect job done the previous evening—opportunities seemingly lost, without second chances.

It was no secret among investigators that hospital pathologist Dr. James Johnston didn't wish to perform the autopsy. "This is above me," he told police. A histopathologist with expertise in tissue examination, not forensics, Johnston pleaded with officers.

"The man practically was in tears--he was telling them to get a forensic specialist," an attendant who helped with the autopsy remembered. Officers insisted he go ahead. At ten a.m., with Becky dead some six hours, Johnston began his work.

Assisting was Dr. Keith Cunningham who had handled the 1970s political murder autopsies, experienced with sexual crimes. Bermuda had no rape kit, so Johnston and Cunningham used standard supplies to gather oral, anal, rectal, hair, and urine samples.

Later, some officers cited Bermuda's racial sensitivities when they defended their decision not to call a forensic pathologist. They pointed out that they had not called in an outsider in the murder of a local man, James Caines, who was black. Thus, they argued, they might have been chastised for calling one for Becky, who was white.

But, not only did Caines' murder happen three days after Becky's, as

Caines lay dying in his mother's arms, he named his killer. Becky's murder would not be solved as easily.

Although, without doubt, it would have been preferable to bring in a forensic pathologist, later accusations that autopsy reports were inconclusive or flawed proved false. Evidence of exactly what happened existed on the day that Becky died. That fact, unfortunately, would turn out to be both the good and the bad news.

Meanwhile, members of news media complained that they had to rely "largely on unofficial sources." The *Royal Gazette* protested that Bermuda needed "enough information to quell wild and exotic rumors" in the wake of Becky's murder. Such silence, "only causes public uncertainty, followed by wild speculation…" Some of the rumors, an editorial suggested, "have been downright racist and divisive which is entirely undesirable."

A Canadian newspaper report that police had found semen from two different men went unconfirmed. As the Middletons learned later, there was some truth—but also error—in actual findings.

Parents of young black Bermudian men charged police with harassment, protesting "voluntary" DNA samples taken from ten suspects. "I didn't do it. I wouldn't touch a white girl," the *Royal Gazette* quoted one young man.

Becky's murder sent the island reeling. On the same day that Becky's parents took her home, an American tourist fell to his death while being towed in a parachute. Burglars held a Canadian Senator and his wife at gunpoint in a guest house. A few hours later, police were called to that shooting of James Caines mentioned above. Because they suspected a drugs link and a connection with "the notorious white wall crew," a gang still prominent among many in Bermuda, police feared revenge attacks. Unprepared to handle multiple investigations, officials admitted they were overwhelmed.

Lies, both by commission and omission, occurred as Becky's killers remained free.

While police were asking "anyone with information" to come forward--with no one doing so--the *Royal Gazette* reported that Bermuda's well-known turf wars hadn't been interrupted by Becky's murder. Lead Middleton investigators Assistant Commissioner Harold Moniz and Detective Superintendent Vic Richmond were among four police officers who took time out from the murder investigation to hold a "secret meeting" with

Governor Lord David Waddington, protesting the hiring of non Bermudian for the deputy commissioner post. Michael Mylod, tired of Bermuda politics, had announced his plans to leave Bermuda six months before his contract ended.

Jazzy's disbelief

Press conference
Photos Courtesy of the Royal Gazette

Asst. Commissioner Harold Moniz holds reward poster for Becky's killers.
Photo Courtesy of the Royal Gazette

PLP shadow minister Alex Scott, a future premier, told the *Royal Gazette* that officers would resign if the selection process ignored Bermudians. "Our point is that even if they brought in Nelson Mandela right now, it would not be acceptable."

Eight years after Becky's death, a woman who had been a morgue attendant during her autopsy warned she didn't believe Becky was resting. With no one convicted of her murder, "there's been no closure," she said. "Until there is, that child won't sleep."

That woman had more than a passing interest in the autopsy she attended. The attendant hadn't recognized Becky's body in the morgue on the morning of July third.

But when she got home from work, she and her daughter watched a news report of Becky's murder. The woman's daughter cried, "Mom, it's Becky." In fact, Rick Meens lived next door to the morgue attendant, and only hours before Becky and Jasmine left for St. George on Becky's final night out, Becky had been watching television with the morgue attendant's daughter.

"I hadn't thought—," she said. "Rebecca... Of course, that was Becky."

That same evening Jasmine's brother Jordan came over to the woman's house. "We just sobbed," she said.

In Belleville, being prepared for her final ceremony, Becky wore a small blonde wig. Cindy dressed her daughter in her favorite clothes, her sweatshirt and plaid boxer shorts. Cindy placed the wedding rings that had belonged to her and Dave inside Becky's casket.

Belleville United Methodist Church, one of the city's largest, was filled to overflowing. More than a thousand friends filled the church and poured into the streets outside to say goodbye to the "bright, bubbly teenager who was murdered last week while vacationing in Bermuda." The minister placed a pink flower upon the closed, cloth-draped casket, along with the picture of Becky that by then had appeared in media internationally.

Belleville's mayor, the Parliamentary minister, and Belleville's police chiefs attended. "She was one of those people who every day down the hall at school smiled at every single person," one of Becky's friends told a *Belleville Intelligencer* reporter. "I've never been so mad in my life that something like this could happen to such a sweet, innocent girl. We shouldn't be here for this. Becky's legacy should be that the rest of us strive to change society. It's about the need to make things better."

Dave couldn't think about making things better right then. All he could see was the hearse pulling away. "That really puts it all in perspective." First disbelief, then fury.

Rick Meens flew to Belleville for the funeral to be with Jasmine and with Becky's family. For months after that event Jasmine would experience "floating," as though she didn't exist. "Becky dead. Unbelievable. Why," she asked God, "wasn't it me?" A manifestation of survivors' guilt, from which Jasmine would not recover.

For years, Becky's dad, Dave, would see a child Becky's age and automatically think it was her. "When the phone rang, I would think it would be Becky." Then reality would hit, over and over again.

For Cindy the months blurred. "People came over and helped. I wasn't going to give anything of Becky's away, but I found that giving people gifts of her clothing and some of her stuffed animals helped me."

A quilt of brilliant colors hangs in Becky's room; Cindy made it by hand from Becky's clothes.

In Bermuda, Dr. Ian Campbell, a local dentist, warned that Becky's murder should be a wake-up call to "force all Bermudians to face their island's 'social degradation.'" Campbell led a scholarship fund drive to "show the world that the Bermudian community has a heart and is truly sorry for what happened." Within two months, the fund received more than fifty thousand dollars.

"I suspect that the primary motivation is deep sympathy for the survivors of what must rate as one of the most horrible crimes we have ever seen against one of our visitors," Campbell said. "This may indicate that the community is finally ready to realize that individual action throughout Bermuda is necessary if the trend we see is to be halted. Maybe Rebecca's death will result in some good to prevent another Dunlop, Middleton, Herkommer, Caines...."

Dave Middleton contacted Campbell to express his thanks. They remain best of friends.

"Very little alarms Bermudians more than a brutal murder, except a brutal murder without an arrest," the *Royal Gazette* warned a week after Becky's murder. "The murder of any visitor is particularly bad news for a tourist resort, but the brutal rape and murder of a young woman visitor is bound to attract attention outside Bermuda."

Police promised that the Royal Canadian Mounted Police (RCMP) would examine DNA samples in "an all-out bid to crack the Rebecca Middleton murder mystery." Police said they would not, however, call in Scotland Yard, displaying customary disdain for British "interference."

It was something many in Bermuda felt ever since London seemingly turned its back in 1977.

PART TWO
MASQUERADE

SIX

...Few commentators disagree that the Caribbean will have to come together in some form of federation or common market if it is to survive...Without Cuba, no dice...And there lies the nub of the matter. For better or for worse, the general boycott of Fidel Castro's socialist state will have to give way to the larger interest...But until that day arrives the Caribbean will continue to be the turbulent melting pot—and for that matter, the lush flesh-pot of the Western Hemisphere.

Birmingham Post-- March 13, 1973

Glamour and Politics
March, 1996

JUST THREE MONTHS BEFORE Rebecca Middleton and Jasmine Meens set out for Bermuda, a seventeen-year-old Belleville student, Mark Fyke, had been shot to death during a school trip, his murderer sentenced two years later to life in prison. However, this happened in fast-paced Daytona Beach, Florida, not Bermuda, which boasted tourist safety and tranquility, an island so conservative that bathing suits were permitted only at the ocean and swimming pools.

But this once quiet island, where bad news is best kept secret and where laws aren't at parity with those of Britain, has seen its share of changes since automobiles arrived on the island after World War Two. Once the shrieking of tiny tree frogs seemed the only interruption in hot, sticky summers to the lapping of crystal blue waves on a gentle shore. Now police sirens often break the silence.

Socially and often financially separated from Bermudians, foreigners have long made up a significant part of Bermuda's population, some more welcome than others. The island had been a retreat for British colonials from Africa to Malaya during the Twentieth Century, and the opulence of the island has rocketed since in the 1990s it became the new refuge of tax-free corporations and U.S. offshore funds. Bermuda enjoys the third highest per capita income in the world.

Enormous hotels, encircled by lush golf courses and teal seas, dot the island on which model Twiggy once had a home, the destination of David Frost when he chartered a jumbo jet for a day trip with two hundred friends from Manhattan, and where Queen Elizabeth, Prince Charles, Princess Margaret and Princess Anne have visited with pomp and ceremony. Their royal ancestor, Princess Louise, said to be the loveliest of Queen Victoria's four daughters, who surrounded herself with artists and philanthropists, quietly escaped Canada's frigid cold, where her husband was governor, to winter annually in Bermuda's more temperate environment. Also in the nineteenth century, Samuel Clemmons, also known as Mark Twain, treasured his inconspicuous existence. Even Baroness Sharples, widow of murdered Governor Richard Sharples, keeps a quiet home on the island.

Actors Michael Douglas and Catherine Zeta-Jones joined Bermuda's persona of glamour a few years ago. The Douglas family heirloom, Ariel Sands, once with pink cottages that rented for thousands of dollars a weekend, sits graciously among the hotels on Bermuda's south shore, where beaches that are among the world's most beautiful. The cottages have been replaced with multi unit structures that some complain trade "quaint" for the new trend in tourism dollars, fractional ownership, time shares.

On foliage-draped Middle Road, picturesque Four Ways Inn, an early 1700s cedar-beamed carriage house with a cottage complex that adjoins one of Bermuda's finest restaurants, boasts the visit of former U.S. President George H.W. Bush. A plaque hangs above the corner table at which Bush Senior once sat.

For certain, Bermuda had been less than enthused in the 1980s when former U.S. presidential candidate Ross Perot, next door neighbor of New

York City Mayor Michael Bloomberg, allegedly exploded a large coral reef in otherwise tranquil waters to make his home in aloof Tucker's Town more water accessible.

Oprah Winfrey got turned away from Bermuda. In 2005, she attempted to purchase a grand home near Perot's and Bloomberg's. Parliament had recently ruled Bermudians could sell their houses only to other Bermudians. Enough was enough of foreign purchases. Winfrey bought elsewhere, despite upset Bermudians' challenge of the law that they realized discriminated against themselves, one of a very few efforts to defy government rulings.

Meanwhile, in 2004, Bermuda's relationship with Cuba, where in the 1970s members of Bermuda's Black Beret Cadre (BBC) were rumored to have trained, seemed tighter than ever, annoying the George W. Bush administration, represented by consul appointee Denis Coleman. Problems between the Bermuda and U.S. governments escalated when the Bermuda government agreed to ship old buses to Cuba.

"Government didn't return my calls," Coleman said, packing to leave Bermuda suddenly, citing health reasons. Coleman, a career diplomat, said he could only characterize the Bermuda government's response to his efforts to reach out as "somewhere between ambivalence and disdain. It was certainly a desire…to put some daylight between itself and the…United States…. You have to wonder what is going through people's minds when they don't return the phone calls of the personal representative of the president of the United States."

Despite Bermuda's tourist income nowhere near matching the island's dependence on U.K. and U.S.-based offshore industry, a potentially serious rift between Bermuda and both Britain and the U.S. didn't seem to concern many then. When Coleman left, a *Royal Gazette* cartoon summed up the situation, showing PLP Premier Alex Scott cutting Bermuda's "ribbon" to the U.S. The cartoon showed another ribbon leading to the U.K., already slashed into tiny pieces, floating indignantly in the water.

In 1996, despite a murder that was causing international alarm, Bermuda seemed rarely to catch the attention of its British keeper, the FCO, tasked with assuring "good governance" of this tiny speck in the sea. Like some of the best of parents who blindly take credit for their children's achievements, but miss signs of trouble, Britain often seemed oblivious to its rebellious child's behaviors more than five thousand kilometers away.

Even in 2003 when Bermuda's Deputy Premier Dr. Ewart F. Brown told the tiny country that his party intentionally "had to mislead voters"… or the PLP might not have been re-elected to a second term," Britain remained silent while Brown led a group of eleven to oust Premier Jennifer Smith, who had led the predominantly black party to its 1998 political victory. Neither did the majority of Bermudians register significant concern.

In the early 1990s, Dr. Ewart Brown shook up Bermuda politics with his return, his style aggressive, charismatic—and, some accused, American—threatening more than a few. Although born Bermudian, some challenged Brown's loyalty, resulting in his pledge that he gave up his joint American citizenship to serve Bermuda's government.

Dr. Ewart F Brown
Courtesy of the Royal Gazette

Bermuda's physicians were nervous too. Bermuda's medical association, made up at the time mostly of white men, did all that they could to prevent Brown from practicing medicine in Bermuda—without success. Soon he set up his own clinic in Bermuda, associating with Lahey Clinic in Boston, even with his own MRI.

Brown brought a new way of politicking-- magnetism mixed with obstinacy, and from the time he returned to Bermuda, speculators warned that Brown had a plan to become premier, that no one would stand in his way.

But immediately after Smith's downfall, Brown appeared content to defer to long-time PLP shadow minister Alex Scott, and Brown accepted the deputy premier spot. Three years later, in late 2006, already responsible for both transport and ever-important tourism, Brown successfully challenged Scott, not a first coup for Brown. In the late 1960s Brown had led a student revolt at Howard University, resulting in a five-day takeover of the administration building. In a 1969 quote *Playboy Magazine* published an interview with Brown and other activists that might indicate some formative thinking:

> Did you say "turn into puppet factories"? What in the hell do you think (schools) are now? Castro isn't doing any more harm to the minds of Cuban children than you and your ancestors did to black kids like me when you forgot us in the history books and taught us about a white Jesus and a white Santa Claus and a white world we didn't belong to. At least Castro is instilling a spirit of nationalism and self-respect in young Cubans, while our schools have been human meat grinders."

As it turned out, Brown would change the face of Bermuda politics, tightening the country's relationship with the U.S. and Caribbean, distancing it from the U.K. Brown insisted, despite poll suggestions that a majority on the island disagreed, that Bermuda must get out from beneath the umbrella of Britain.

Unlike most of Bermuda's leaders, who spent most of their lives on the island, the majority educated in Britain and Canada, Brown had headed to the U.S. in the 1960s, after a few years in Jamaica. With a medical degree from Howard University and a clinic in California, Brown returned to Bermuda some four years before Rebecca Middleton and Jasmine Meens' fateful trip to Bermuda.

Quickly Brown and the new American consulate, baseball cap wearing Gregory Slayton, a major George W. Bush fundraiser, seemed to heal the rift left by Denis Coleman. In fact, Cuban issues seemed to be long forgotten by 2008 while Slayton hosted Brown in Washington, D.C., photographed by the

Royal Gazette grinning with President George W. Bush as the U.S. president packed his White House suitcase.

Premier Dr. Ewart F. Brown made it no secret that he'd prefer being prime minister of an independent country. Bermuda needs to "come of age," the *Royal Gazette* quoted Brown in 2008. "Have we fulfilled the potential of those tense, electric, historic days? Could Bermuda not stand on its own two feet? (Or) Have we surrendered to the *quo fata ferunt* mindset?" Bermuda's motto: "Whither the fates carry us."

And while Bermuda's violence and crime escalated, the motto seemed firmly in place.

SEVEN

"A short time before Sir Richard Sharples was assassinated...I warned him: 'You could be the next on the killer's list.' But the genial Governor just laughed and said, 'Oh, come now. Nothing is going to happen to me. People in Bermuda are just too friendly for that sort of thing.'"

John Smith, reporter investigating the murder six months earlier of Police Commissioner George Duckett-- *The People, March, 18, 1973*

The 'Isle of Unsolved Murder'
1972/1973

FOR MOST TOURISTS visiting St. George, a tiny sunlit village named for England's patron saint in 1609 by Bermuda's founder, Admiral Sir George Somers, the "Old Town" would seem to have no connection with violence and tragedy. Never did either Rebecca Middleton or Jasmine Meens, greeting the town crier on a brilliant Wednesday morning when he made his regular appearance in the square outside the Old State House, realize the danger that lurks beneath the guise of many tourist spots.

Only the most curious of visiting foreigners wander behind historic St. Peter's, built in 1612, the oldest Anglican church in continuous use in the New World, where the graves of Bermuda's UK-appointed Governor Sir Richard Sharples and his aide Captain Hugh Sayers of the Welsh Guards provide gloomy witness to Bermuda's years of volatile racial revolt. Even after Emancipation in 1834 until the 1960s, black and white societies remained separated by law. Blacks were barred from the best of hotels, required to sit downstairs in cinemas, prohibited from using the same lavatories as white people, and forced to sit in the back during Church of England services.

Inquisitive visitors to St. Peter's graveyard today also find that on the opposite end of the church gardens from those majestic twin granite headstones marking the graves of Sharples and Sayers, town slaves and free blacks lie still divided for eternity from free and wealthy whites. Not only physical separation. Black people were expected to know their place, even in death.

Since the 1950s, rioting has been interspersed with subtle unrest, and by the late 1960s, the influence of America's Black Power movement had spread to Bermuda. In fact, some of Bermuda's Twenty First Century politicians, current Parliamentary ministers, admit that they once were young members of Bermuda's Black Beret Cadre—a 1970s offshoot of the Black Panthers—that to this day some suggest might have been associated with the 1973 political murders.

The island of unsolved murder, some declare. By the 1970s, along with the political murders, Bermuda police files remained open with more than twenty other mystery murders. "Panic started in 1943 when millionaire Sir Harry Oakes was battered to death in his bed," London's *Sun* reminded British readers, shocked by the Government House murders. "Later the woman secretary of the man who found Sir Harry's body was murdered." In 1959, three women died after being attacked. "The body of one—London typist Miss Dorothy Rawlinson—was dumped nude into the sea. In July, 1971, the body of 24-year-old Mrs. Jean Burrows from Chatham, Kent, was found floating in a harbor.

Bermuda's escalating violence was compounded further when Britain's state-run airline made Bermuda a stop for flights to Jamaica and Panama in 1973, opening floodgates for marijuana from the Caribbean and cocaine and heroin from Central America. Not consulted by the airline, Bermuda's government had been furious. Premier Sir Edward Richards told Governor Sir Richard Sharples that the airline's behaviors might result in the United Bermuda Party (UBP) taking the island to independence so that it could control airline routes.

Only a few days after Premier Richards' warning to Sharples, snipers shot the governor to death. The assassinations of the Queen's appointees temporarily delayed talk of independence, and the Panama route was halted later that year. But drugs didn't leave with the flight's termination.

Still on Bermuda's conscience when the governor and his aide were shot down in March, 1973, was another murder—exactly six months earlier—of Bermuda's U.K. appointed Police Commissioner George Duckett, lured outside to change a light bulb, shot to death on his porch. These three expatriate murders, the U.K.-appointed governor, his aide, and Bermuda's police commissioner, earned Bermuda its dubious distinction of being alone among Britain's territories in recent times to have had its royally-appointed leaders assassinated, a secret many still prefer not to share.

Then, less than a month after Sharples' and Sayers' murders, supermarket employees Victor Rego and Mark Doe were gagged and shot to death during an armed robbery, reportedly to gather funds for revolt. Doe had switched shifts with his brother so that he could attend a church service the next night. That store, Shopping Centre, still stands on Victoria Street in Hamilton, marking the boundary between prosperous Bermuda and the island's infamous "back of town," known for its poverty, drugs and violence.

British author Mel Ayton, who has reviewed Scotland Yard reports of the investigation into the 1970s political murders, declassified in 2005, confirmed that police believed others were involved, along with the two men who Scotland Yard and Bermuda police identified. One of them, Erskine "Buck" Burrows, a trusty at Casemates, had endeared himself to the commissioner and worked at police headquarters. He confessed to the killings. Witnesses identified Burrows' friend, Larry Winfield Tacklyn, allegedly running from the Shopping Centre murders. But police didn't follow through with an arrest of a "third man." According to a 1973 Government House memo, officials asked Canadian police to keep a watch on the suspect, but he was never extradited. When he returned to the island a few years later, the arrest warrant for the man, with political ties, "mysteriously" had gone missing. The suspect later joined a sect in Israel.

In Bermuda, it sometimes seems, a bird or two in the hand are worth another in the bush.

In London on December first, 1977, while Erskine Burrows and Larry Tacklyn awaited the gallows, with many Bermudians holding their breaths, Frank Hooley, MP for Sheffield, pleaded with the U.K. Parliament to give "urgent consideration" to the impending hangings. "We are the guardians of the human rights of all citizens in the United Kingdom and of our dependencies overseas…No right can be more fundamental than the right to life itself."

The scheduled hangings had aroused acute public controversy in Bermuda, Hooley reminded, "so much so that members of the Bermudian Parliament, members of the Progressive Labor Party, have travelled five thousand miles to London to press that this Parliament should debate the matter."

That petition asking for clemency, presented to the Queen, signed by six thousand people, said Hooley, "in the context of Bermuda is equivalent to six million signatures if collected in the population of the United Kingdom."

Despite that plea, Bermuda's white-controlled Prerogative of Mercy Committee refused to recommend the two men convicted of the political murders be spared the gallows, and Bermuda's white premier, Sir David Gibbons, refused to call a special Parliamentary session.

There had been no hangings in Bermuda for more than thirty years, Hooley reminded. "…There is reason to believe that if that is done, it will create a very serious racial tension in that territory…it would be a very grim irony if the results of these executions were to lead to disturbances in which there might even be further loss of life," a statement that proved on the mark when the two tourists and a hotel employee burned to death when rioters set fire to the Southampton Princess, believing the hangman stayed there. By the next day, riots were island wide.

"Some people will regard it as rather cynical if this House could not spend three hours at least to consider a matter concerning the life and death of two people in a dependent territory when we have, from time to time, perfectly properly, been critical of the behavior in relation to human rights of many individual governments throughout the world."

Foreign Secretary David Owen replied that he'd sent the matter to Bermuda's governor. There were no grounds for challenge, Owen said, citing a 1947 "hands off" policy recommended by then Colonial Secretary Arthur Creech Jones, "which has been followed ever since."

Another member, Jeremy Thorpe, MP for North Devon, suggested that the House, "ultimately responsible for its territory, might suspend the executions while Bermuda's Parliament had time to reconsider capital punishment legislation." A move to halt capital punishment had been rejected by Bermuda's Parliament in 1975; however, many suggested an emergency session could have led to passage of an immediate end to the practice, and instead, sentence the men to life imprisonment.

Britain, Thorpe reminded, "had affirmed that capital punishment was cruel and inhumane."

Again, Owen refused to allow further discussion.

In Bermuda, where Premier Sir David Gibbons refused to call Parliament together, furious crowds gathered at dark in Victoria Park in Hamilton, a "People's Parliament." If the government didn't speak for them, they would speak for themselves. Horrified by the Bermuda Appeals Court's final decision, Lois Browne Evans spoke to the crowds before she rushed to Casemates, where Erskine "Buck" Burrows and her client, Larry Tacklyn, hung a few hours later.

Nowadays, one won't find the bodies of Burrows and Tacklyn in any of Bermuda's churchyards. Their families were not permitted to bury them. Instead they lie in a yard outside long-abandoned Casemates Prison. Before it closed in the early 1990s, Casemates might have compared unfavorably to an eighteenth century European dungeon.

Thus, when Bermuda's white leadership and its territorial parent, Great Britain, seemingly turned a deaf ear to its black majority population, with the British Parliament refusing to help spare the lives of the two men accused of the political murders, that fiery rage that erupted in three days of rioting, burning, and death cast an indelible mark on Bermuda's soul.

Most would agree, as Bermuda's brochures proclaim, the island is "another world"—resulting in alternate realities for tourists on holiday, for off-shore business people who often conduct their affairs at the finest of restaurants, for their spouses with busy days tending to their privately schooled children, for reclusive wealthy white Bermudians, often found at the Royal Bermuda Yacht Club and exclusive Tucker's Town—and for black Bermudians—those with power and money and those without either.

But Lois Browne Evans would have none of those rules and manacles.

Born in 1927, Browne Evans grew up in Bermuda's "back of town," her family's home not far from the island's dump, where burning garbage spewed noxious fumes, and poor black Bermudians retrieved food and supplies discarded by hotels and shops.

Though her family wasn't poor, Browne Evans watched as black children who were unable to pay the required shilling per week (education was compulsory until sixth grade but not free) were teased and sent home.

With a rigid social system depending on race and money, the British-appointed governor led with his personally selected executive council. Women couldn't vote until 1944, even then only very few with significant land holdings. Few blacks, male or female, owned enough land to qualify.

A powerful group of white males, referred to as the "Front Street boys" or "Forty Thieves," owing to their multi-generation ownership of the most valuable land and businesses in Hamilton, led Bermuda, hanging onto their wealth jealously.

When the first of Bermuda's political parties, the Progressive Labor Party (PLP), formed in 1963, Bermuda's bank lines and churches remained racially divided. Movie theaters had only been desegregated in the late 1950s, thanks to a strong, but peaceful, protest that some preferred to call "a tempest in a teapot," forcing other businesses to follow. Later dissatisfactions wouldn't be expressed with such polite restraint.

Formed to unite the black community, the PLP abhorred "colonialism," its central principle -- independence from Bermuda's British masters. "Colonialism is a cancer," said the 1968 PLP election platform. The mixed-race United Bermuda Party (UBP) formed a few years later, a response to the PLP, and maintained government control.

Browne Evans' philosophy of the 1960s, termed socialist and sometimes even "Marxist," attracted Bermudian youth, as well as members of the Black Beret Cadre, according to one of her biographers, Randolf Williams. As her power grew, more than one person was expelled from the PLP for disagreeing with her. She had been called by "any number of names... ranging from 'pioneer, trail blazer...to rabble rouser, and even a female devil,'" wrote Williams.

In 1956, her first murder defense, Browne Evans persuaded prosecutors to reduce the charge against a taxi driver who admitted killing his girlfriend, from murder to manslaughter. Her second case defended the accused in the murder of one of the three women raped and killed along the picturesque south shore in the late 1950s, the "Murder Mile" killings. She took the first diminished responsibility argument before Bermuda courts, but to Browne Evans' shock, a foreign psychiatrist testified that her client could understand right from wrong. She convinced the jury to call for mercy, a first in Bermuda for a black man.

However, protests from Front Street, demanding execution, resulted in the governor changing his mind, announcing the man would hang. Browne Evans gathered a petition. In the end, he went to a mental institution in the U.K.

Incensed by racial abuses, Browne Evans never minced her words, and an admonition to young people during a 1960s political rally would become part of her legacy. Some ten years earlier, a white Bermuda physician had suggested that unwed pregnant girls, the majority black, should be sterilized. Bluntly, she told listeners that she didn't care if a young man spent his time "fornicating in the bushes because at least he was going to give birth to another Bermudian." Browne Evans later claimed she intended to call upon Bermuda's black youth to put aside drugs and become involved in politics. Three decades later, according to Williams, she explained that she got the terms "fornicating" and "adultery" confused.

Nevertheless, Lois Browne Evans became a leader who gave hope to the black community. Since her return from law school in Britain during the mid 1950s, she accomplished a litany of firsts, despite incredible adversity: among them first female, first black female to be called to the Bermuda Bar, first black female Parliamentarian, first female Opposition leader under Bermuda's 1968 Constitution.

Thirty years later, the PLP achieved its goal: the party of those "Front Street Boys" had been trounced. Lois Browne Evans led her party in celebrating a solid victory. "A New Bermuda," victorious PLP members cried when they took over government in November, 1998, only weeks before the trial of Rebecca Middleton's accused murderer, Justis Smith, was set to begin.

It had been Browne Evans' dream to lead the PLP as premier, but many speculated that her heated disposition likely led to the choice, instead, of her protégé Jennifer Smith.

A few months later, with a PLP-led change in Bermuda's constitution to allow the Bermuda government, instead of the British governor, to select the attorney general, Lois Browne Evans was appointed to the post. No doubt, although the governor remained tasked with "internal and external security," and where the senior judge—the chief justice of Bermuda's Supreme Court—remained appointed by Britain, with little sway from the government of Bermuda, a locally-appointed attorney general was a major step away from British control.

Incredible accomplishments. Lois Browne Evans succeeded despite an environment in which blacks were treated abhorrently and women, black or white, were accorded no more than second class, or less, status. No doubt, racism and sexism had molded Lois Browne Evans into a strong advocate for black Bermudians.

Meanwhile, to the surprise of a few, Browne Evans, who had long protested the bestowing of British titles, happily accepted the title of "Dame." And some would wonder whether her racial attitudes, and those of some of her colleagues, had moved beyond righteous indignation to its own form of bias.

For LeYoni Junos, born in the 1960s when racial injustices had finally led to rebellion, her island appeared to her nowhere near as hostile as the words of Lois Browne Evans seemed to suggest.

LeYoni didn't understand racism as a child. "I didn't grow up experiencing it, at least not like people a generation before me." When she started elementary school, "happy go lucky," she didn't realize integration was new. "They don't really teach you that in school." While studying in England, she learned European and American history, "but not the history of my own culture."

LeYoni admired Lois Browne Evans for her vigor and leadership, but she didn't much like politics. Her work with Amnesty International and on Bermuda's human rights commission consumed her. She kept to herself, immersing herself in nature, books, music, her pets, and fighting against international violence and sexual mutilation of women, viewing herself as a daughter of Bermuda, and a "universal person."

Born Leonie Jones, named after her father, Leon Jones, a well known local singer, she'd changed her name some ten years before to reflect her artistry and nature. A singer and actress, LeYoni played Dorothy several years ago in the Bermuda Dramatic Society's *Wizard of Oz*. Throughout the 1990s, dedicated followers gathered at Bermuda's hotels to hear her sultry jazz.

Human rights activist Stuart Hayward has known LeYoni since she was a child. For Hayward, LeYoni's view of the word was "unique…refreshing."

Le Yoni Junos, the author learned, was the same chocolate-skinned beauty who waved in the early 1990s when she visited a neighbor, sharing her love of nature and her island home. We'd become reacquainted in 2003, not long after I'd returned from nearly a year's medical hiatus in the U.S. To my surprise, LeYoni hopped out of a delivery truck, grinned, and handed me a load of dry cleaning. She hoped to be leaving this job soon to work in victim support with Bermuda's police. She'd make enough then to pay her mortgage with just one job, a relief. She didn't mention what had happened to end her Amnesty post.

Rick Meens, Becky's caregiver when she was murdered, and Becky's father, Dave Middleton, who I phoned in 2001, haunted by what seemed injustices in Becky's murder case, both told me that I should speak with LeYoni.

Now in January, 2004, nearly eight years after the murder of Rebecca Middleton (whose murder had by no means slipped into the shadows, as much as many wished it would), we closeted ourselves in a cubby at the back of a printing store, her second of three jobs, having just left her night shift at the Salvation Army.

LeYoni told me of the rooster she'd found when we met in the 1990s, half dead. He was doing superbly now, she said, residing in her bathroom, and on occasion visiting the hen caged outside, sitting on eggs that weren't going to hatch. To save its life in the cold, LeYoni slept with the fowl during Bermuda's winter months that, much to the surprise of many unsuspecting tourists, who erroneously associate the moderate climate of Bermuda in the Sargasso Sea with the islands far south in the tropical Caribbean, bringing high winds, rain, and damp, usually unheated houses.

In fact, the Sargasso Sea, so named because of a peculiar forest of seaweed, called *sargassum*, which drifts lazily over the entire span, is perhaps the strangest and most notorious sea on the planet. At the heart of the Bermuda Triangle, where ships and aircraft have disappeared in deadly calm, the area contrasts with the seas around it, investigator Gian J. Quasar writes. At the heart of the Bermuda Triangle, some 1200 miles north of Puerto Rico, its currents are largely immobile, yet surrounded by some of the strongest undercurrents in the world. Anything that drifts there becomes locked amidst the expansive weed mats. Moreover, the Sargasso Sea rotates slightly itself, transforming as currents change with seasonal weather patterns.

Like this tiny island it surrounds, the sea becomes an isolated mass where disharmony appears invisible.

LeYoni held out a photograph. She had recently returned from her first trip ever to the Library of Congress in Washington D.C. "I was so excited that I took a picture of myself." Standing alone in front of the great steps, with a huge Lewis and Clarke exhibit hanging on the front door, LeYoni beamed.

To her surprise, she'd found shelves of materials about Bermudian slave Sarah (Sally) Bassett, who gave her granddaughter poison to kill the slave master, blacksmith Francis Dickinson of Southampton Parish. In June, 1730, Bassett was convicted of witchcraft and executed on an inordinately hot June day, right outside of Hamilton.

"A regular 'Sally Bassett Day,' that's what they still call days like that one," LeYoni said. "On her way to the stake, legend says, Bassett shouted, 'No use you hurryin', there'll be no fun 'til I get there.' When Sally Bassett's ashes cooled, they say, the national flower, the *Bermudiana*, grew from them."

A few years ago, at the manicured round-about at Crow Lane just outside Hamilton, said to be the site of Sally Bassett's fiery death, LeYoni and her colleagues at Amnesty International reenacted the shameful scene, just one of many examples of Bermuda's long history of whipping and executing slaves.

"I wondered why she did that, and then it suddenly hit me. I wouldn't be surprised if the slave owner had raped Sally's granddaughter. No one ever thinks of those possibilities. Sally Bassett took the rap for it all, and they burned her at the stake."

In Bermuda, one finds either splendor or struggle--very little in between. Like the majority of Bermudians who labor to pay high mortgages, to buy gasoline at nearly eight dollars per gallon, or to purchase groceries at prices that encourage the use of starches, LeYoni's life consisted of racing from one job to the next, snatching scarce time to duck into a corner and bury herself in those books that changed her life.

"Did you ever see *Beauty and the Beast*, I mean the animated version? There's a place where she's in the beast's castle, and he takes her into this room. There are walls and walls of books stretching all the way up to this high ceiling. She was like in heaven. That's just me."

LeYoni found *Bury My Heart at Wounded Knee* at a garage sale when she was eighteen. "I didn't know what a Native American looked like. They have these stereotypes on television, mostly white people playing them. Now here were these dark-skinned people with very distinct features. In fact, they looked like my grandmother. It was an awakening for me, reading that book."

A year later, LeYoni discovered *The Passover Plot*." From the jacket, she located Dr. Hugh Schonfield in London. "Well, I got on the phone and asked directory assistance for his number. I spoke to this man, and I told him I wanted to thank him for writing this book. I told him that it had really changed my life." She was planning to go to England, she said, "So I asked if I could call him, and he said okay." LeYoni went to his house and had tea. "I think he was eighty-something at the time. He had lost his wife and was still mourning for her. He was a sweet old man, and here's a little black girl telling him that he had opened my mind to so many things."

Despite her staunch Salvation Army upbringing, LeYoni had many questions about the origins of Christianity. "At first I dropped the book. 'Oh, this is the devil,' I said. Then a year later I went back looking for it." The book talked about how Christianity shares doctrines borrowed from earlier religions, she said. "I had to open my mind, because as long as you're closed, and you're afraid to read this stuff, you don't allow yourself to get educated. You're afraid God's going to strike you down because of what you've been taught." In Bermuda, she said "if we didn't go to church--blacks and whites alike--we'd be whipped. It was actually beaten into you. But if I had been born in China or somewhere, I would have been taught Confucius or Buddhism, or whatever. And I would be just as adamant about it, because it is ingrained. But it doesn't mean it's true, and it means I've got to examine things for myself."

"I want to tell you how it first started for me." LeYoni Junos' intensity swallowed the tiny room. The night of Rebecca Middleton's murder "I had gone down to Blue Hole, across the harbor from Ferry Reach, to pick up my car. Since I was down that way, I decided I'd go to the park."

She'd glanced uneasily across the sound toward darkening Ferry Reach as she locked her car, creeping through thick terrain toward a small pool, once the site of a dolphin show. LeYoni loved to wander through this nature reserve, dancing between roosters, chickens, and tiny birds. This night she shuddered, glancing at the sinister clouds hustling above her. Unusual for LeYoni, she kept peering over her shoulder, worried that someone with "less than good intentions" would appear.

"I could have been in trouble because no one would hear me. I asked myself, 'Why are you thinking all these negative thoughts?' It's not like me to be thinking that way. I'm the type of person, I've hiked in England, and I've lived in Dominique, in Hawaii. I pay attention, but I'm not usually fearful." LeYoni sprinted to her car, locked the doors, and hurried straight home.

She awoke early the morning of July third. As she drove to work, LeYoni Junos heard the first radio report of a young white female tourist murdered at the end of dark, isolated, heavily wooded Ferry Road, just across the inlet from Blue Hole Hill.

"Rebecca Middleton probably was on her way down to St. George when I was at Blue Hole, because they had gone to Heritage Night." When she heard of the young woman's death, she said, "I knew immediately. My gut went back to that experience."

It wasn't her job as Amnesty International director in Bermuda or that she was a member of Bermuda's Human Rights Commission, she said.

"I just knew what I had to do."

For the most part, folks don't declare themselves in Bermuda. It's far safer to "lie in the tide." Perhaps that is a result of being a British colony with its rules of politeness. More likely, Bermuda's long history of racial divide has taught many the consequences of speaking out. Bank foreclosures and other financial and social disciplines are long traditions.

"Like grouper, they wait," the saying goes. "Whichever direction tide flows, so must they." That it's the way things are supposed to work on the tiny "Isle of Rest," or as some still prefer, "Devil's Island."

PART THREE

The Queen -v- Kirk Orlando Mundy

EIGHT

...Bermudians have a traditional aversion to gossip. Even after petty local crimes, police have complained about a lack of cooperation... The Scotland Yard team, who have used the term "Wall of Silence" seem to be preparing for a long, dogged spell of police work..."

Daily Telegraph - -March 15, 1973

'Safe...'

July 9, 1996

SIX DAYS AFTER Becky's murder, with a ten thousand dollar reward in place, Dean Lottimore--the man had who had "high fived" one of the men who rode off with Becky, then took Jasmine home before heading to Ferry Reach where Becky lay murdered--"remembered" who the suspects might just be. Questioned hours after Becky's murder, Lottimore had denied that he recognized the pair.

"The best person that fits my description is one of the bank robbery guys," Lottimore told police. He had known Kirk Mundy for "a long time, like from hanging out on the roundabout on St. John's Road." Mundy used to fix bikes with his friends. "Kirk used to just pop in, speak to us guys and then leave. Then he went overseas...within the last three, four years ago, I started seeing him again. I feel strongly that it was him who was riding the bike." Lottimore said he kept the secret because he couldn't prove they were involved, "and I was basically scared."

Dean Lottimore told police that he lived in St. George with his girlfriend, their three-month-old son, and her grandparents. On the morning of July second, he recalled, he hung around Hamilton most of the day. The twenty one-year-old unemployed former kitchen porter had left his job two weeks before.

Like Coy Fox, who had needed the ride to Ferry Reach Park on the night of the murder of Rebecca Middleton, Lottimore "did a hustle" the morning of July second to earn a few dollars, helping a friend with a container off-load. He'd tried to find his friend "Booger," but he wasn't home. Then he checked with the security company where he had applied for a job. A woman told him to check back the next day.

On to Bermuda Regiment headquarters. "I was to meet my color sergeant, but he never showed up. I sat off and talked to a couple of mates, and then I left by myself." Just after two a.m. July third, Lottimore stopped at Swinging Doors, a notorious Court Street club where violence is hardly unknown, before he headed home. He drove into St. George at three a.m., carefully maneuvering on the slick roads, a few drinks admittedly under his belt. A pretty routine day.

Lottimore told police he remembered Mundy's shoes—"a pair of white sneakers with a blue *Nike* symbol on the side." At the impound, Lottimore identified the bike that belonged to Mundy's girlfriend, Keasha. "That's got to be the bike, and come to think of it, I have seen Mundy riding that bike…It had to be Kirk. I know his voice." Lottimore told officers Mundy "was doing the talking, talking to the girl, Rebecca."

Actually, Dean Lottimore remembered both men. "I think that the pillion passenger was a guy named Justis Smith…" Lottimore had gone to secondary school with Justis Smith's brother. He'd been "picturing the faces" of the two on the bike, "and it has been on my mind all weekend, and those are the two who come closest to the description. Justis is slim built too, and he is shorter than me." Lottimore admitted that he had been at the Smith home to visit Justis' brother either Friday or Saturday. "I asked his brother Jefferson if he is going to the Culture Shock Show at Somerset Cricket Club. I never exchanged words with Justis, but I saw him."

Two days later, when police challenged them, Sean Smith and Tajmal

Webb also changed their stories. They were scared, Sean Smith said. Webb told police it was none of his business.

Both men admitted they knew Kirk Mundy, who, Sean Smith said, did not want to make eye contact when he stopped the night of Becky's murder. Furthermore, Sean Smith told police, "he (Mundy) had his hand out of one of his shirt sleeves, and the sleeve was over his shoulder so that part of his body was exposed." Seon Smith said he asked Mundy why a cloth was hanging over the license plate, and Mundy said because the bike wasn't licensed and insured.

"When they rode off, I said to Tajmal, 'Isn't it strange that they would put a cloth over the license plate knowing that they had to go across the causeway?' Webb agreed, 'Yea, that was stupid because there would be more of a chance to be pulled over by the police.' Then the next morning my mother called me and told me that there was an incident in St. George. She said that the incident was a rape and a murder, and it didn't click with me."

Meanwhile, Bermuda police waited another day after those identifications to arrest Mundy and Smith. Dave Middleton and Rick Meens wondered aloud whether police would have made any arrests whatsoever if Lottimore finally hadn't spoken up.

On July tenth, police had no trouble finding Justis Smith, as was his habit, loitering behind a church near his Deepdale Road residence. Despite his sullen glare, Smith got into the cruiser without objection. Police advised Smith that he was under arrest for the murder of Rebecca Middleton.

"Ya, I'm safe," he replied.

Kirk Mundy posed no problem either, reporting to the Somerset police station on schedule for his weekly visit, a condition of his bail. Detective Constable Peter Clarke asked whether he objected to providing a blood sample.

"None at all, Pops," Mundy replied.

Did he wish to make a statement?

"Sure."

Did he want a lawyer?

"It's cool."

Police took both to King Edward VII Memorial Hospital where Dr. Keith

Cunningham documented recent scratches on Smith's arm. Mundy, too, had wounds, but attributed them to his Sunday motorbike crash.

Justis Smith declined the offer of a lawyer, offering to tell "the whole story:" He and Mundy went to Moonglow, drank beers, left about three a.m., passed two men standing next to a broken down orange Toyota who said help was on its way, greeted a man in Flatts and rode back toward Hamilton with him. The other man left, he and Mundy sat outside Smith's house until his mother complained. He went inside. "That's it," said Smith.

Detective Inspector Carlton Adams repeated an offer of a lawyer.

"I don't think I need a lawyer, but, ya, I'll call him." Smith telephoned Archie Warner, a well known defense attorney who now practiced with Lois Browne Evans, who continued to express publicly her belief in Larry Tacklyn's innocence, nineteen years after Tacklyn's trip to the gallows. Elizabeth Christopher, another seasoned criminal attorney, joined Warner.

Back in Somerset, Mundy's story differed from Smith's. Mundy denied going to Moonglow the night of July second. He'd spent that night with his girlfriend, he said. He couldn't remember what he was wearing; there was nothing special about the night.

"Then what is it that stands out in your mind to remind you that you were at your girl's house all night on Tuesday, July second, 1996?" Inspector Peter Clarke asked.

"Because she is pregnant, so I spend most of the time with her."

"Do you know where Ferry Reach, in St. George's Parish, is located?"

"Of course."

"When last have you been to Ferry Reach?"

"I couldn't even recall."

"Did you go to Ferry Reach during the early morning of Wednesday July third, 1996?"

"No."

"So if another person told the police that they were with you in St. George on Tuesday night the second of July, 1996, what would you have to say about that?"

"Wrong person."

He arrived at Keasha's about eight p.m. on Tuesday, Mundy insisted. "Frankly, that's it." He recalled leaving Keasha's house sometime after lunch Wednesday, "cause her old man came home for lunch."

Meanwhile, Mundy's girlfriend, in another room, offered a different version. Keasha Smith told police she hadn't seen Mundy until the early hours of Wednesday. "I asked him where he had just come from, and he said from Moonglow, down St. George. I asked him who he went with, and he said Justis—that he was towing Justis." Keasha Smith described the clothes Mundy wore that night, "yellow and black long pants... a gauzy type... and a short sleeve net shirt (with) a lot of holes." She admitted the motorbike he drove and crash helmet were hers. "The helmet is not at my house now. I don't know where it is."

The following day Detective Inspector Stuart Crockwell and other officers accompanied Keasha to her house with a search warrant. Police found the helmet behind a chair.

Keasha denied that she had received jewelry from Mundy, other than an engagement ring in January, 1995, which she still wore. They planned to marry about two months prior, but "I cancelled because I seriously thought about it and decided I wasn't ready."

When Mundy heard Keasha's version, he appeared unperturbed. "Must have been if she is saying that's the time I got there. Oh yes, yes, yes, yes, because that's the night I saw those guys broke down in a car there?"

Perhaps just in time, Mundy's lawyer Mark Pettingill arrived, halting questioning.

Police waited outside while Pettingill, a partner with Mundy's bail lawyer, Richard Hector, warned Mundy that if he'd left DNA evidence, police would know he was lying. Mundy smoked a pack of cigarettes while he gave Pettingill his revised version of what went down the night of Becky's murder.

"Will that work?" he asked Pettingill. Then Mundy went to the bathroom.

When he returned, with Pettingill by his side, Mundy told police he wanted to tell them "everything." He had taken Rebecca Middleton to Ferry Reach, Mundy admitted, but he had nothing to do with sexually assaulting Becky or her murder. Justis Smith, he said, was the culprit. In fact, Mundy promised he'd show police the murder weapon and testify against Smith.

The next day Mundy led police to the swing bridge to a knife that he said Smith had tossed as the pair fled St. George. A police diver found it right where Mundy said it would be.

Two months later, in late September, armed with a search warrant, police found three steak knives in a kitchen drawer at the home of Justis Smith—in a box with one knife missing.

"I bought those steak knives a long time ago. I believe in the States, but I can't be too sure," Justis Smith's mother, Barbara Smith, told police.

Kirk Mundy had told her that he and Justis went to Moonglow that night, Justis Smith's mother admitted. "Afterwards, when I heard the news of the girl's murder in St. George, that's the Canadian girl who was killed. I asked them if they had seen anything, and they said 'no.'"

She said she "just left it at that." Sometime after four a.m. she heard them "talking loudly, and I said something to them about it being late." She denied reports that she'd found bloodstained clothing. "Justis never talked to me about the murder." Nor, she claimed, had she ever asked him about it.

Carrying the knives out of the house, police thought they looked suspiciously like the one divers pulled from the water beneath the swing bridge. Police were relieved.

By now the kidnap, rape, torture, and murder of young Rebecca Middleton had caused international angst. It seemed Bermuda would put this murder to rest.

Two days after Becky's murder, standing beneath the casuarinas under which Becky died, LeYoni Junos believed she felt Becky's presence. She touched the tree closest to the road, covered with flowers, a Canadian flag, teddy bears, and messages. LeYoni made the murdered child a promise she intended to keep.

So when she read of Kirk Mundy's and Justis Smith's arrests in the murder of Rebecca Middleton, LeYoni felt no relief, only conflict. With murder still a hanging offense in Bermuda, she disagreed with Amnesty's opposition of capital punishment.

"When I heard on the radio that they found this girl's body in Ferry Reach, I knew immediately, my gut went back to that experience in Blue Hole the night Rebecca Middleton and Jasmine Meens went to St. George…I had a professional responsibility, but it also went back to that experience in the park."

LeYoni called a meeting of Amnesty's board of directors. Becky's had been a vicious murder, she reminded, a classic human rights violation that shocked her on many levels. It had happened in LeYoni's home, not something she could or would ignore. In the case of such a brutal rape and murder, as well as torture, LeYoni believed that if the men were found guilty, the punishment fit the crime.

LeYoni told Amnesty board members that she recognized how important the organization's fight against the death penalty had been. "But, I said, 'This week of murder has really had an effect on me, and I wouldn't feel comfortable—I didn't know who did it—but I would not feel comfortable fighting for the life of the individual who killed this girl…I feel a pull for the victim's rights, and I couldn't march down the street…I wouldn't interfere if they got the death penalty.'" She would step down as Amnesty's director, she said.

Board members asked LeYoni not to resign. "They said that it was 'a democratic organization, and things are voted on.'" So LeYoni stayed on.

"They recommended that I watch this movie that was playing at the theater (*Dead Man Walking*). Actually, I went, and I watched…but it truly confirmed my beliefs…I thought, 'If this boy hadn't received the death penalty, he would have lived on as an ass hole—not admitting what he'd done!' Because he knew he was going to die for it, it played on his mind so much that eventually he confessed, and I think he died a better individual—at heart. So that didn't help me change my mind."

With her glowing smile, dreads to her waist, and tiny nose ring, LeYoni Junos was remarkably unforgettable. And because others didn't forget her either, she got her comeuppance when she did the unthinkable.

LeYoni Junos failed to "lie in the tide."

NINE

...For the half million tourists who go to Bermuda on holiday each year, the island is an expensive paradise with magnificent beaches, narrow winding roads, and Technicolor flowers....Bermuda's sleepy atmosphere is deceptive...in the past five years there have been two major outbursts of rioting, plus a number of unexplained violent crimes....

The Guardian--March 12, 1973.

Another Nail on Becky's Coffin
July 12, 1996

KIRK MUNDY'S ATTORNEY Mark Pettingill approached two of the lead officers investigating the Rebecca Middleton murder, leaving serious crime headquarters. It was just after 5 p.m.

Pettingill told Detective Superintendent Vic Richmond and Inspector Stuart Crockwell that Kirk Mundy's role "in the Rebecca Middleton matter...amounted to nothing more than being an accessory after the fact." Furthermore, his client would give evidence against the person who he accused of killing Becky, Justis Smith. Kirk Mundy, Pettingill promised, would "wear a wire" and get Smith's confession.

Richmond told Pettingill that he was on his way to meet Attorney General Elliott Mottley and others for a meeting about Becky's case. Richmond assured Mundy's lawyer that he would pass on that message.

On Saturday morning July thirteenth, viewers packed Magistrate's Court where police brought Justis Smith and Kirk Mundy in separate, unmarked cars. Outside a crowd gathered behind the gates.

As Mundy's lawyer headed into court, Crockwell handed him a pink charge slip. "You got what you wanted," Crockwell told Mark Pettingill.

Smith looked down, scratching an arm as he heard the judge state the charge against him, premeditated murder.

Mundy, hanging onto a walking stick, blaming that Sunday bike accident, heard his charge…"well knowing that Justis Smith had murdered Rebecca Middleton did receive, relieve or assist Justis Smith." Accessory after the fact to Smith's charge of premeditated murder. Unlike Smith, Mundy had escaped a murder charge, only a minor scrape.

As police led them out, Justis Smith hid his face behind a white towel, Mundy wore a baseball cap and his viper sun glasses.

"You could have knocked me over with a feather," Mark Pettingill said.

Only hours later, Bermuda's Senior Crown Counsel Brian Calhoun, who had offered assurances Dave and Cindy at Bermuda's airport when they flew Becky's body back to Canada a week before, switched on his mother's television in Toronto to hear a newscaster announce that only one of the two men arrested for the crimes against Rebecca Middleton had been charged with murder. Moreover, neither had been charged with sexual crimes. Calhoun was enraged. Unbelievable. He'd expected both men to be charged and tried together. Let the jury decide.

Few doubted the influence of Crown Counsel Khamisi Tokunbo, a protégé of Lois Browne Evans. Bright, motivated, professionally respected, and Bermudian--significant on this tiny island where space is an important commodity and many locals worry that foreigners will consume their jobs.

Some locals identify Tokunbo both by his birth name, Calvin Simmons, and by his African name, which he chose when he became an adult. Khamisi, he told the *Bermuda Sun*, means Thursday in Swahili, and Tokunbo, "one who is born overseas." His middle name, Mawuli: "there is a god."

Tokunbo began his career as a public works mechanic, left for the U.S. to complete an economics degree, then onto London for law. After a brief stint in private practice, including a year with the lawyer who got Mundy's bail, Richard Hector. Tokunbo joined the attorney general's chambers. Just months before Becky's murder, Tokunbo had successfully prosecuted a killing in which a lesser sentence was given to one man in return for his testimony against an alleged accomplice.

With cane for support, Mundy arrives at Magistrate's Court
Photo Courtesy of the Royal Gazettete

Word inside the attorney general's chambers was that Tokunbo had agreed with his boss, Attorney General Elliott Mottley that this was the way to go in the murder of Rebecca Middleton. Give up one to get the other. Police didn't object, at least not loudly enough to make a difference.

In early September, with Mundy and Smith back in court, Mottley admitted in Supreme Court the RCMP had not yet returned DNA results. But, the attorney general publicly announced, he was ready to proceed without awaiting the results. Next, Senior Crown Counsel Brian Calhoun announced the date for a Magistrate's preliminary review in the case against Justis Smith, October twenty first. Kirk Mundy would appear in Supreme Court on that same date.

In Belleville, Dave Middleton marked his calendar and booked airline tickets for himself and his younger son, Mark, who agreed to go with him.

Facing murder charge, Smith hides his head beneath a towel
Photo Courtesy of the Royal Gazette

But to the surprise of almost everyone, Kirk Mundy made an unexpected earlier trip.

On the sixteenth of October, 1996, Rick Meens answered his shop telephone to hear lead investigator Vic Richmond instruct him to go to Supreme Court right away--Mundy would plead guilty to the charge of being an accomplice, not murder.

Richmond told Meens, "Smith did it."

Rick Meens didn't believe that Justis Smith acted alone, and he told Vic Richmond so. "No one I know believed Mundy didn't do it, either," Meens argued. Jasmine's father had twenty minutes to get to court.

He'd been in shock after Becky's murder. For months, Rick Meens sat alone in parks, depressed and blaming himself. One could hardly be shocked that both he and Becky's family would miss media reports that only Smith had been charged with murder, with Mundy no more than an accomplice.

Moreover, those holding charges could have been changed at any time—until Mundy went to trial.

When Rick Meens arrived at Supreme Court, proceedings already had started. Khamisi Tokunbo was reporting "the agreed facts," while Mundy looked on. Sickening details, Mundy's lies regarding his whereabouts the night of Becky's death. Somewhere Meens heard, "consensual sex." Becky "fondled and played with his private parts and whispered in his ear…she wanted to have sex with him." Smith was the murderer, Tokunbo quoted Mundy. His fear of Smith was Mundy's explanation for his early insistence that he was with Keasha the night of Becky's murder. Mundy, after all, had assisted police, Tokunbo reminded.

Powerless, Rick Meens listened to lawyers and the judge banter over Mundy's sentence. Tokunbo recommended only three to four years.

"I'm sorry," Mundy uttered from the cage.

Bermuda's Chief Justice Austin Ward, terming the crime a "gruesome murder," accepted the accomplice argument. Mundy's conviction made him eligible for seven years in prison. Ward gave Mundy five. If Mundy cooperated by testifying, Ward reminded, he could apply to have his prison time reduced.

Rick Meens looked around the silent courtroom. "I couldn't say a thing." He rushed to telephone Dave Middleton, who had just gotten off the phone with Vic Richmond.

"He (Richmond) told me this was the way to go," Dave told Rick. "That way they'd give up one to get the other."

No one had told Rick Meens or the Middletons that Attorney General Elliott Mottley began rushing the paperwork on the eleventh of October, and the court indicted him on the fourteenth to rush Mundy to court on October sixteenth.

Why would a judge approve an arrangement based on such a bizarre tale of consensual sex?

And why would no one mention Mundy's stepped up court date, especially given its international implications, to Bermuda Police Commissioner Colin Coxall or Governor Lord David Waddington?

To Mark Middleton's horror five days later, Becky's brother found himself waiting outside a small courtroom, standing right next to Justis Smith.

Smith's small frame astonished Mark. No doubt Becky would have given him a fight. Revulsion, disgust. This was his first and last trip to Bermuda, Mark Middleton promised himself.

To Dave's surprise, Smith's lawyers waived a Magistrate's Court preliminary hearing, a normal procedure, but Bermuda officials hadn't kept the family apprised of what to expect.

With Senior Crown Counsel Brian Calhoun prosecuting, Justis Smith stood silently as a judge formally charged him with Becky's murder, finished in what seemed to Dave and Mark Middleton only seconds.

Suddenly Smith shouted from the cage. "Kirk Mundy is a liar and a coward. It is he who stabbed the girl and he who raped her. Now he and the police are trying to frame me for it, and that's not right."

Brian Calhoun found Smith's words startling. Usually the accused are silent, he thought. He'd never bought Mundy's story, and Justis Smith's words supported Calhoun's view that one man alone could not have done all that was done to Becky.

However, by December third, Calhoun would be off Smith's case, in intensive care following two heart attacks, rushed overseas by medical transport for bypass surgery. Justis Smith defense lawyer Archie Warner's heart attack followed soon afterward. Some who found themselves amusing suggested Justis Smith's court case would better be managed at Johns Hopkins in Baltimore.

Meanwhile, Mundy had escaped murder charges, leaving Justis Smith alone to stand trial for premeditated murder.

It seemed that a second nail had appeared on Becky's coffin.

PART FOUR
THE 'MOST CURIOUS' OF EVENTS

TEN

...For years, tranquil and gentle...dotted with women in fine muslin clothes, businessmen in knee-cap hugging Bermuda shorts and elegant visitors from the ships in the harbor in their naval whites. Nothing, it seemed, could disturb the order of things...But... the young black population of the island has been subjected to the propaganda and influence of Black Power politicians, both from within and outside the island...Never again can life here seem like one long garden party...

Daily Express-- March 12, 1973

Bad News, Worse News
October 18, 1996

"SEMEN ONLY IN the vagina? Only Mundy's? What are you telling me?" Scenes of Crime's lead inspector Howard Cutts shouted at the voice that had dropped the bombshell.

When Cutts heard the news confirmed on October eighteenth, two days after Kirk Mundy's plea, he was too horrified to speak. "I'll have to call back." He sat frozen in his chair for nearly twenty minutes before he could dial the phone. The faxed report a few minutes later confirmed the RCMP's findings—no DNA from Justis Smith.

Police had expected to find semen from both Mundy and Smith, among the reasons police and the attorney general had been confident in charging

Mundy as an accomplice. Use Mundy to get Smith. Now with only DNA evidence from Mundy, and Justis Smith charged as the principle killer, officials believed they had an overwhelming problem.

Government Analyst Kevin Leask wrote in a 2004 email: "This whole debate seems to have arisen from overconfidence in a tentative result." From samples gathered at autopsy, Leask had conducted "preliminary testing" on oral, vaginal and anal swabs, reporting semen in all orifices. But soon afterward, Leask discovered that his supplies were outdated. A repeat study using supplies from the hospital lab, he said, showed "yeast cells, which are similar in size. With good staining solutions, (yeast cells) turn a different color than spermatozoa, but they had appeared the same with the old stains I had on hand." By August sixteenth, he said, he had reported to police that there were problems with the evidence.

However, finding a particular person's DNA doesn't necessarily mean that person committed the crime; not finding a particular person's DNA doesn't necessarily mean he didn't... But police panicked.

DNA results, without Smith, surprised police far more than the findings did Mundy, who reminded officers that he had admitted having sex, and his condom might have broken. Police did flabbergast Mundy, though, when they told him that forensic evidence showed the knife police recovered from beneath the swing bridge couldn't be the murder weapon, a conclusion based on Dr. James Johnston's speculation during a casual conversation with Scenes of Crime lead investigator Howard Cutts-- incorrect, other experts would testify-- that Becky's wounds didn't match the blade size.

"Kirk Mundy even gave them the knife," Mark Pettingill recalled, "and now police didn't believe they had it."

While police pondered their dilemma, unsuspecting media reported that "Mundy, a Jamaican national, is expected to be a key witness against Smith." However, with no DNA from Justis Smith, police and the attorney general now worried their plan had fallen apart.

Behind the scenes, Senior Crown Counsel Brian Calhoun, who recalled losing more than a few nights' sleep over the way the Rebecca Middleton case appeared to be going, later told his colleagues that he feared that he had come close to losing his job. Attorney General Elliott Mottley reportedly termed Calhoun's behavior insubordinate if he refused to prosecute Kirk Mundy as an accomplice after the fact to Becky's murder. From the start, Calhoun argued that both men should be prosecuted together, let the jury decide, he maintained.

Lawyers in the attorney general's office, also afraid of losing their work permits, reportedly stood silently by while Calhoun challenged the attorney general. Calhoun knew that if he were fired he'd be entitled to a hearing before a public review board, where his objection to charging Mundy only as accessory would become public, something Calhoun believed Attorney General Elliott Mottley most certainly didn't wish. The Rebecca Middleton murder was making international headlines and had to be handled quietly.

Mottley reportedly backed down, ordering Calhoun to take Justis Smith's case to Magistrate's Court for preliminary hearing. Instead, Mottley assigned Khamisi Tokunbo to prosecute Mundy.

Later Mottley would claim otherwise. He recalled first hearing the "theory" that two men were involved only six months after the murder, when he met with police. Even then, said Mottley, the view that two men were involved was merely speculation.

Police Commissioner Colin Coxall first heard of Mundy's plea during his routine weekly meeting with Governor Lord David Waddington. Now with a drug war, malcontent officers, and service reorganization on his plate, and with Becky's case obviously going awry, Coxall summoned his officers.

They had argued with Elliott Mottley and Khamisi Tokunbo, Lead Detective Superintendent Vic Richmond insisted. But Mottley and Tokunbo, Richmond said, refused to budge.

Officers later admitted privately they failed to go to Colin Coxall, one claiming fear of Elliott Mottley, others of Coxall. Those of foreign origin, of course, panicked that their work permits would be pulled.

During the first of three meetings between Coxall's and Mottley's teams, several months after Becky's murder, police for the first time handed murder photos to Senior Crown Counsel Brian Calhoun. "This girl was held down! No way that the tiny mark on each hand counted as defense wounds." Calhoun slammed the table, leaping to his feet. "If her hands had been free, they would have been cut to shreds fighting off the knife. That's a forensic fact. This is a classic two-man murder."

The police commissioner agreed. Until now, Calhoun had found himself the lone member of the attorney general's team insisting two men viciously murdered Becky. Mottley and Tokunbo continued to argue evidence that two men participated was insufficient. Junior attorneys, along with police, inside and outside of those meetings, tread lightly, fearful of repercussions.

During a second meeting, Coxall reached Miami-Dade forensic expert Dr. Valerie Rao by speakerphone. Both Coxall and Calhoun erroneously had assumed Rao had been called immediately after Becky's murder. When Coxall learned that she had not, he sent scene photos and reports to her.

Rao agreed that two men likely murdered Becky. If she were called, she would testify to that effect, Rao told the meeting.

Rao's statement didn't sit well with Mottley, who, along with Tokunbo, insisted there was no proof that both men killed Becky. Put your statement in writing, Mottley told Rao.

Attorney General Elliott Mottley (left) and Police Commissioner Colin Coxall faced off behind closed doors.
Photos Courtesy of the Royal Gazette

Rao preferred to testify in person.

Not good enough, said Mottley.

Richmond, Cutts, Tokunbo and Calhoun sat quietly as Coxall and Mottley adjourned to another room. Next, loud noises, banging on furniture, shouting.

Finally, after a third meeting, Mottley backed down. He agreed to charge both Smith and Mundy jointly with murder. But the horse had departed the barn many months ago—well before anyone closed the doors.

"Like Teflon," one police officer said, "nothing seems to stick to Mundy." This time, Kirk Orlando Mundy's luck didn't hold. One year and two weeks after Becky's murder, July seventeenth, 1997, Mundy appeared in Bermuda Supreme Court to answer charges for that November, 1995, armed robbery for which he was on bail when he and Justis Smith drove off with Becky.

Today Mundy faced Senior Crown Counsel Brian Calhoun, who wasn't impressed when Mundy again offered to testify against his accomplice.

Just like in Becky's murder, Mundy had fled from the scene on a motorbike with his accomplice. This time, they'd made off with some forty thousand dollars after pointing fake guns at security van drivers, one of whom, it turned out, was in on the plot. Phony weapons or not, Mundy had committed armed robbery.

"There is a very serious problem in this country with armed robbery. It's growing in intensity, it's growing in frequency," Calhoun told Supreme Court Chief Justice Austin Ward, the same judge who sentenced Mundy the year before. "An example must be set."

Mundy received sixteen years for armed robbery, added to the five years he earned as "accomplice" to the murder of Rebecca Middleton. Crown Counsel Brian Calhoun felt weak relief. Kirk Mundy would be off the streets for twenty one years—or less, given Bermuda's propensity for early release.

Two weeks before Mundy's armed robbery sentencing, Becky's family quietly observed the first anniversary of her death. A poem appeared in the Centennial High School yearbook, the one that should have held Becky's graduation photograph. Written by Becky's friend, Diana Jericevic, *A Requiem* celebrated Becky's life but remembered the pain, "to us who lost a friend."

In Bermuda, Diana Casling, who had worked at the *Royal Gazette* during the summer that Becky was killed, now an attorney, led a rally on the steps of City Hall, called "Day Against Violence," with poetry readings, personal testimonies, and speeches by Premier Pamela Gordon, Opposition Leader Jennifer Smith, and Hamilton's mayor. Sponsors sold tee shirts, different colors representing rape, incest, domestic assault, and murder.

Hundreds visited Ferry Reach, placing more teddy bears, flowers, cards and a new Canadian flag upon the two casuarinas under which Becky was murdered.

Meanwhile, Bermuda Police Commissioner Colin Coxall had made so many enemies among Bermuda's criminals that guards carrying semi-automatic weapons protected Coxall and his family round-the-clock to prevent his meeting a fate similar to that of murdered Police Commissioner George Duckett.

However, it wouldn't be violence that took Bermuda Police Commissioner Colin Coxall down.

Another July with drug traffickers gathered in their usual corners during searing afternoons and humid nights, soon to get a bombshell.

ELEVEN

"Would not the best tribute that we could pay to our late colleague the Governor of Bermuda and his ADC, who died with him, to institute in Bermuda a really tough regime from the security point of view?...Would it not also be in the interests of the people of Bermuda as a whole...so that the tourist traffic, on which they depend so much, should not be scared away?"

Rear Admiral Morgan- Giles to Britain's Parliament
--March 15, 1973

'Operation Cleansweep'
July 7, 1997

BERMUDA POLICE COMMISSIONER Colin Coxall waited until the night before his major drug bust took place to brief Bermuda Premier Pamela Gordon and Home Affairs Minister Quinton Edness. First a street attack, *Operation Cleensweep,* then, immediately after dealers were off the streets, a top-down attack on the illicit narcotics infrastructure.

Much to the surprise of Premier Pamela Gordon, in office only a short time, her cabinet, senior police officers, and just about everyone else, U.S. drug enforcement officials had, without their knowledge, been conducting surveillance. The operation to attack street drug sales had taken about four months to plan and carry out. Safety of DEA agents was paramount, secrecy vital. On such a small island just one leak could mean disaster.

The day after the briefing, on July seventh, 1997, plain clothes DEA officers came down on the drug dealers. Within a few days, accused street sellers packed Westgate Prison.

Attorney General Elliott Mottley endorsed the operation. Handling all of the prosecutions, Senior Crown Counsel Brian Calhoun accomplished a record number of convictions for street drug sales. Traffickers were off the streets, media and the public alike were more than pleased. A few worried that arrests would crowd the prison. The new governor, Thorold Masefield, approached Coxall about extending his three-year contract, set to end in 1998. Coxall agreed to stay. Bermuda's new police commissioner had impressed more than a few in Bermuda.

When Colin Coxall arrived in April, 1995, he found police still recording interviews in longhand, buildings falling apart, a criminal intelligence system sadly lacking organization and equipment, and only six or so officers out on the street, with five times that number behind desks.

Preliminary to Coxall's appointment, in 1994, with Bermuda's drugs problems and violence escalating, the FCO commissioned its inspector general, Lionel Grundy, to work with Governor Lord David Waddington, who had served as Home Secretary in Prime Minister Margaret Thatcher's government, to correct the situation. Grundy reported police "incompetence, waste, and apathy and a burgeoning drug business." He and Lord Waddington agreed that violence, drugs, and gaps in money laws threatened Bermuda's standing as a leading financial center. Bermuda's second industry, tourism, also was declining.

Reminiscent of Bermuda's murdered Police Commissioner George Duckett, who handled violence head on, Colin Coxall came with credentials previously unheard of in Bermuda police: eleven years managing London's police force as deputy commissioner and acting commissioner; a former Scotland Yard detective chief superintendent, leading a reorganization of more than forty thousand officers; assigned to inspect forces in Singapore, Malaysia, Hong Kong, Amsterdam and other countries in Europe. By Coxall's second year in Bermuda, the island's crime had been reduced some forty percent.

Some in Bermuda, though, when they heard of Coxall's appointment, interpreted hiring a white commissioner and his new deputy, Michael Mylod, former assistant chief constable of Hampshire, England, as an example of black disenfranchisement. PLP leaders carried a five thousand-signature petition to Lord Waddington. "It appears from his behavior pattern that the governor despises Bermudians," the *Royal Gazette* quoted one community member, Stanley Morton. The PLP proposed that the governor's $126,000 salary be reduced to one dollar, a move that didn't pass. Waddington replied that he had the greatest respect for Bermudians. "I also have the greatest respect for decisions taken by a democratically-elected government."

Coxall, as was his style, ignored politics and set about reorganizing police, calling immediately for DNA, fiber testing, photography, drug analysis, arson, ballistics, soil analysis, and forensic entomology (using insects to time death) analyses—until now foreign to the small island. Because drugs made their way to Bermuda by cruise ships or yachts, Coxall called for policing at sea. The island's tourism and financial industries were "too competitive to risk lack of confidence in the ability of Bermuda to provide a safe, peaceful environment," Coxall warned.

A tourist stabbing during a robbery near a hotel resulted in officers and reserves moved out from behind desks to the beat. With a top heavy force-- redundancies set protests into motion.

Within three months of his 1995 arrival, Coxall had released a service strategy that UBP Environment Minister John Irving Pearman termed "refreshing." Later, however, Pearman would find Coxall's diligence highly disconcerting.

At the same time that he chose Colin Coxall to lead police, Governor Lord Waddington seconded Elliott Mottley, Q.C., a criminal lawyer from Barbados, to serve as Bermuda's attorney general. Open murder cases had filled Bermuda's books for several decades, prosecution rates abysmal. Mottley promised the governor that he would personally prosecute all murder cases.

Black and from the Caribbean, Mottley's appointment caused little furor—unlike that of the white officers from the United Kingdom, which to some Bermudians represented hated "neo-colonialism." Attorney General Elliott Mottley's service appeared free of controversy—until the murder of Rebecca Middleton.

Despite Becky's murder causing serious international damage to Bermuda's touted reputation for safe travel, it seemed that with Colin Coxall in place and Elliott Mottley keeping his promise to prosecute all murders, residents and visitors alike felt safer. A decline in violence, the *Royal Gazette* suggested, "seems to us to stem from a very simple fact--the public now knows that the police service means business." Or so it seemed—until those events the newspaper termed among "the most curious...in Bermuda's political history."

Bizarre complications from the bust. Police found some fifty checks in the hands of known drug users, allegedly signed by UBP Minister John Irving Pearman, one of the Bermuda's most powerful politicians, a former deputy premier, tourism, youth and sports, and home affairs and labor minister, who also headed company boards and at one time the Employers' Council. He had served on the Royal Pitt Commission, investigating the cause of the 1977 riots. Now police put under surveillance the minister who not long before had praised Coxall's service.

Four days after Coxall's Cleansweep success, the police commissioner met with Governor Masefield to alert him of the allegations involving Pearman. Masefield told Coxall that he would make Premier Pamela Gordon aware.

Coxall handed Masefield a confidential report, which was passed on to the premier. Much to Coxall's shock, Pearman or his lawyers received a copy of the report.

In a move that astounded police and politicians, Pearman reacted by going public in the *Bermuda Sun*, saying that police were investigating him in a "sex and drugs" allegation. Coxall, Pearman charged, had conspired to destroy him. Pearman threatened to resign from the UBP and sit as an independent if Coxall were not sent packing, a move that could very well bring about an early general election and, with it, loss of government control.

Premier Pamela Gordon immediately called a press conference, saying Irving Pearman had her full support. Home Affairs Minister Quinton Edness, overseas at the time, made a public statement upon his return, standing behind Colin Coxall and setting up battle lines.

By early August, the Pearman affair had split the UBP Cabinet. Gordon watched the PLP gaining momentum. The last thing the UBP wanted was an early election. Unity was imperative.

Two weeks later, in what the *Royal Gazette* termed a strange public demonstration, the home affairs minister changed his stance. Quinton Edness and Coxall met at the Monte Carlo restaurant near Hamilton City Hall, once a favorite lunchtime gathering spot, with tables so close that they allowed for few private conversations. Edness raised the matter of a succession plan. When Coxall suggested that several years would be required to prepare a Bermudian to take the police commissioner helm--certainly not news to Bermuda--Edness stormed out, terming the lunch a turning point in his relationship with Coxall. Some believed that Edness engineered the argument to explain his change of mind.

For whatever reason, the end of Edness' support meant the end for Colin Coxall's service to Bermuda. Four hours later, Governor Thorold Masefield summoned Coxall to his office, saying that Edness demanded his immediate dismissal "for refusing to draft a succession plan." Stunned, Coxall refused.

The next day, Deputy Governor Peter Willis told Coxall to be off the island in forty-eight hours—a move that is not unique in Bermuda when foreign workers meet with bureaucratic disfavor.

At his lawyer's recommendation, Coxall rushed a letter to Edness apologizing for any offense he may have caused, along with a quickly-drafted plan of succession. No response. Governor Masefield extended the deadline for Coxall's resignation by one week. Coxall gave up his job. Only with legal help did he manage to stay until October to wrap up his business.

The UBP's decision to close ranks in support of Pearman and to force Coxall to resign didn't end well. Media reported "jitters."

"People are convinced that Colin Coxall was a large part of the solution for Bermuda… despite his huge successes, he was pushed out of Bermuda for purely political reasons," a *Royal Gazette* editorial suggested. "Because there are unanswered questions, many Bermudians and many in the international company sector no longer believe Bermuda is governed in an upright and straight forward manner. As we understand it, those in the tourist business fear future offenses against visitors, and those with offshore companies are already being approached by other jurisdictions who are pointing out Bermuda's failures."

When Coxall left, artist Peter Woolcock's *Royal Gazette* editorial page cartoon showed a swarm of rats celebrating his exit.

Letters of complaint followed. "Well, once again, the drug dealers are out on the roads--same faces and a few new young ones. If I can see them why can't the police? Not only do they sell drugs, which I have seen for myself, but they litter as they sit or stand all day long. Political parties should work with the police, not against them. What a joke all this has been...."

Governor Masefield squirmed, issuing a statement that Coxall's dismissal had nothing to do with the Pearman affair or the drugs crack down; rather, government had lost faith in Coxall.

The *Mid Ocean News,* an aggressive twice-weekly, argued that Coxall's resignation indeed was forced by Operation Cleansweep, not because of any "erosion of confidence in his abilities." Governor Lord Waddington and former Premier Dr. David Saul publicly supported Coxall's work. "I personally think he was a very fine commissioner. Bermuda recruited a first class officer," Saul said.

Reportedly Governor Thorold Masefield was called to London and castigated. Pearman, never charged, insisted checks were for work done around his house. Pearman died a decade later, never again serving in Parliament, and with the PLP now in charge.

Coxall's only fault, said community leader William M. Cox, "was that he thought the government was serious in saying it wanted a war against crime."

"If achievement is any yardstick," *Royal Gazette* editors wrote, "then his thorough overhaul of a police service in just two years must surely count among the most impressive fetes ever seen in an island where indolence and inertia are the police service's chief characteristics."

Had Coxall been allowed to continue his work, many believed that Bermuda would by now almost certainly be relatively drug free, a hope that Coxall once held for the picturesque island.

Coxall's Christmas mail tells him that it is not.

With Coxall's departure, Jean Jacques LeMay, a Canadian who had replaced Michael Mylod as deputy commissioner, suddenly found himself commissioner. He hadn't been in Bermuda when Becky's murder happened a year earlier. With crime on a major upswing, he had a full plate.

LeMay told the media that recruitment drives, despite insistence that police matters could be managed by locals alone, had failed. He would immediately begin overseas recruitment. PLP Home Minister Paula Cox termed LeMay's statements "extraordinary" and "discourteous to the government." At the same time, from the Foreign and Commonwealth Office, police inspector

Lionel Grundy predicted that, given the benign neglect police suffered for decades, it would take six to ten years to bring Bermudian officers up to internationally recognized standards.

Meanwhile, packing to leave Bermuda, Coxall didn't forget the brutal Rebecca Middleton murder. Coxall contacted his long-time associate, famed criminalist Dr. Henry Lee, with whom he had worked to set up forensic contracts, asking him to investigate blood spatter evidence in Becky's case. Dr. Lee suggested to Coxall that police also contact forensic pathologist Dr. Michael Baden.

Not long after television cameras caught Coxall holding an umbrella on a rainy October night, boarding British Airways for his return trip to England, Inspector Norrell Hull, an officer from the West Indies assigned to Becky's case from the start, headed to an overseas conference conducted by Baden. Hull had instructions to accomplish more than note taking.

During a quick break Hull detailed Becky's case to the famed forensic pathologist who was known for his work with the Lindbergh kidnapping, John Kennedy's assassination, the Jon Binet Ramsey murder, and hundreds of other major cases. Baden was intrigued. He agreed to review Becky's case.

By Christmas, 1997, the second holiday season for the Middleton family without Becky, two top U.S. forensic scientists now had joined Miami Dade forensic expert Dr. Valerie Rao, whose DNA analysis in 1997 duplicated the RCMP findings—no DNA from Justis Smith. By far, not the only evidence against the pair, all three agreed.

Another bombshell a month later in the Rebecca Middleton murder case—a result of those three meetings between the now departed from Bermuda police commissioner, the attorney general, and their men.

Kirk Mundy, missing his viper shades and wearing his orange prison uniform, to the surprise of most everyone, arrived on January ninth, 1998, under police escort to Supreme Court. In the cage next to Mundy stood Justis Smith, still in remand at the boys' detention center.

The attorney general had filed a new indictment against both Kirk Mundy and Justis Smith—a joint charge of murder.

Privately, the move was not without conflict in the attorney general's office. Sources inside the chambers whispered that Senior Crown Counsel

Brian Calhoun refused to file the indictment, claiming he had argued that he couldn't, in good faith, sign the document.

Mottley swore the affidavit claiming that "new" forensic evidence from Drs. Valerie Rao, Henry Lee, and Michael Baden showed non-consensual sex, that Becky had been carried to the street, and that two men were involved.

To say now that new evidence was the reason for filing joint charges? A misrepresentation of the truth?

"I was hopeful that Mundy would volunteer to be a witness…against Justis Smith," Mottley told the media. "To do so would operate to his benefit when being sentenced for the crime of being accessory after the fact." Never, Mottley would say, would he have "countenanced an arrangement" to promise no new charges.

Now the lawyer who thought he'd gotten Kirk Mundy off the hook in 1996, Mark Pettingill, rushed back to court, arguing that the new murder charge was an abuse of process. "Two separate charges can't be produced on the same defendant and incident." He warned the charge could serve as an "international embarrassment" for Mottley.

Because Pettingill would have to testify in Mundy's appeal to halt the murder charge, Pettingill handed the case to his colleague, former Bermuda Attorney General Saul Froomkin. That Froomkin, Canada's "honorary consulate," accepted Mundy's case took some Canadians by surprise, including Dave Middleton, who had been concerned that Becky's country had done little to support efforts for justice.

Then another new face, Solicitor General William (Bill) Pearce, fresh from Vancouver, Canada, who Mottley had selected from ninety applicants for the job, found himself mired in the Rebecca Middleton murder prosecution, urging that Bermuda not let a suspected murderer get away. No deal had been struck, Pearce insisted. Impossible--because evidence showed Mundy had lied. Thus, how could Mundy possibly be called to give evidence against Justis Smith?

"…Right-thinking people here and abroad would be shocked to think that Bermuda's justice system failed to bring Mundy to trial and virtually allowed him to get away with murder by his deception," Pearce argued.

Mundy's new attorney, Saul Froomkin, though, argued that Mundy had been given an irreversible deal in 1996. "Unless my lord can find credible evidence that Mr. Mundy lied…"

Perhaps the judge recognized exactly that? Bermuda Supreme Court Justice Richard Ground confirmed on February sixth, 1998, murder charges would stick,

However, the Middletons' hopes would be short lived.

Double jeopardy, said Bermuda's Court of Appeals six weeks later when members threw out the joint case. Mundy, as accomplice, had been accused of assisting Smith, charged with premeditated murder.

*Kirk Mundy makes a suprise return, this time charged with murder.
Photo Courtesy of the Royal Gazette*

*Justis Smith still in remand at the boy's detention center.
Photo Courtesy of the Royal Gazette*

How could an accomplice to murder later be charged with murder?

Back in the attorney general's chambers, Senior Crown Counsel Brian Calhoun reportedly warned not to appeal. If the attorney general took Mundy's case to the Privy Council--and if this highest court agreed with the Appeals Court that a murder charge against Mundy amounted to double jeopardy--Mundy would have anointed protection from murder charges. Alternatively, if they sat tight with Mundy for a while, leaving the option for appeal open, Mundy wouldn't be home free.

But the attorney general's office began preparing for its appeal to the Privy Council. When the document reached Bill Pearce, the new solicitor general complained that it was weak and failed to address major points. At least, Pearce offered, allow him to present the appeal to the Privy Council.

Mottley refused, according to Pearce, assigning the job to a junior lawyer.

On the sixth of July, 1998, two years and three days after Becky's slaughter, Kirk Mundy received his free pass. London's Privy Council refused even to hear the case.

Now Mundy could testify in the Justis Smith trial, take the rap, and go unpunished, protected by double jeopardy rules, rumored to be a Smith defense ploy.

When Dave Middleton heard Privy Council's decision he told the *Royal Gazette* that he was "sick and tired of people trying to get away with murder. If justice was not done, the whole island has to live with the tragedy. What we have here is a teenage girl who has been raped and murdered. And you have two characters, who, with the help of their lawyers, are doing a pretty good job of trying to squirm their way out of it…I'm very disappointed. I think Mundy should be tried for murder, he was very much involved. The bottom line is that my girl was murdered. I think there are only two suspects here, and these two seem to have been nailed down. There's no evidence that anybody else was involved. When it gets to trial," Dave Middleton predicted, "the evidence will speak for itself."

Most thought the evidence did exactly that.

PART FIVE
The Queen -v- Justis Raham Smith

TWELVE

The habit of drift onto the streets...accounts for the group... designated the "Court Street boys"...They come...from anywhere in the back of town areas and by reason of the prevailing mobility (almost everyone over 16 owns an auxiliary cycle...or some other means of transport) from elsewhere in Bermuda...They need an outlet but find none—except in clubs where they gamble and drink...Rabble rousers, purveyors of grievances, peddlers of dope... have thus a ready-made audience...."

Wooding Commission Report—Bermuda Civil Disorders 1968

The Trial of Justis Smith
November 23, 1998

A CAGED WOODEN BOX held Justis Smith when, finally, more than two years after Becky's murder, Smith's case got to Bermuda's Supreme Court. Smith, leaning on the wall, resting his head on his hands, at times seemed to doze. On the right side sat strangers in maroon velvet cushioned chairs, the jury. The press filled the harder, wooden seats on the left.

Becky's father, Dave Middleton, described the judge as "a little man, a frail little man…introverted, I wouldn't say he was particularly healthy. He seemed to have no self confidence."

Wigs and black robes, the old courtroom's small size, creaking cedar, stale stench, Justis Smith lazing in the box, all lent the aura of an imaginary place, a horrible nightmare for Cindy Bennett. Becky's mom tried to cope by keeping a sunflower-covered diary, Becky's favorite flower, recording the legalese spouted between prosecutors and defense attorneys. She sat next to Wayne, dazed.

Now nearing the end of November, with the Sargasso Sea turning an angry purple, international media and curious locals crowded Supreme Court to watch this long-awaited trial.

For Dave Middleton, lead defense attorney John Perry "appeared more like a Steve Martin or Johnny Carson than a Johnnie Cochran." His behaviors caught the attention of the media and judge alike.

Born in Jamaica, Perry had spent twenty-two years as a defense lawyer when he led Justis Smith's team, brought from England by the Smith family. Reportedly, a local church picked up at least part of the cost. A familiar face in Bermuda courts to this day, Perry often flies into Bermuda to defend some of the most notorious of Bermuda criminals.

"It is not uncommon for Perry to goad a witness into a verbal sparring match which, at times, can result in the witness becoming so confused he does not remember his original testimony," the *Bermuda Sun* wrote. "Compound this with his theatrical gestures—dropping into his chair after he makes a point, slouching, vigorously shaking his head when he disagrees with the prosecutor, and muttering under his breath. Over the past year, he added a new prop to his bag of tricks—glasses, which he whips off in moments of disgust. He is a tough opponent."

"You'd have to have seen his mannerisms," Dave said. "His hair fell into a curl that he dramatically swept out of his eyes. His court presence was unbelievable."

Even Perry's wife added to his decorum, Dave recalled. "Everybody had to notice her. She'd be sitting there for a while. Then she was off for shopping sprees and out to lunch."

On the first day of court, Judge Vincent Meerabux bowed to Perry, telling him, "I've heard of your work." That remark stunned Dave Middleton. From that point, Dave believed, Meerabux allowed Perry to run the court.

Lead prosecutor Bill Pearce had been a trial lawyer for some thirty years when he arrived in Bermuda, another hiring that drew protests—a white foreigner. Pearce had tried cases in the Supreme Court of Canada, the Privy Council in London, and in the Yukon Territory. But he had never prosecuted a murder case. Now Bill Pearce found himself prosecuting the most controversial murder case to hit Bermuda since the political murders in 1973. A few weeks after his arrival in Bermuda, during Mardi Gras in February, 1998, Bill Pearce and a police officer assigned to assist him, Terry Maxwell, secretly headed to New Orleans to meet with Dr. Henry Lee.

Dave Middleton described Pearce as methodical: "Like Perry Mason, Pearce hooked together details. Then, as though playing a chess game, he followed case law to its ultimate objective." Sandra Bacchus, assistant prosecutor, "was a hard working, go getter," Dave said. "As the trial went on, her role grew." Justice Vincent Meerabux, to Dave Middleton, "looked like a man excited to be in charge."

Born in Guyana, once a territory of Britain with problems that diminish those in Bermuda, (as was Richard Hector, who got bail for Mundy), and a judge in Guyana during the 1970s, Meerabux' expertise was in drafting law, which he'd done in Bermuda until he was appointed to the bench in 1993.

Dave wondered who appointed Meerabux, "I thought perhaps he just happened to walk by the door when they were deciding on the judge. He'd have to pump up his pompous attitude on the bench. When it got to trial, he knew the outcome," Dave said.

"I never heard Justis Smith say a word," Dave recalled. "I can't remember hearing a plea." Smith made no eye contact. "Frankly, he makes me nervous. He even looks dangerous. Even when Meerabux asked him where he was (when Becky was killed), he didn't answer."

Becky's parents heard first-hand how their daughter tried to speak but couldn't, and the terrible scene at Ferry Reach. Among the first to testify, Dana Rawlins broke down when he described for the jury how he found Becky struggling to breathe, crying, in the middle of the road.

Coy Fox, now working in a supermarket, described "blood all over the place and knife wounds." Fox told how Becky seemed relieved when they found her. "No, no jewelry except her watch." When Dean Lottimore arrived,

Fox said, "It appeared that he knew the people who had done this, you know because his reaction."

Sean Smith told how the cloth covered the bike's license plate.

"Did you see blood on Mundy's clothes?" John Perry asked.

Sean Smith said he did not.

"You're lying, boy" Justis Smith shouted from the dock.

"She (Jasmine) looked frightened. I was trying to keep her calm. As much as she was responsible, I was responsible too," Dean Lottimore told the court. He admitted that he went directly to Ferry Reach after he dropped Jasmine at her house. Lottimore identified Mundy and Smith as the men who took Becky.

Jasmine Meens followed Lottimore, glancing at Justis Smith, leaning against the dock. At one time she feared Smith. Now to Jasmine he just looked meek.

"Why did you get on one bike and Rebecca the other?" Sandra Bacchus asked.

"I stood closer to Dean Lottimore, so I said, 'You go on that bike.'"

Smith's lawyer, Archie Warner, charged that Becky was "fairly drunk," Jasmine's and Becky's judgment impaired. He suggested Jasmine lied when she told the court how Becky showed Smith the necklace that police never found. Jasmine seethed when Warner suggested that the girls flagged down Lottimore, that the ride offer from Mundy and Smith was made only once, and that Becky immediately jumped on the bike.

"She wasn't in a hurry to get on the bike," Jasmine argued, glaring at Warner.

A reporter observed that Jasmine "picked at her well-manicured fingernails."

"Of all the things to take notice of," she recalled. "Archie Warner kept asking me questions, changing around what I said. He got away with that."

Detective Terry Maxwell, who had been assigned to help Bill Pearce prepare the case against Justis Smith, told the court that he had gone back to Ferry Reach to sketch the murder scene. Maxwell also measured travel time from Mullet Bay, where Mundy and Smith picked up Becky, to Ferry Reach, then to the Smith residence.

"This was being done on the twenty third of February, 1998?" Perry's question seemed reasonable.

"That's correct."

"Quite a long time after the incident, isn't it?"

"That's quite correct, my lord."

"Who instructed you to do this plan?"

"The attorney general."

"Why wasn't this done in 1996?"

Maxwell said he had no idea. He was not a part of the initial investigation.

Perry bristled. "Were you in the Supreme Court when a belated attempt was being made by the prosecuting authorities in 1998 ….?"

"Yes, I was present then."

"Yes, and did you hear the following words, 'Right thinking people may think Mr. Mundy has got away literally with murder.' Did you hear those words said in court?"

"No, my lord."

"You didn't hear the words said by the solicitor general?"

"My lord, this is totally irrelevant," Bill Pearce interrupted. "My friend has been grand standing from the first day of trial to bring home to the jury the fact that a mistake was made in July of 1996."

"Not a mistake, a cock-up," said Perry.

"A cock-up, whichever he wants to call it." Perry's purpose, Pearce charged, was to show "that Mr. Mundy has got off with a five–year sentence… So if Mr. Mundy got off, therefore, Mr. Smith should get off. Now, that has nothing to do with whether Justis Smith is guilty of this offense."

Dave felt relief as Bill Pearce took the floor, calm, meticulous. "If the jury is continually to be subjected to my friend's speeches for the rest of this trial--if the jury at the end of the day is influenced by that factor in coming to their solemn decision as to whether Mr. Smith is guilty of the murder of Rebecca Middleton--that would be a very serious mistake."

Meerabux turned to Perry. "The question of repeated outbursts….are you doing that often?"

The comment startled Dave Middleton. Did Meerabux not observe Perry's dramatics?

"I'm not saying you did it to this particular witness, Mr. Perry. I know there is something called baiting."

"My lord, we defend," said Perry. "We use all legitimate tricks in the book. I am doing no more, I intend to do no less."

Meerabux said nothing more, the games continued.

Security guard Wendall Burchall told the court that when he saw two men speeding by on the bike, both slim and wearing dark clothes, "The piece of cloth caught my eye…I was saying, 'I hope it don't get in his wheel.'"

Lawyer Archie Warner, who argued that Burchall wouldn't have been able to see the men, termed the piece of cloth dangling from the back of the bike "a piece of string." Sandra Bacchus assured the record was corrected.

"When you drove them to St. George on that evening, how did you expect them to get home?" prosecutor Bill Pearce asked Rick Meens.

"Normal. I expected them to call me to come down and pick them up."

"What happened later that evening?"

"It was after three a.m. that Jasmine came into the house and notified me that she had been waiting down the hill for Rebecca."

"How did she appear?"

"Pretty normal. She was fine. She was obviously concerned about Rebecca, but other than that…"

"Were there any signs that she had been drinking that evening?"

"No, not really."

Smith defense lawyer John Perry interrupted. "With respect, how can my friend ask this question?" Jasmine had said she was drinking.

"You asked my opinion," Meens said.

"Be quiet," Meerabux ordered.

"What did you do after that?" Perry asked.

Meens recounted his and Jasmine's search and his call to police about six a.m.

"And was there any response by the police?"

"The initial call, no." He told of the second call, telling him to go to the St. George police station. "I remember asking the officer if they had found Becky, and he just kept saying, 'We need you to come to the police station.' I asked her if she found her, and I said, 'Is she okay?' Because, you know, I had been thinking that because of the lapse of time, Rebecca…."

"Try and just raise your voice a little bit," Pearce requested.

"What I was thinking is possibly she had been raped, which I think would have been anybody's concern being the lapse of time. So I asked if she was okay. They just kept saying 'We need you to come to the police station.'"

Driving by the airport, "we heard it on the—well, most Bermudians…" Rick Meens' voice broke—"I'm sure you can understand. That's when I heard it on the radio, so from that point on we drove—I drove to Ferry Reach."

"Get him some water, please." Meerabux offered.

"I really thought I was dreaming. I literally had to go back a second time because I didn't believe it."

On the trial's fourth day, police escorted Justis Smith to the murder scene at the end of Ferry Road, along with jurors, the judge, prosecutor Sandra Bacchus, defense lawyer John Perry, and Dave Middleton. They stood beneath the two casuarinas that still held mementos for Becky, hiked up the old Railway Trail, now a path for joggers, then headed down the short path to the ocean side at Whale Bone Bay, where Mundy told police he washed himself. Next onto Mullet Bay Road, where the girls had met Lottimore, Smith and Mundy. Finally the group gathered at the swing bridge, where divers found the knife.

As Dave Middleton leaned on the bridge, Smith's attorney John Perry stood nearby. "We were looking at the bridge, I was standing next to him," Dave recalled. "Perry told me, 'Well, you know, I am a lawyer, but I have two daughters.'" Perry warned Dave Middleton, the case was a "cock-up."

For Dave Middleton the whole process was a lot more disastrous than that.

THIRTEEN

"Thank Allah, then the people of Bermuda for helping me…"

Larry Tacklyn—referring to his acquittal for the Government House murders, a month before he was found guilty, with Erskine "Buck" Burrows, for the Shopping Centre murders.

Recorder to the Rescue
November 30, 1998

A WEEK INTO SMITH'S trial, a court reporter appeared, requested by Bill Pearce for the Middletons who were astonished that Bermuda functioned under such an antiquated system. Defense lawyer John Perry appeared content with the monosyllabic testimony required of witnesses whose testimony judges recorded with their quills, word by word. Perry complained to Justice Vincent Meerabux, he didn't believe the stenographer would speed up the process. Judges would have to take their own notes anyway.

Neither was Meerabux convinced. "I have queer living habits," he said. "I read at four o'clock in the morning…I like to wake up, prepare, and get on with my business."

Meerabux inquired how soon the transcripts would be ready. "I'm a finicky judge. I don't like people tapping on my door…I will sit here and someone will have to lock the building up. If you are willing to pay for the overtime for the backup staff to stay around. I'm not here to lock up court."

If his demands were not met, he said, "I will just ask you to tell this court reporter to take a walk."

Wayne Bennett watched his wife next to him, Cindy's face taut. Things that in most places are so taken for granted, in Bermuda become a hurdle. Wayne shuddered as he heard Meerabux say that proceedings "have commenced, now some Christopher Columbus has got the idea that we must have proceedings be recorded."

Next, they debated number of copies. Prosecutor Bill Pearce was happy with one, Meerabux requested one, Perry wanted two.

Then, to Wayne's amazement, Perry pointed to a juror, who was sitting in the public front row. Perry sent her to the jury box. "I notice these things. I've already informed competent people to do things." Perry suggested that a platform be built.

Dave Middleton wondered if the people of Bermuda knew the international reputation of the man who now termed Becky's murder "a deliberate, specific act done with care." Former chief medical examiner for New York City, chief forensic pathologist for the New York State Police, an FBI, DEA, and U.S. Department of Justice consultant, Dr. Michael Baden had chaired investigations of the deaths of President John F. Kennedy and Dr. Martin Luther King Jr. By request, he had examined the remains of Tsar Nicholas II, Alexandra, and the Romanov family in Siberia in the 1990s, examined the deaths of Medgar Evers, Yankee Manager Billy Martin, Marlon Brando's son Christian, and thousands of others worldwide for defense attorneys, prosecutors, and human rights groups.

In Dr. Michael Baden's opinion, four hands held Becky down, tortured and raped her, then deliberately stabbed her to death.

To those words, Perry assumed the stance of a rooster in charging mode, accusing Baden of conspiring with police to claim that two men killed Becky.

When they contacted him, "What did (police) call you? Dr. Baden or Michael?"

"Dr. Baden."

"By the end of the conversation…Michael?"

Not the case. Norrell Hull, the officer who spoke to him at the conference and who coordinated the case with Baden, was very formal.

"I mean did he say to you, for example, this …is about a year and three months after the incident? You realize that, don't you?"

"Yes, sir."

"I mean did he say to you, for example, 'Dr. Baden of O.J. Simpson fame, we have a problem,' like he said on Apollo 11? You remember that well-known saying in Apollo 11?"

Baden agreed that he remembered.

"That's the one that went up?"

"Yes."

"You remember when the astronaut said to NASA, 'We've got a problem,'… do you remember that saying?" asked Perry.

"I remember more things that Johnny Cochran said than I do about Apollo 11."

Perhaps, Perry suggested, Hull wanted to "fill a little gap?"

It wasn't unusual to be contacted more than a year after a crime, Baden countered.

"To support a two-man theory?"

"To evaluate the cause of death, to attempt to reconstruct what happened at the time of death."

"Dr. Baden, the cause of death was established on the third of July, 1996."

"The medical examiner can be of help in trying to reconstruct what happened at the time of death, and that was the type of question Chief Inspector Hull asked me."

"Are you telling us that an important issue like this, which involved the brutal--let's not mince words about it--the brutal killing of a young visitor to these islands, that the request made to you to give some opinion wasn't done formally?" It was a setup, Perry insisted.

"He asked me what my opinions were. He didn't tell me what the end product should be. That would be inappropriate…"

What prompted Baden to write that letter?

"…because I thought there was a possibility there was a bite mark…"

Perry got much more than he intended. He flipped his curl and leaped to his feet. "You missed my point."

"Counsel cannot cut off," Pearce objected.

"Give the answer, what is the answer?" Perry appeared off balance.

Baden repeated, a possible bite mark.

"Just a minute, please!"

"Let him finish," Pearce said.

"I'm sorry, I'm in charge." Perry's face reddened.

"Would you agree with me that in your October letter, you did not… include that Mr. Smith was involved?"

Baden explained he had referred to Justis Smith in a previous letter.

"Dr. Baden, read that letter to yourself, please, in its entirety…where you say that it is your opinion that Mr. Smith was involved?"

"I say on page two."

"Do you understand English?"

"Yes, sir. It says at the top of page – the first partial paragraph, the top of page two."

"Top of page two." Meerabux muttered, searching for the section. "In which I state, 'Mr. Mundy claims they stopped at Ferry'"--

"Stop, stop!"

Perry peered. "I asked you, Dr. Baden, and please don't pussyfoot around, be careful what you say…."

Baden turned toward the judge. "He doesn't want me to say."

"Not he doesn't want me--" Meerabux didn't finish his sentence.

Baden tried again. "If I can go to page two… 'He then walked to the water, washed himself.'"

"No, no, no." said Meerabux. "Go to the next paragraph." Baden tried to help the judge, now crimson faced.

"That is not your opinion." Meerabux' tone intensified.

"I'm including that in my opinion."

"No, no, no. No, that's not your opinion." Now nearly a squeal. "It doesn't work that way." Meerabux took a deep breath. "Do you understand?"

"Yes, sir."

"Your opinion," said Meerabux.

"Okay, my opinion. 'The absence of dirt,' this is my opinion."

Meerabux and Perry seemed satisfied.

No dirt on the bottom of Becky's feet, no blood between the blood-soaked grassy area where the major stabbing occurred and the road, where she was left to die. No disturbed turf to suggest that she crawled or was dragged.

"The torn clothing, the circumstances, the autopsy findings, all indicated the sexual intercourse was not consensual."

Meerabux interrupted. "I beg your pardon, no, no, no."

Perry peered over his glasses. "What I suggest to you is that this is an exercise of the prosecuting authorities and yourself desperately thrashing around to find some support for a two-man theory. And you of O.J. Simpson fame have been brought in like a gunslinger to do your deed."

"Wrong," said Baden.

"Yes. And your next proposition is that at least two persons were involved in the attack?"

"Yes."

Perry approached Baden. "Let me put my case to you straight. My proposition to you is this: You have completely abandoned the objectivity which should attach to the opinion of an expert. You, I suggest, have adopted—"

Bill Pearce objected. "My lord, this is not an appropriate line of questioning."

Baden remained composed. "He's calling me a liar. He can call me a liar if he wants."

Flanked by police and his attorney Elizabeth Christopher, Justis Smith returns to scenes of Becky's murder.
Photo Courtesy of the Royal Gazette

Dr. Michael Baden and Dr. Henry Lee draw international attention.
Photo Courtesy of the Royal Gazette

Perry persisted. "I'm calling you worse than that, Dr. Baden."

To Pearce, Perry said, "Your witness may, like Paul on the road to Damascus--he may see the light and change his mind. I'm giving him the opportunity."

Still unruffled, Baden told Perry, "I say I'm stating what is forensically obvious, and I am not abandoning objectivity, I'm just giving an opinion that apparently you don't care for."

"I'm going to suggest to you that your conclusions are bogus."

"That's your job."

"...And I'm going to put this to you: That you have adopted the position of a paid lackey to the prosecution authorities?"

Baden had had enough. "Sir, if this is permitted in Bermuda, that's fine. It would not be permitted in the United States, if I may answer your question. I am not a paid lackey, I gave my opinion.

"In fact, my opinion disagreed, as you pointed out, with a number of the other experts... My opinion is based on my knowledge, my expertise, my review. I don't make my opinion conform to what other people have said. I've given the best. You may disagree with it. I may be wrong, but (it is) the best of my opinion, based on all the evidence that I have reviewed."

Perry badgered. "You see, what you have done is to avoid the objective facts, and you have come up with some bogus conclusion."

Pearce objected. "My friend is giving his final argument. These kinds of abusive questions are not permitted in this jurisdiction."

Pearce was wrong, the pattern continued.

Now, though, Perry's overconfidence got in his way. On the night she was killed, Perry charged, Becky was "highly under the influence of drink."

"Under the influence," Baden agreed, but not "highly."

"Dr. Baden, it was 257 millimeters--milligrams, rather, per one hundred millimeters of blood." Perry's tone was condescending.

"I think that was in the urine..."

"It doesn't make any difference where it came from," Perry argued.

"Of course it makes a difference." Baden smiled.

"That's the blood alcohol content in her body?" Perry's voice dropped.

"No, the urine content is not the same as the blood."

"Of course it's not." Perry composed himself.

"It doesn't have the same significance," said Baden.

"Are you saying she was not highly under the influence of drink?"

"She was under the influence," Baden said, "the degree of influence would depend much on what others saw when they saw her that evening. The same amount of alcohol has different effects on different people."

Perry switched to the absence of Smith's DNA. "Are we agreed that there is no forensic evidence to connect any other man?"

"Or by everything?" Baden asked.

"Everything."

"Forensic evidence establishing that the knife found in the water came from the Smith kitchen. That's forensic evidence…"

Perry sighed, and then launched into an exercise of logic regarding apples falling from trees, without interruption from either Meerabux or Pearce.

In the end, Baden agreed with Perry's solution to the apple question. "Do you want to know why I agree?" Baden asked.

Perry admitted he would.

"Because I have faith in your representation, and it's almost twelve o'clock," Baden told Perry. This time, Dr. Michael Baden had commandeered lunch.

Becky's mom, Cindy, more exhausted each day, thought Justis Smith's father, Richard, appeared tired too. Frequently she'd see him sleeping not far from her in the small courtroom.

Dave Middleton, meanwhile, thought how confused Meerabux seemed. Years later, Dr. Michael Baden would agree, saying Meerabux did not appear in good health, perhaps worthy of investigation because of questions of the court's competence.

Justis Smith's defense attorney, John Perry, the star, seemed to be in his element, Cindy thought. How many "Hollywood" characters would be born from her daughter's death? Becky seemed lost in the judicial jockeying.

The courtroom took on a sinister silence after the lunch break when Dr. Michael Baden detailed the murder of Rebecca Middleton. Even John Perry did not interrupt.

"One person holding…the other with one hand holding her head, while the other cut(s)-- many little jabs, about fifteen jabs--not to kill her but to get her to cooperate….Scrape, scrape, scrape, scrape, scrape…the space of the scrape marks, which, in my opinion, match exactly the elevations on the serrated knife, and do not match at all the roughness of the roadway."

Baden said he didn't know if the stabs came from the front or behind. "But two arms had to hold, or we couldn't get those six cut wounds on the neck without doing more damage...stab wounds on the top of the head (and the blows), attempts to make her cooperate."

Already raped before she made a desperate attempt to escape, she was caught, tortured, then she received those fatal wounds, Baden said. "That's the best I could reconstruct."

"Are you sure you're finished?" asked Perry.

"If I haven't covered anything, I'd appreciate your raising it."

"I'm not going to help you, you tell us." Perry complained that Baden's report did not include the word "nonconsensual."

"I guess I thought it was redundant."

"Or is it because you are now trying to make your case of a two-man theory, (after) you have nailed your colors to the mast?" Perry's theatrics intensified. "You have changed, Dr. Baden, you have left it out, and I want to know why."

"You get me nervous by shaking your head back and forth."

"I'm sorry, the truth will out, Doctor."

Perry persisted. "Tell me something. Do you think it's possible for a man to rape a woman while she is seated on the grass?"

"I think it's very possible to have a woman perform oral sex on a man."

Perry twisted, slid to his chair, then rose. "Please don't belittle this poor girl's memory. The girl was raped."

"She suffered very much," Baden said. "...what I meant to imply with sexual assault--including forcing her to do oral sex, as well as the anal sex."

"Forget about this complete side issue about oral sex. How could a man rape a seated woman?"

"To say, 'Do this', and 'Put this in your mouth,' when she doesn't want to."

Meerabux reminded Perry that U.S. law of rape encompasses oral sex and other acts.

"Go over with him step by step. Pick it up with the vagina," said Meerabux.

Perry attempted a different tact. "It is an inhuman thing, I hope you'll agree, an inescapable inference" that Becky was raped by Mundy. "Could the gripping have happened then?"

Baden glared. "Mr. Perry, you accuse me of coming here just to adopt whatever the Crown says about this case. I came, I looked over the photographs.

I looked at the autopsy report…If all that I was to do was to adopt what other people said, then you don't need me here, you know."

"Dr. Baden, you are really making it up as you are going along…You were brought in to support the two-man theory, isn't it?" Perry repeated. "Let's see if we can get into the real world, Dr. Baden. Would you accept the normal approach of someone who has committed a crime—I know we have eccentrics and everything--but the normal approach is to hide, not to go public. Do you accept that?"

Depends on the circumstances, Baden said. "Some perpetrators want the body to be found. Actually, murder isn't logical." There was a risk while Becky was being sexually assaulted in the verge that a car would come along, and the headlights would show the driver the assault in progress. "People do stupid things, especially when they murder people. I agree with you, it's stupid, but I can't get into the perpetrators' minds."

Dave Middleton glanced at Justis Smith, his head in his hands. Smith appeared bored.

FOURTEEN

"The motive…was to make the people, black people in particular, become aware of the evilness and wickedness of the colonialist system…just ordinary people like ourselves who eat sleep and die… We need not stand in fear or awe…Finally, the motive was to reveal black people unto themselves…standing with tears in their eyes, crying for a man who, when he was alive, didn't care if they lived or died…yet when many of their own people pass away, there is sometimes barely a tear shed…"

Confession of Erskine "Buck" Burrows for the Government House murders--June, 1976

Facts, Law, and Ad Hominems
December 1, 1998

"MEMBERS OF THE JURY, space yourself out a bit more," Judge Vincent Meerabux ordered the next morning. "I know you have difficulty with the legs, but as I examined last night… I don't know, but we will see."

An invigorated John Perry returned to Dr. Michael Baden. "You agreed yesterday that the bruising on the upper arm could--yes, those bruising could have occurred during Mr. Mundy's penile penetration of Ms. Middleton's vagina."

Cindy felt waves of nausea.

"Not quite, you misstate what I said…to a reasonable degree of medical certainty—ninety-five, ninety-eight percent--that she was held while being stabbed by another person." Only a one per cent chance that there weren't two people.

Perry exhaled. "Dr. Baden we are really going to be here a long time if you are going to go back on what you say."

"Mr. Perry, you can't threaten him that you are going to keep him," Meerabux warned.

Perry repeated his question. "Yesterday, he said 'Could have happened that way.' That was your answer."

"He just said one percent." The judge squinted at Perry.

"He didn't say anything about one percent yesterday."

"He is saying that this morning."

"I know he's saying that this morning…."

"If I suggested to you that of the thirty-five stab wounds, five--and five only--are to the left side of the midline, what would you say to that?"

"First, there aren't thirty five stab wounds, there are seventeen stab wounds. I can't talk while you're talking."

"Seventeen what?" The judge struggled to keep up.

Perry, said Baden, was trying to make him testify to something that forensic science could not say--whether the knife attack came from the front or behind. "That's forensic pathology 101. We can't tell."

Not so, Perry argued, the knife has an orientation. "There is one side of the blade and one side without the blade, so you can see?"

"I'll make a deal," Baden offered. "I won't argue law with you, and please don't tell me…You can't assume the knife is being held the way you'd like it to be held, especially if there is more than one person involved, who may be exchanging the knife between them."

Perry argued, "People in fear or stress, they are behaving in a way which ordinary normal people behave. They don't adopt a position which is different. All I'm asking…."

"No you're wrong," Baden said. "Murder is not logical. If we are going to kill somebody--we are not going to kill somebody as if we are normally holding a knife and a fork…We don't know what a person does who is emotionally, sexually, and physically very much under stress or very much attacking another person. There is no normal way to hold a knife when one is killing somebody."

Poised as if he were assisting with a table setting, Perry asked Baden, "Are you prepared to hold the knife?"

"Yes, this is one way to do it."

"Now, stab to the back with the knife in the same position. Yes!"

"…But I don't need to." Baden changed the knife's angle. "Sir, I don't know if you have ever murdered anybody with a knife, I haven't."

"If I did, I wouldn't call in a pathologist." Perry bowed.

"I haven't murdered anybody," Baden continued. "And people do peculiar things when they are in frenzy. This is a frenzy murder."

"You know, my lord, the laughing and the talking and all—it's difficult…" Baden turned toward Meerabux, who seemed not to hear.

"You find yourself in the position you are disagreeing with a lot of people, aren't you?"

"Mr. Perry, I came here to give my opinion." Baden said. "I did not try to tailor my opinion to anybody else's opinion. My opinion may be right, it may be wrong,…I have not attempted in any way to tailor my opinion or to be a lackey to somebody else… Honest people can disagree."

"…Do you accept that you find yourself in the position of disagreeing with a lot of people? Yes or no."

"All my life, I've disagreed with a lot of people."

"In this case?"

"I agree with some people, and I disagree with some people on minor points, Mr. Perry. That this poor woman was viciously, sexually assaulted and cut and stabbed is clear to my mind. That two people are involved is clear from the autopsy findings, the trace evidence and the circumstances…She came on a motorcycle with two people."

"Stop the speech, please!" Perry demanded.

"No, he has to allow him to answer the question." Sandra Bacchus stood. "Mr. Perry, I am now on my feet. That is simply unfair. Just because perhaps Dr. Baden is not saying what Mr. Perry wishes him to say doesn't mean that Mr. Perry can curtail his response. This is the way that it's done, and it's the only thing that is fair to the witness, the jury, and to the judicial process."

"And to the court reporter," Pearce added.

"If everybody agreed one hundred percent," Baden said, "I would be concerned that this was all discussed and arranged beforehand, because science permits and encourages disagreement...."

Perry persisted. "Do you agree that you were brought into this case one year and three months after fundamental decisions had been made as to the prosecution of this case?"

"I'm trying to help you," said Baden.

"Would you be quiet, Doctor," Meerabux shouted.

"I'm sorry." Baden was taken aback.

Meerabux refused to allow Baden's report to be entered into evidence.

Years later Dr. Michael Baden would tell Greta Van Susteren on U.S. television that he found the handling of the investigation into the murder of Rebecca Middleton a travesty. It was "unconscionable," he said, "...a blot on the criminal justice system of Bermuda—a tragedy and an outrage,"

Dr. Baden would have an opportunity to re-visit another Bermuda judicial decision in 2005 when the death of a U.S. businessman visiting Bermuda, found hanging in the closet of a guest house, from a rail lower than his height, with his family reporting photos of bodily injuries on his abdomen and sides, was ruled a suicide. In 2010, the victim's father told this author the family remained dissatisfied with Bermuda's handling of this case.

It was lunch time, Bill Pearce reminded, and he had some private matters that he wished to discuss with autopsy pathologist Dr. James Johnston who had just left the stand.

John Perry requested that his own pathologist evaluate the knife. "She can do it at the lunch adjournment. I've never seen a problem with these exhibits."

"Where will she take it?" Meerabux asked.

"It can be in the courtroom."

"Perhaps the clerk will be here," Meerabux said.

Pearce gave permission.

"I am obliged," said Perry.

Meerabux nodded. "Permission granted."

The knife was lying on the table when Dave Middleton returned early from lunch—unattended, in its plastic bag.

Justice Vincent Meerabux appeared weary when court resumed for its afternoon session, His first order of business, the photos of Becky with Jasmine Meens, Russell McCann, and Jonathan Cassidy, taken just before she was murdered.

The photos, said Bacchus, were important to verifying that she wore the missing ring and gold chain, perhaps allowing the jury to consider "why possibly some harm was done to this girl, aside from the sexual assault." Bacchus pointed to a photo of Becky leaning toward Jonathan Cassidy. "If you see under the top part of the shirt, I believe you will see evidence that she was wearing a white undershirt."

Meerabux agreed there was "some material—I don't know what it is. Kind of a windbreaker, or what?"

An undershirt, Bacchus said. "No such undershirt was discovered at the scene. Furthermore, you've heard some evidence with respect to the cloth."

Meerabux interrupted. "This is it. The defense has conceded one, there was a serious sexual assault committed on the victim, an unlawful act took place that evening...You are bouncing, you are dancing around. Well, dance around the time line..."

The judge glowered at Bacchus. "You have to get principal and secondary participator...Already my understanding, you have Mr. What's-His-Name, Mr. Mundy, whose name seems to be popping up from time to time in this trial...."

Meerabux glanced at his watch. "It's a quarter past already....I don't know how you're running your case, but having got (aggravated sexual assault) thrown into the pot, now to throw in business that was never considered...I don't know if it was considered...Now you are throwing in theft and robbery because there was violence there," Meerabux rambled.

"Look at the evidence," Meerabux said. "I notice there has not yet been an attack on the scene itself... Whether or not there was contamination at the scene, I don't know...I assume that is then sterilized and put up-- whatever you do here in Bermuda, whatever ribbon, I don't know, that was that. Alright...But to throw it in with robbery, I don't know. Why not have a sleep on it? Let us all have a sleep."

"That's what I was going to suggest," said Pearce, who noticed Meerabux tiring.

"We have a long day, all right? I don't think anyone deliberately is trying to wear me down, but there is a saying, 'Either we rush out or we run down.'"

Bacchus tried one more time, "We allege, and you will hear, that the girl showed the chain to the two guys, so just sleep on that aspect if I could ask you, my lord."

"I want you to sleep on it and wake me up tomorrow morning. Alright. So we are adjourned."

The exhausted judge left at 4:20 p.m.

"Did you see any jewelry on Ms. Middleton?" Sandra Bacchus asked Scenes of Crime Lead Inspector Howard Cutts the next morning.

"Only a wrist watch, undamaged, showing the correct time." Cutts said he examined it, then returned it to the family. No tests for trace.

"Were there any other items of clothing on Ms. Middleton?"

"No, only the shirt and the bra."

The investigation itself was "rooted in total inefficiency," John Perry charged. "Detective Cutts, you said about the sixth of November you were handed a roll of Fuji film, what year was that? This is 1998."

"This year," Cutts conceded.

"Now, Inspector Cutts, don't misunderstand me, I'm not criticizing you, as such. But it does appear, does it not, that the underlying retrieving of items in this case has been wholly inefficient, do you accept that?"

"No, sir."

"No?"

"Absolutely not," Cutts returned.

Was he, then, "behind every officer" marking evidence?

Cutts agreed he was not, but skilled officers supervised recruits, discarding only "irrelevant" evidence.

Perry twirled. "But the relevance of an item might not become important at the date of the retrieval, perhaps later down in the investigation--that's right, isn't it?

"If—it could be, yes."

"Yes, an item which may be infinitesimal at the beginning becomes highly relevant somewhere during the investigation, that's right, isn't it?"

"Yes."

"So how could you say that these training officers could make that determination when they are not even involved in the investigation?"

"Because I have every confidence in the officers who were leading the search." Some evidence, he added, had been at the scene for some time. "An item such as Kentucky Fried boxes… were not, in my opinion, relevant."

"What I am saying is that everything should be picked up, everything should be labeled, and it may well be entirely agreed that somewhere down the investigation some things can be disregarded." Perry's voice sounded soothing, far removed from the aggressive John Perry who had questioned Dr. Michael Baden. "Sun glasses, who picked up the sun glasses?" Perry asked.

Cutts didn't know.

"Where?"

He didn't know.

There were also old condom wrappers that he picked up but discarded after checking for fingerprints, Cutts said.

"On the eleventh of July, Kirk Mundy tells police he went to the beach to wash himself…not known to the police on the morning of the third of July…, information required to map the actual crime scene. Do you follow that?"

"I disagree."

"You disagree? Well, what can I say? So if a condom were found on the beach with semen in it, don't you think that might be relevant to determine whether that was Mundy's semen or not?"

"No."

Perry need say no more.

Becky's mom fixed her gaze upon the knife that Marine Police Officer Chris Taggett held in front of the jury. He found it in eight feet of water near the shoreline at the swing bridge--just where Kirk Mundy said it would be. "I didn't see any marks or stains on it."

"A number of boats are moored in the area," Perry suggested. "Small boats, larger boats, different size boats…used by people along that area?" Perhaps boaters had carried the knife as part of picnicking gear?

Unlikely, suggested Miami-Dade police knife expert Robert Hart. The knife found in the water and those from the Smith household kitchen "came from the same manufacturer at approximately the same time…Molded plastic handles were the same size, color, texture, composition. All blades, the same size, finish and serration patterns, all ground in the same manner, to the same degree of sharpness. Blade stamp markings, the same size, spacing, style…" Not only that, all four blades showed the same degree of damage. They were stamped with the same tool, and, all four knives were stamped within five and fifty stampings of each other," Hart told the court.

U.S. forensic examiner Michael Kelly followed, confirming that eight cuts on Becky's shirt matched the shape and size of this knife, as did the cut to her bra.

Who could doubt that the knife was the one that her killers used?

Lead prosecutor Bill Pearce handed the judge hospital pathologist Dr. Keith Cunningham's report of injuries to both of Smith's forearms at the time of his arrest. But, Smith's defense lawyer John Perry argued, there was no proof they came during a struggle with Becky, especially without fingernail scrapings. Pearce countered that the injuries were consistent with the time frame of Becky's murder.

"Some recent, some days old. This examination was when?" Meerabux asked.

On the tenth, a week after the murder. Even without the fingernail scrapings, Pearce argued, "at the least, these injuries call out for an explanation…" The scratches fit Dr. Baden's expectation that any perpetrator would have had scraping, scratching injuries. We are not talking about highly-charged evidence or something that will overwhelm the jury. We are talking about scratches."

Meerabux thought aloud. "At some point, (Justis Smith) was within the vicinity and with the same person who admitted that he was an accessory after the fact to murder. There is no evidence that the motorcycle had blood stains, but neither here nor there, one can say. There is no evidence that he had blood stains. There is no evidence from the fingernails of the victim that his flesh was on her nails. There is no extra identification evidence that he was there. That leaves us with the knife."

Bill Pearce argued that there was one more major factor that made the report of the scratches relevant.

"What other thing? You tell me."

"There is the statement of Justis Smith that he was with Mundy from three o'clock continuously..."

"...He was there at the scene," said Meerabux. "So the link is-- you have the time, you have inferences (of the scratches), and now the question of the knife... the knife came from the same manufacturer as the knife from Smith's mother's home, and that's as far as it goes. This is where we are about this recent dark-scabbed injury. What else do you have?"

"All relevant evidence ought to go in," Pearce said.

"Mr. Perry," Meerabux invited, "what do you add to this, recent injuries?"

"No evidence of a struggle involving Smith," Perry said.

"But in my direction to the jury on circumstantial evidence, I will give a very strong direction on speculation—do not get involved in guessing, guesstimating," Meerabux said.

Perry chided. "It isn't right to have a piece of evidence come in which has no probative value and then wait for directions to the jury. The proper approach is to exclude it...."

"Mr. Perry is still standing, and I'm still thinking. Perhaps it was the doctor's fault," Meerabux mused. "Sometimes I wonder if an experienced doctor--when they write these reports--why do they not address or focus their mind on certain things they put in the report. They just drop these things." The judge appeared petulant.

"Where does that leave the Crown?" Perry's voice rose.

"That's the danger," Meerabux agreed.

"Of course it is. That is the danger," said Perry.

"I am going to rule. I have to rule." Meerabux leaned back. "The prejudicial effect far outweighs the probative value, I will not allow it."

Dr. Keith Cunningham's evidence of scratches to both of Justis Smith's arms was out.

Now December tenth, the trial's third week, criminalist Dr. Henry Lee focused the first slide of Becky's brutalized remains. Lead prosecutor Bill Pearce cautioned that explicit photographs might be upsetting. "The public ought to be warned."

"I don't think I need to warn members of the public," Justice Vincent Meerabux said.

"I entirely agree with your lordship," defense attorney John Perry agreed. "I don't think the public should be warned." Rather, the pictures should be tilted to face the jury.

"What is your occupation, Dr. Lee?" Bill Pearce asked.

"Chief criminalist for the state of Connecticut, director of forensic science laboratory of Connecticut state police, commissioner of the department of public safety, chief fire marshal for the state, professor for seven different universities, law schools and medical schools."

Lee showed his first picture of Becky as she lay dead, almost naked. Lee pointed to the sickening blood patterns ...A "floating pattern, just like if you spill some coffee on the kitchen table, you start running according to the gravity. Goes to the lowest point...which means her body has to be in a horizontal position."

Onto the next, Becky's upper torso.

Dave's fingernails tore into his skin. A friend of Cindy's wrote in her diary as Cindy waited outside, choosing not to listen to the morbid testimony.

No blood drops on the grass, nor smears on the pavement, said Lee, suggested Becky didn't walk or drag herself to the road. Rather, Becky sat upright, "not standing—more likely sitting."

"At the time the wounds were inflicted?" Pearce asked.

"Don't lead," Perry admonished.

One of the stains splattered in "all different directions, consistent with impact spatter." She received major injury, battery, at this first location.

"Subsequently, she was moved. Again, excessive bleeding. Afterwards her body was transferred to the middle of the road."

If she had walked, there would have been "vertical drips or a blood trail. There was neither," said Lee. "If she crawled by herself to that location, there would be more than a tiny amount of vegetative material. We should see more damage...blood drops too. So we eliminate that possibility." In Lee's view, if one person alone had dragged Becky, there would be smear or skin abrasions, which photos didn't show. "By the process of elimination-- it's not walking, not crawling, not dragging and back carrying."

Everything suggested "two people carrying and depositing Rebecca Middleton in the middle of the road."

"What is your final conclusion, doctor?" Pearce asked.

"My final conclusion...this scene has three separate locations." The first attack, then she tried to run away, walk away, or even crawl away, he said. At the second spot, "she received additional stabbing. Some in the back, some in the front, excessive bleeding. Subsequently, her body was transported, more likely carried, by two persons into this final location." The third area, a "staged scene," something that he'd seen many times. "Somebody stage a traffic accident type of scenario, left in the middle of the road."

Perry adjusted his spectacles, removed them, replaced them. He peered at Lee. "It hasn't been put to you this morning, I notice but it is right, is it not, that you gave evidence at the O.J. Simpson case for the prosecution?"

"No, defense," said Lee.

"You gave for the defense?"

"Yes."

"You're sure for the defense?"

"I was there," Lee answered, "in fact for six-and-a-half days."

Perry ignored a few chuckles.

"Dr. Lee, you told us that you made your first report in 1997?"

"That's correct, sir."

"That is over a year following this incident, do you know that?" What conversation did he have with Inspector Norrell Hull?

Lee, like Baden, wouldn't be intimidated. "I did not have any lengthy conversation because I am so busy. I work sixteen, some eighteen, twenty hours a day, seven days a week. I don't have much dialogue with people, just continue working." He had only brief conversation with Hull.

"What I want to know is did he tell you what the police were hoping to achieve?"

"They want me to investigate this case…Can I issue a report based upon the blood-stain pattern? That's all reconstruction."

"Dr. Lee, please answer my question."

"I did, sir."

Perry repeated. "Did Chief Inspector Hull tell you what the investigation was hoping to achieve?"

"I don't know. I don't recall any lengthy conversation…If you attend any of my workshops, you're going to see there are hundreds, sometimes thousand students. If everybody started lengthy conversation, I can't even walk out of a lecture hall."

Perry changed the subject. "On the assumption that Ms. Middleton did walk from the grassy area to the road, her walking would have liberated some of the soil and vegetation, would it not?"

But she didn't walk, Lee argued. If she had, she would have walked in her own blood and there would be more vegetation caked on her soles.

Of course, there was a possibility that Becky had walked, Perry insisted.

No, Lee repeated. "You have to consider a totality…Don't just look at one tiny bit of evidence. Look at the whole picture. I only can tell the scientific facts, scientific truth, I'm not here to argue any minor point."

Perry pressed. "You didn't conduct any experiment, did you, to see how much vegetation or soil would have been acquired and remained on her feet in the conditions of July third, 1996?"

"Nobody can duplicate that," Lee said.

"Just answer my question, please."

"I already answered your question"

"No, listen to the question carefully."

"You say, did I conduct? I say no, I did not conduct."

"Exactly, exactly. So you are not, Dr. Lee, in a position to know how much soil or vegetation would have attached to her feet if she did walk, would you?"

"Nobody can tell you."

"What do you mean nobody could tell you?"

"You can tell? Can you tell?"

"I'm a lawyer."

"I'm a scientist."

Perry's furled his eyebrows. "I'm putting the questions to you, you don't ask me questions."

Lee didn't retreat. "Based on my experience of thirty-eight years, she was carried."

But Lee didn't know Becky's weight, Perry reminded.

"Don't care. Nothing to do with my interpretation."

But some vertical blood spatters could be consistent with Becky standing at some point. Perry wouldn't concede.

"No," Lee answered.

"No?"

"Yes."

"I suggest to you that it could."

"Well, I'm the expert."

Perry twisted, inhaled and peered at Lee. "It's vertical, isn't it?"

"It's consistent with an angular impact, so a downwards angular impact."

"Doctor, is it vertical or not?"

"I tell you already. It's downward angular impact."

"My question was that there was no evidence found of blood on the ground at scene two."

"Thank you, make it clear," said Lee.

"That's what I said to you." Perry's annoyance was palpable.

"No, you just said marker two," said Lee.

"No, I said on the ground." Perry said.

"I'm not going to argue with you," Lee told Perry. "I can only come here to deliver this blood pattern interpretation to you. No more, no less to the court of law, that's it."

Perry showed Lee a photograph, suggesting it showed dirt on Becky's hands.

Very little, said Lee. The photo had been enlarged, Lee explained. Therefore, the amount of dirt might appear larger than actually present. "… You can see that the printing's different. That's why I'm the expert."

But Lee's opinion disagreed with original investigators, Perry argued.

"If somebody has no special training, they can be fifty years old and only investigate ten, twenty homicides. Compare somebody… that investigate six thousand cases, you're going to have differences."

Wouldn't seeing the site give better information than a photograph?

"Not necessarily. In my career I see a lot of investigators make serious mistakes. He cited the Jon-Benet Ramsey or Vincent Foster deaths, among the thousands for which agencies sought his opinion.

"And what I am going to suggest to you, that when Ms. Middleton was on the ground, she was still bleeding?"

Lee smiled. "I agree with you wholeheartedly. Finally we agree on something!"

"That's a road rash, isn't it?" Perry pointed to the scrapes on Becky's shoulder.

"No."

"What do you say it is?"

"Something sharp. This is motion with a force..." Lee suggested. ..."something that has...pointing tips, could be a serrated knife."

"I knew you'd say that," Perry sneered. "What I am going to suggest to you, Dr. Lee, is this. That having been approached by Chief Inspector Hull, you have, in effect, tailor-made your testimony."

"No."

"To the case which you know the Crown is presenting."

"I think that's an insult. I have never tailor-made my testimony. Nobody can buy my testimony or tailor me. I only report scientific fact. I have no emotional involvement or vested interest or revenge. Believe me, thirty eight years in my career, one thing I have is my integrity, sir."

His testimony delayed for two days, Dr. Lee had been frantic. "I had another situation involving a serial killer that couldn't wait," Lee recalled. "Justice Vincent Meerabux refused to allow me to leave Bermuda, even briefly. He threatened to hold my passport, but I left anyway. When I came back, I thought he would hang me. But he didn't... Perry shouldn't have been allowed to treat witnesses as he did. Obviously, they don't want a foreign expert telling them what to do."

In all of his experiences, Lee said, he never had one like in Bermuda. In one of his textbooks, Lee explains such behaviors:

"The lawyer with the strongest case will argue the facts, one with less strength will argue the law, and the one with the weakest case will use *ad hominems*--that is, go after personalities."

FIFTEEN

"The present Constitution does not, of itself, make for good government, and I believe than an elected government which has to face the responsibility of dealing with law and order is likely to be more sensitive to, and respond more swiftly to, events.... Bermudians have been adept at having their cake and eating it; the time has come when they have to consider whether this is giving them indigestion...."

--Secret Memo Acting Governor Ian Kinnear to Secretary of State, FCO—May 1, 1973(National Archives, London)

'A Gigantic You-Know-What'

December 11, 1998

"THE CROWN SEEMS TO BE LOOKING with ten different faces in this matter. Ought not Mundy to be called and let chips fall?" John Perry demanded. "Answer the question, Mr. Pearce."

"Putting a witness forward who is not credible would create not only an ethical issue, but the assumption that Mundy's testimony is necessary, which it is not," Justis Smith prosecutor Bill Pearce argued

"I've been wrestling with this case and a lot of things." Justice Vincent Meerabux rifled through papers on the bench. "The difficulty is that the court is now going to be asked to call a witness who is regarded not to be credible. I think, in one case, the defense has called him a liar, already the Crown is saying he's not a credible witness…It's a difficulty I'm in, a difficulty in relation to this case."

"It's a difficult issue. I recognize that," Pearce agreed.

"Created by the prosecution," defense attorney Archie Warner chimed.

Meerabux muttered something that neither Dave nor Rick could hear.

John Perry beamed. "One of my abiding disappointments is that although I studied Latin—"

"You recognize it as Latin?" Meerabux smiled.

"Is it Latin?" Perry replied.

"It is."

"I dropped Latin like I dropped music," Perry beamed back at Meerabux.

Bill Pearce ignored their banters and calmly began his final summary.

But the judge's next question--whether there was enough evidence to charge Justis Smith with premeditated murder--caught Pearce by surprise.

"An abundance of evidence…overwhelming." Pearce's voice elevated. "First, deliberation…continual stabbings of a deliberate nature, designed to inflict grievous bodily harm… There is an opportunity to decide whether to stab again or to desist."

"But why was Mundy never charged with premeditated murder?"

Perhaps another missed opportunity? Bill Pearce said only that he wasn't in Bermuda at the time.

Meerabux' next question surprised Pearce even more. "So who is charged with premeditated murder?"

"Smith," Pearce answered.

"He and he alone?"

"He and he alone in this case."

But how was Mundy involved? "You brought Mundy, and I'm trying to get Mundy."

"I don't have to," Pearce said, because Bermuda law holds two participants equally culpable. "They're considered in law to be partners in crime. It makes no difference if Mundy made the stabs or Smith… They are acting in concert.…"

Was there evidence to place Smith at the scene? Meerabux quoted Perry: "There is no blood, no semen, no hair, no bit of flesh, no saliva, no evidence to put Mr. Smith at the scene of the crime."

The expert testimony that the murder weapon that came from the same batch as in the Smith household provides direct evidence, Pearce reminded. Moreover, witnesses across the island—the security guard, police, the men with the broken down car, even Justis Smith's mother—put them together.

"In most murders you don't have direct evidence," Pearce reminded. "The key witness, of course, is dead, and more often than not you have to rely entirely on circumstantial evidence to prove the case. So there is nothing unusual about this case. The test is whether on circumstantial evidence the defendant can be proved guilty."

Furthermore, Smith's lies showed "consciousness of guilt," Pearce said. "Smith tells us that it was just an innocent excursion to St. George to have drinks and come back home…We know on the facts that that's not a true statement…Yes, they went riding around, but they also stopped…at the Mullet residence. They talked to the two girls, and Rebecca Middleton got on the bike, left with the two of them, and they went to Ferry Reach. We know that. It follows Smith was there. There is no other person that could have been there.

"The reason Justis Smith deliberately omitted talking about stopping at the Mullet residence--the reason he deliberately omitted the fact that Rebecca Middleton embraced him and they talked—that she showed him the necklace—how he had to get off the bike to allow her to get on, and him to get on after—It goes to a guilty conscience. He knows those are incriminating facts, and he's deliberately left them out of the statement. Now from that lie," said Pearce, "inferences can be drawn."

Meerabux returned to Mundy. "He says he goes off to wash himself in the water for five or ten minutes after having sex. It did not dawn on the police that this man may have been washing off blood? Even after all this, Mundy was not charged with murder or rape?…It looks like a gigantic you-know-what with the police department," Meerabux said. "What time was a call to the hospital?"

"That's four a.m. or thereabouts," said Pearce. "What was happening at the scene is between 3:05 and 3:20 a.m. They were with Becky only twelve or thirteen minutes. If someone else killed Becky then from where did this phantom person materialize--out of the mist?... So this phantom person is not only someone that happened to be there, but a total stranger with the same predisposition as Mundy-- to inflict torture and murder this woman, then to carry her to the middle of the road. Some total stranger...

"Then this total stranger disappears into the mist again, and according to their theory, they pick up Smith along the way...He was just having a nice little walk about Ferry Road? There is no person in this world who could possibly believe that."

Pearce recalled that day in court many years later. "God, I was so upset, the whole scene was preposterous. A set of knives from the same batch as the murder weapon, cut marks on Becky's shoulder that matched the knife, examples of strong direct evidence.

"We had Smith in spades," Pearce believed.

Meerabux asked. "How do you put the weapon in his hand?"

The testimony about the knives, Pearce reminded. More than twenty shop keepers had testified that this type of knife wasn't sold in Bermuda.

"What are the odds of that? Then, what are the odds of that other person-- the mystery person who brought an identical knife to the ones in the Smith household-- throwing the knife from the bridge or from a boat within a few days of July third?"

Pearce reminded that Becky's underwear had semen in the crotch, suggesting her panties were put back in place after Mundy's attack.

"If Mundy first raped Becky, then who would be the logical person to have cut off her clothing and to have continued with the sexual assault? That would be Smith."

Also, reminded the prosecutor, "Even though Smith's semen wasn't found at the scene, there is evidence of two condom wrappers in the vicinity, so it's consistent with one of two things: Either (Smith) used a condom...or Rebecca Middleton resisted, and he didn't have sexual activity, it was merely an attempt, or he couldn't perform.

"But what we do know is that after Mundy had sex, her clothes not only were removed from her body, there were injuries inflicted...to control her, to force her to do something that she did not want to do. As Dr. Baden said, oral sex--or things such as, 'Let me rape you or I'm going to hurt you even more'...And who would be the person most logically to do that? Again, it points to Smith."

Becky's skirt had her own saliva on it, likely held over her mouth, to prevent her from screaming. "Again, you can't be cutting, performing sexually, and doing all of these things with one person. We are talking about two people.

"Even after the assault, the bike license was covered. A lame attempt is made to explain that the bike isn't registered. It's obviously there to avoid detection. They were trying to get away, to hide from their crime. That's consistent with the knife being thrown out at the swing bridge, the first available body of water."

Significant, too, no evidence that Smith tried to get away from Mundy. "The moment that they turn off to Ferry Road, a crime is being committed by both of them--detaining a person against her will... It was up to Smith to ask Mundy to stop the bike and say, 'Let me get off. I'm not going here. I'm not going to have anything to do with this.'

"But he didn't. He stayed with him...the entire time...Indeed at the end of all of these dastardly acts, he gets on a bike with the license covered, and again Justis Smith makes no attempt to distance himself from the acts...All point to the fact that he had the intention to kill along with Mundy."

Justis Smith, by his own words, had confirmed his presence, Pearce said. When Sean Smith, whose car Mundy and Smith passed broken down on the bridge, testified that he saw blood on Mundy's clothes, "Justis Smith shouted from the cage, 'You're lying boy.'

"If Smith hadn't been there, how would he have any opinion whatsoever regarding blood being on Mundy's clothes?

"The piece of cloth covering the license place was consistent with Becky's missing vest. She had it before, and she didn't have it or her jewelry after."

"She had jewelry, and it wasn't found?" Meerabux asked.

"It wasn't found...There are several offenses being committed, deprivation of liberty..., theft of a necklace, ring and vest..., sexual assault, and aggravated assault in terms of controlling injuries. Then, fatal stab wounds.

"Because Smith did not distance himself," Pearce said, "the act was committed during unlawful detention. That makes Smith a party to the crime, even on its lowest threshold."

Nonetheless, the prosecutor suggested, evidence supported a higher threshold—"that Smith intended to cause her death...Overwhelming evidence--not just some evidence, places Smith at the scene....At the very least (Smith) provided the knife to Mundy. That would make him guilty of murder... Bermuda's law of equal culpability."

"Was Mundy ever charged with premeditated murder?" Meerabux asked.

"No," Pearce said, wondering how the judge after more than two weeks could ask such a question.

In Dave Middleton's estimation, Bill Pearce had laid out a strong case against Smith. Mundy an accomplice? With a law on the books that holds two persons equally culpable? Who had been tiptoeing when charges were set, and why? Only one man charged with murder, and only the murder charge? No mention of kidnapping, rape, sodomy, theft, despite glaring evidence?

The judge continued his banter. "At some point, say you have the socializing taking place, and then the socializing went a bit deeper in the offense."

"What offense?" asked Perry.

"A serious sexual assault," Meerabux continued. "And then at some point along there, something happened, triggering the common purpose to kill."

"Where is the evidence?" John Perry challenged.

..."Mr. Pearce will no doubt put some flesh on that." Meerabux sighed.

"Flesh, he doesn't even have a skeleton...not a shred of evidence."

"Can you tell me why Mundy was never charged with premeditated murder?" Meerabux asked Smith's defense lawyer John Perry. "...Mundy and your client on the same motorcycle...the inference being, since they are on the same motorcycle...Then they were like Siamese twins."

"We know they are not Siamese twins. There is a problem." Perry scowled.

"I'm trying to use colorful language." Meerabux grinned.

"They are not Siamese twins. That's exactly the point....Your lord, you are perfectly right." Perry demurred. "They could only get to the point if they were Siamese twins."

Meerabux frowned, "Again, the premeditation. Since they are Siamese twins—"

Perry sprung to his feet. "But they are not, yes!"

Meerabux rambled. "We know that Mundy was there, we know that there was a ghastly act. Hence, there must be premeditation by Smith to do those ghastly acts, because the acts themselves-- when you look at the stab wounds-- it supports the view it cannot be a casual affair there at all. There were nineteen stab wounds, it has to show there was deliberation—"

Perry swirled and interrupted. "I respond in a sentence before the break."

A break? Again, Perry's in charge, Dave thought.

"This is an exercise in a question begging chain of reasoning," Perry said.

"Are you finished?" Meerabux asked.

"Yes."

Meerabux, appearing drowsy, declared a recess.

The whole problem with the case, Smith lawyer John Perry insisted when court resumed: "There is no direct evidence putting Smith at the scene. The Crown…can only do so by inference."

A two-man theory meant that Justis Smith could not be the (lone) perpetrator and the only man charged with premeditated murder.

"Now that's why we say, my lord, that this involves an abuse of the process…." The court already had accepted Kirk Mundy's guilty plea as an accomplice, and yet Crown witnesses, Drs. Michael Baden and Henry Lee, had testified two men kidnapped, raped, tortured, sodomized, and murdered Becky.

Not only that, Perry argued, there wasn't sufficient evidence to give the case to the jury.

"Preposterous," Bill Pearce shouted. A jury should decide whether there was enough evidence to convict Justis Smith of Becky's murder, not the judge. "Verdicts are decided on trial evidence, it's as simple as that."

First muttering, then silence while Judge Vincent Meerabux acknowledged John Perry's call for dismissal. He'd rule on Perry's request the following Monday, Meerabux promised.

Now Friday, Bermuda did what Bermuda does best on weekends, very little, except for at least one soon-to-be former resident, who was busy packing.

Bermuda buzzed when on Monday, December thirteenth, residents learned that Attorney General Elliott Mottley had made an unannounced departure on Sunday.

Most speculated that Mottley's discomfort with the trial had gotten the best of him. Of course, on the small island, where secretaries type legal reports and have on occasion been rumored to whisper results, some surmised Mottley had gotten heads up and headed for the airport.

When court resumed on Monday, though, Meerabux had made no decision. Instead, he sent the jury home, to return on Wednesday.

Cindy, staying at the Hamilton Princess, ran into fellow guest John Perry in the elevator. She didn't speak.

Listeners packed Supreme Court on Wednesday. Justice Vincent Meerabux took fifty five minutes to review the evidence, confirming, Dave thought, the absurdity of John Perry's request to dismiss for lack of evidence and abuse of process.

The judge ordered Justis Smith to stand.

Cindy had a bad feeling. She left the courtroom.

The jury foreperson, following orders from Justice Vincent Meerabux, announced, "We find Justis Smith not guilty of premeditated murder."

A maudlin silence—then cheers.

Dave Middleton and Rick Meens watched as Justis Raham Smith, now twenty, left the dock. Two young men sitting behind Dave stood up and cheered.

"Sit down," Dave snapped.

Smith supporters applauded in the public gallery, while Middleton friends sat in stunned silence. Although Meerabux had announced his decision to both teams of lawyers before the ruling, Sandra Bacchus appeared devastated. One lawyer who came to observe said that he'd never forget watching one of Smith's lawyers filing his fingernails while they waited for Meerabux to rule. Many jurors were in tears.

By now most of Bermuda and overseas knew that Elliott Mottley was gone. His Sunday departure was surprising to most, especially considering a recent

Royal Gazette report that Mottley had promised to stay until the following March to transition the new attorney general—Lois Browne Evans.

With the Browne Evans' appointment not yet made and Mottley gone, Bill Pearce found himself acting attorney general. Immediately, Pearce appealed Meerabux' ruling.

Cindy had doubted Bermuda's legal processes from the beginning, Meerabux' ruling only a confirmation. To many, it seemed, Becky had gotten lost in the trial—her murder minimized, comparable to Cindy's having lost her purse in Bermuda, instead of her beautiful daughter, her baby.

"I am very disappointed with the way it went and am not at all happy with the decision," Dave told reporters. "I don't think it's fair. We know what happened. We know who did it. It was not the way we expected to go. I haven't figured it out yet…a little numb. More disappointment…the feeling you are left with is 'the bad guy wins.'"

Regarding Elliott Mottley's sudden departure, Dave said, "people can draw their own conclusions…The last time I spoke to Mottley,…he was going to prosecute the case, he felt they had a very good chance of conviction. Not too long ago, I found he wasn't prosecuting the case. He was the man at the top, now he isn't here."

From the day that Dave Middleton arrived in Bermuda to bring home his murdered daughter, he said, "people have said that this type of crime needs to be addressed. I think we have a number of people here who think this didn't happen. It really did happen. There is going to be no rest until the persons responsible for Rebecca's death are brought justice. I think that is in the interests of everyone in Bermuda."

Bill Pearce expressed his sympathy for Becky's family. "I'm sure they are disappointed in the justice system in Bermuda, both with respect to Kirk Mundy and Justis Smith."

That was putting it mildly, Cindy thought, but she agreed that Pearce and Bacchus "did an excellent job with the hand they were dealt."

Richard Smith hurried out of the courtroom. "Everyone knew (Justis) didn't do it. I know how they (the Middletons) feel. I feel sorry for them. If the law was done right the first time, they wouldn't have this problem."

"You better lock him up," Rick Meens shouted at John Perry. "That's what you want to do. Keep him under lock and key. If he wasn't there, he should walk, but nobody can tell me he wasn't there…Why did Smith do it? Why did Mundy do it? Is this child's life worth five years?"

"Free at last, free at last," a crowd of young men cheered as police escorted Justis Smith to freedom. Rick Meens passed by another group shouting, "Free Kirk Mundy."

"The prosecution cocked this case up," Smith's lead defense lawyer Perry told reporters, wondering aloud why a deal was made with Mundy. Perry requested a police escort for his departure. "Is it safe?" he asked. "It's wicked what has happened in this place," a reporter quoted Perry.

In Bermuda, Canada, England, and the U.S., followers of the case were flabbergasted.

Meerabux told the press that he believed prosecutors failed to link Smith, to show premeditation, to put Smith at the scene, and provided no confession. Plus there was the Mundy problem. Even the knife found at the swing bridge that matched the set found in the Smith home, he insisted, provided "inconclusive" evidence.

Now main characters from Bermuda's 1973 political murders crept into the fray. Two months before the disastrous outcome, the PLP had finally taken control.

And the harder the new government tried to quiet the uproar, the louder it became.

SIXTEEN

And so it is for tourists…Bermuda's sleepy atmosphere is deceptive (and) masks an island where political and racial tensions are bubbling in a very ugly fashion just below… and strains that threaten to ruin this holiday paradise…

The Guardian—March 12, 1973

Repercussions
December 16, 1998

WHAT COULD BE MORE upsetting to a tourist destination with already frayed nerves than out of control media? News that Justis Smith had gone free in the murder of Rebecca Middleton dominated media across North America. Bermuda, too, dissected the ruling, registering shock when CNN alighted on the island from the U.S. to detail how the case went awry. *City Confidential*, an A&E network series, filmed *Death on the Rock* which exposed unpleasantries that the Queen's "Jewel in the Atlantic" would have preferred to keep to itself.

Toronto freelance writer Jules Elder's column in the *Toronto Sun* three days after Christmas suggested that both Becky and Bermudians deserved better. "There have been howls of dissatisfaction following the acquittal of Justis Smith and (Kirk Mundy's) five-year sentence… The justice system was inept, as well as the police."

As holiday advertising filled newspapers, the Bermuda tourism ministry tried to assure visitors that Bermuda was still a safe destination. Most seemed certain that eventually interest in the murder of Rebecca Middleton had to go away as efficiently as had the political murders of 1973. Instead, voices grew louder.

"This is a Christmas where many of us will have mixed feelings as we celebrate the season against the backdrop of a murder trial that most of us will never forget," the *Bermuda Sun* observed. "Rebecca Middleton's horrific murder, the trial that followed, the grief of her family, the confusion many of us feel as to how all of this transpired the way it did, and concern about our criminal justice system, all stand in contrast to Christmas and what it represents. The murder offends our sense of justice."

Former Premier Pamela Gordon, now Opposition leader, called for an inquiry. "We view with alarm and concern the recent turn of events in the Rebecca Middleton case," she said. No one could ignore the "heartfelt pleas of Rebecca's parents, to whom we offer our sincere sympathy."

Premier Jennifer Smith, to the consternation of many, remained silent. Dave Middleton suggested that people direct letters to her or to Governor Thorold Masefield. "If she got thirty thousand letters, she would have to sit up and take notice."

Two days after the trial ended, Public Safety Minister Paula Cox and Deputy Governor Tim Gurney met with Dave Middleton and Rick Meens. "I told Paula Cox…people can give all sorts of excuses, but until things happen, they are just that," Dave said. Bermuda "lost big the other day. There is an opportunity while everything is fresh to resolve the justice system now."

He had no intention of letting the matter die, Dave told the deputy governor. He'd seen a lot of people who were good at pointing the finger at others when things went wrong, but not with getting things done. Gurney promised to watch the situation.

Paula Cox, Dave recalled, "was supportive, but noncommittal." When Dave asked that a memorial be placed where Becky died, Cox replied that if they did that for Becky, they'd have to do it for everyone, Dave recalled. "That might not bother some people, but it stuck with me."

Publicly, Paula Cox endorsed the call for an inquiry, telling Bermuda, "If we are going to maintain a sense of integrity to our process, there is clearly a need for justice both to be done and to be seen to be done."

A *Royal Gazette* editorial labeled Meerabux' decision not to allow the

Smith case to go to the jury "reasoned and sound." Meerabux "was within his rights…It was a courageous act and the right decision," an editorial proclaimed.

Judicial experts would disagree.

In Belleville, Police Chief David Klenavic told the local newspaper, "Whoever committed the murder has gotten away with it."

Doug Parker, general manager of the Belleville Utilities Commission, worried, "I don't know how Dave's going to cope. Being a father myself, I know that would be a terrible thing to have to deal with."

Catherine Glover, Becky's high school principal, reminded how important it would be "for students that some kind of justice is done…Now it seems as though that's not going to happen."

Back on the island, calls escalated for an inquiry into what went wrong. Walton Brown, political science professor at Bermuda College, termed the decision "the straw that breaks the camel's back." The collapse…"was just one in a series of investigations into serious crimes which have come up short."

Even Justis Smith's lawyer, John Perry, publicly called for an investigation, ready to lay blame on police. "The people of Bermuda must ask themselves what's gone wrong. This unfortunate young woman came to this beautiful island for a holiday, and she ended up dead. It appears that nobody has paid the penalty." A "cock-up," Perry repeated.

From Barbados, former Attorney General Elliott Mottley denied his decision to leave Bermuda only days before the Smith acquittal had anything to do with the controversy surrounding the handling of Becky's case. He needed to return to his busy law practice, he insisted.

Justis Smith was lying low, his mother said. The media reported he was locked in his room, although some locals claimed they saw him partying with friends in Bermuda's clubs. When a *Toronto Sun* reporter tried to interview Smith, a gang of young men blocked his path.

Several weeks after his release, Justis Smith appeared in the public gallery of Supreme Court to watch the trial of an accused bank robber. When he left court, a *Royal Gazette* reporter approached Smith. When the journalist persisted, Smith turned around, mimicked holding a gun, pretending to pull a make-believe trigger. "Bang, bang," said Smith, jumping on a motorbike with a friend, heading toward "back of town."

Justis "just needs time to get back and get settled in," Smith's mother told reporters. She denied rumors that her son had been threatened.

Dave Middleton and Rick Meens knew that he had. As they stood with friends outside a Front Street restaurant, a man approached them within the hearing of many and offered to take care of both Smith and Mundy.

"We are not violent people," Rick Meens replied, "and we don't plan to become so now."

A week after the trial ended, Bermuda's troubles increased exponentially--a website appeared, dedicated to justice for Becky and a boycott of Bermuda. Bad for an island professing to be a tourist paradise.

Michael Vigodda, a Canadian who knew the Middleton family, set up the website that within just a few days received some twenty thousand hits. Emails deluged the attorney general's chambers, occupied by Bill Pearce. Volunteers in the U.S. and U.K. signed up to help the website take off in other countries.

It seemed that Bermuda could ignore the problem no longer. Finally, a week after the website appeared, Premier Jennifer Smith made her first statement, agreeing that the boycott was "of considerable concern." She urged a swift appeal of Meerbux' decision and promised to use her "good offices" to assure that there was no "undue delay."

PLP Tourism Minister David Allen charged that the website distorted "what Bermuda is all about," calling Bermuda "a very civilized place where 99.9 percent of tourists are treated very well." Allen termed the island's image since the case collapsed "a temporary setback" that could be overcome by promoting Bermuda in Canada. That comment ruffled more than a few feathers.

"That is just so cynical it's beyond me," Michael Vigodda said from Canada. "Maybe he thinks he's paid to think this way." Vigodda believed that it had taken the website pressure to get the premier to comment. "It's sad that the Middletons have never received such a statement through their entire ordeal, but that (the website) should receive it instead." On that basis, he said, "we've not received it happily." Jennifer Smith's statement, he said, "neither says anything we want to hear, nor says much at all."

At the same time, a radiant review of Bermuda appeared in the *Globe and Mail*, Canada's national newspaper, a piece Vigodda labeled "tactless." Vigodda promised that complaints would go to Buckingham Palace…to U.K. Prime Minister Tony Blair, and to then Canadian Prime Minister Jean Chrétien. "Ms. Smith is not dealing with a bunch of terrorists making demands here," Vigodda said. "She's dealing with reasonable people who are trying to get a supposedly honorable government to do something honorable."

Officials of Bermuda's Women's Resource Center reported phone callers frustrated over the collapse. One attorney told Dave Middleton, "People in Bermuda tend to beat their chests for a few weeks, and then it's put to rest."

Not this time. Within three months after Smith walked from remand, the fallout from the case hit the island where it hurt—in decreased tourist numbers, both from Canada and the United States.

Perhaps Vigodda would turn out to be correct. In fact, U.K. Prime Minister Tony Blair likely heard exactly what happened in Bermuda regarding the Rebecca Middleton murder case—perhaps over breakfast with his wife, human rights lawyer Cherie Booth.

While North American media reported the conclusion of the Smith trial with incredulity, the Canadian government took a passive approach—despite thousands of telephone calls to Ottawa. Canada's Department of Foreign Affairs told media that it was unlikely that it would pressure for an official inquiry.

Why would the Canadian government work to free a couple who were held in South America on drug charges, Dave Middleton wondered, but not stand up for a child killed in another country? The Canadian government's attitude never changed. The geographic giant rumbled briefly after the FBI and volunteers from the U.S. rushed to assist in the disappearance of Americans Natalee Holloway in Aruba and newly-married George Smith from a Mediterranean Sea cruise ship in 2005. Canadian Consulate General Pamela Wallen, headquartered in New York City, expressed interest in the case in 2006, promising to write a letter of concern to the Bermuda government. However, she left office, and her successor did not follow up.

Becky's mother trusted Detective Constable Terry Maxwell, the police officer who assisted Bill Pearce in preparing the case against Justis Smith, a support to her and Wayne throughout the trial.

On this tiny island, it's not unusual for folks on opposite sides to socialize, judges entertaining defense attorneys in their private homes, and parties including all sides. And Maxwell was, in fact, a close associate of Kirk Mundy's former attorney, Mark Pettingill, who also served as lawyer for Bermuda police. Both considered the other a friend, sometimes, Maxwell and Pettingill agreed, "like brothers."

Cindy didn't know what to expect when Maxwell, hours after the case collapsed, suggested she and Wayne meet at a hotel for dinner with Mark Pettingill and his wife. Afterward, they met in Pettingill's office. Although Mark Pettingill hadn't been associated with the Smith prosecution, he could provide keen legal observations of what went wrong, things that Becky's parents, who'd never before been in any kind of courtroom before their daughter's murder, would not be likely to observe.

Pettingill told Wayne and Cindy Bennett he had been shocked by Justice Vincent Meerabux' decision to halt the case against Justis Smith. He had no doubt that Pearce, with Maxwell's help, had built a solid case. Of course, Pettingill couldn't discuss that "elephant in the living room"—the Mundy plea—off limits owing to privileged information rules.

The evidence in the Justis Smith case, though, had been there, all public information. The media has missed very little. It took simply putting that information together, Pettingill explained. However, the chaos, confusion and emotion that followed the verdict suggested few people had done so.

That night, back at the Hamilton Princess, Cindy slept little. The next day, on her way to a local television station, despite Cindy's dislike of the spotlight, she carried in her purse a list of questions for Bermuda.

"Becky's smile was like the sun, it didn't discriminate. It shone for everyone," Cindy Bennett began.

More than a few locals complained the girls shouldn't have gotten on the bikes with the young men. But Cindy told how Becky displayed characteristics that many in Bermuda protested were in short supply—Becky was trusting and unprejudiced. She and Jasmine had entrusted the cab drivers to pick them up as the dispatcher promised three times, and when they didn't, Becky trusted the young men to take her home, a fatal error.

"That smile and sunshine went out of our lives. The ache in my heart never goes away. I had peace of mind with Becky going to Bermuda, which has long been known as a safe place with high standards.

"Coming here on July fourth, 1996, we were in shock. All we could think of was to bring Becky home. When we left we were assured things would be looked after in 'the right way.'

"In Canada we put trust and faith in our police. Here our trust was betrayed. Things didn't go as we expected. No one deserves to be treated the way Becky was."

Choking back tears, Cindy warned the tiny country, "No community deserves to be treated in (this) manner... An unjust system makes victims of everyone." It was time for Bermuda to deal with what had happened. "Not a single day goes by that we don't think of Becky. Please don't let Becky's death be in vain." Steadying her voice, Cindy looked directly into the camera. "Think carefully," Cindy warned.

Elliott Mottley has gone. Why didn't he prosecute Justis Smith? Were key police assigned to Becky's case? Why did only one police officer, Howard Cutts, testify in the Smith trial? Who made that decision to charge Mundy as an accessory, and why prosecute without DNA evidence? Why was the case dropped in Bill Pearce's lap, without the help of other senior prosecutors? Was evidence handled efficiently? Who brought the second round of charges against Smith and Mundy for murder? Why did Elliott Mottley leave Bermuda so suddenly? Why didn't Chief Justice Austin Ward serve as judge in the Justis Smith murder trial, "given its magnitude and controversial history?" Finally, why "in a modern jurisdiction, is the current system of court reporting by judges' hand so antiquated?"

The only public response to Cindy's questions came from Chief Justice Austin Ward, himself: "Who sits on cases is not a matter for anybody outside to decide."

When one examines Bermuda law, though, it isn't difficult to answer most of those questions, particularly who appointed Justice Vincent Meerabux, reportedly a member of Ward's church. Likely Chief Justice Ward recommended Meerabux to Governor Thorold Masefield, the official decision maker.

Cindy added one more question: What happened to the tape of Kirk Mundy, who had agreed to be wired to get a confession from Smith? That tape had never been made public.

As it turned out, police files held a possible answer. The officer who taped

Mundy and Smith alone in a cell together copied the original and gave both to Maxwell, according to the officer's report, tightly sealed from public view.

In 2004, Maxwell said the tape was blank. Pettingill argued he could hear some noise. Without video, Smith might have signaled to Mundy. The Middletons and Rick Meens continued to wonder why police would copy and label a blank tape.

Police denied Dave Middleton's and Rick Meens' requests for a copy.

It had been a nightmare, a *Royal Gazette* editorial agreed. "First and foremost for the family of Rebecca Middleton, who, like everyone else, still do not know what happened on the morning of July third, 1996, and its aftermath. This has surely been a nightmare for the attorney general's chambers and the police service. Charged with the investigation and prosecution of a vitally important case…nothing seemed to go right from the start…One of the most important cases of the decade…" Beyond that, "Bermuda has been made a laughingstock in Canada."

Dave Middleton corrected the comment. "I know exactly what happened to Becky from the testimony that we were allowed to hear. Becky was kidnapped, tortured, raped, and her clothes replaced. Then she was attacked again and murdered."

What he didn't know, he told the press-- the reason rape charges weren't filed. Innocently asked, Dave Middleton had no idea how loaded this question would become. With no freedom of information legislation in Bermuda, and Supreme Court documents locked up, few thought to ask: How many physicians does it take to determine that Becky was raped, tortured, beaten, sodomized, and left in the middle of Ferry Road, perhaps to be run over by a vehicle, and to die? Weren't the reports of three physicians—Dr. James Johnston, Dr. Keith Cunningham, and Dr. Henry Pearse—enough to dispel the words of a known criminal, easily shown to be lies?

Instead, not only did some take the word of Kirk Mundy, but they continued to promote the story as true—that Becky had gone with the men to have consensual sex. When that didn't work any longer, some white lies would become sinister.

Cindy and Wayne left Bermuda the day after her television appearance. At home, Cindy received a letter from her friend, Robert Paul, and his family.

"You've displayed remarkable courage, integrity and grace throughout this whole ordeal," Paul wrote. "Our family has been following the sordid series of events as they unfolded in the media. When we received your message, it was hard to hold back the tears while only faintly trying to understand the torment in your life. There are, I am sure, many, many people who feel as we do, and that, I hope, can be a very small bit of comfort to you."

Paul's father-in-law had taught at Bermuda College a decade before, "and we spent a lot of time in Bermuda. When these two murderers were apprehended, my father-in-law bluntly stated that 'the poor parents of this child are in for a lot of suffering because they will never be convicted in Bermuda.' I did not believe him for a minute, although I was somewhat aware of the darker aspects of the island.

"Now it appears…that there will be no justice for your daughter or yourselves. That people can be so uncaring and willing to defend the obvious total miscarriage of justice is disheartening and basically immoral, if not evil. The words of Smith's lawyer are beyond the realm of all human compassion."

Referring to Vagodda's website, Paul wrote, "One thing that I think cannot hurt is the boycott—especially for this tourist-sensitive island. The one thing these people get excited about is their tourist income…(By the way, my best friend is a captain with Air Canada, and he feels sick about this every time he lands his plane in Bermuda)."

Legal efforts seemed hopeless. Cindy, who initially opposed the boycott, changed her mind. She wrote to the Pauls: "A few years ago I said there is 'no justice in this world.' The onus is on the people of Bermuda to open their eyes and see what is happening right in front of them. With burying their heads in the sand, they are only hurting themselves. It is time for Bermuda to wake up to the fact this could have happened to any of them and is more likely… now that this affair has ended in such a mess."

When it seemed to the Middletons that Bermuda events couldn't get much more bizarre, they found out otherwise. Two weeks after Smith walked free, *Royal Gazette* reporter Tim Greenfield faxed Dave Middleton in Belleville to tell him that an employee of Bermuda immigration had threatened to remove a foreign political reporter who had written about the "Boycott Bermuda" website.

Laverne Furbert, a member of Bermuda's immigration advisory council, complained that *Royal Gazette* reporter Raymond Hainey "took 'perverse pleasure' from the bid to keep visitors away from the island."

Hainey, a Scotsman, had annoyed Furbert when he reported that the *Globe and Mail* travel piece on Bermuda had "backfired" because of its timing. He had "no respect for Bermuda or Bermudians" and a "disdain for the Progressive Labor Party. By his recent articles concerning the Rebecca Middleton murder, it seems to me that Hainey is taking some perverse pleasure in the fact that some unknown Canadian named Michael Vigodda has created a web page to discourage Canadians from choosing Bermuda as a holiday destination.

"Do we need to have a reporter writing for our own daily newspaper who continues to debase the Bermudian people, insult our premier…, discourage tourists from coming to our island, criticize positive travel features in international newspapers about Bermuda and take the word of an unknown Canadian like Michael Vigodda to be gospel truth? I personally will be writing a letter to the minister of immigration and will send a copy to Mr. Hainey and this newspaper asking that Mr. Hainey's work permit be not only reviewed, but revoked."

Editor Bill Zuill said he stood by Hainey and was concerned by the threat to his work permit "simply because she disagrees with our reporting." Zuill said he welcomed Furbert's comments and would publish them in full. But "you can't have freedom of speech for your own views on the one hand and then threaten somebody else's freedom of speech on the other."

Dave Middleton suggested that perhaps Furbert should re-examine her comments. "To even suggest that someone lose their livelihood because they have a different point of view is very drastic." If the Middletons had responded with the same thinking, "we would be trying to shut down Bermuda…The facts are the facts. We had an awful murder down there, and so far no one has really been brought to justice."

If Furbert had been successful, this wouldn't be the first time someone had been shipped home suddenly for what might seem minor infractions. In the early 1990s a housing authority director was deported for skinny dipping in the ocean behind his house. (A policeman hiding in nearby bushes spotted and reported him).

A few years ago, a Bermuda immigration official summoned a young food server to government headquarters because she was wearing a navy blue blazer on a cool, rainy day. Accused of impersonating a manager, the server and the restaurant's owner were chastised. She wore a navy blue sweater until she left Paradise shortly afterward.

A foreign bank employee not long ago criticized Bermuda in general terms to her colleagues. With a return ticket kept on file at immigration, as is Bermuda's policy for foreign hires, removal was prompt.

A hotel senior chef thought he'd made a joke when a waiter asked him which dish should be served to Premier Dr. Ewart F. Brown. The chef's response—"the one with the arsenic"—not amusing. Gone in two days.

In what might seem to be an effort to put out the flames, Hainey's next story covered the plea of a Toronto journalist who called for Canadians to "go easy on Bermuda."

Hainey left Bermuda shortly afterward for Australia. Years later, back in Scotland, Hainey wrote to former Police Commissioner Colin Coxall, who knew about repercussions in Bermuda first hand. "Miss Middleton's murder is still unfinished business as far as I'm concerned."

Hainey wasn't alone in that thought.

Part Six

A Not so Independent Inquiry

SEVENTEEN

Bermuda depends on the tourists, yet if it is unable to solve its racial problems in a peaceful manner, it will risk cutting off its economical lifeblood. Sadly, the very nature of tourism, with its multi-million dollar hotels and the fast spending Americans who patronize them, makes this peace process the more difficult.

The Guardian--March, 12, 1973

Past Chances upon Present
Spring 1999 to Summer 2000

BELLEVILLE'S HEAVY SNOWS had melted, and as bare twigs blossomed, the Middletons dealt not only with Becky's loss, but with the injustices of the last four years. Then, a bombshell—a Bermuda Supreme Court justice—the same one who in January, 1998, had tried to clear the way for Kirk Mundy to face murder charges with Justis Smith— overturned the "no case to answer" ruling by Justice Vincent Meerabux. Justice Richard Ground ruled that Justis Smith should face a new trial.

Ground, called to the bar in England and Wales in the mid 1970s, had served as attorney general in the Caymans in the early 1990s before he came to Bermuda, earning respect often difficult to achieve in tight knit island circles.

Ground hadn't missed the horror of Rebecca Middleton's murder and the injustice that followed. The Court of Appeals, three roving judges from the Caribbean, upheld Ground's decision and ordered retrial of Justis Smith.

Despite his "cock up" claims and call for an inquiry, Smith's defense lawyer John Perry jumped back into the fracas, leading the appeal to London's Privy Council--the same high court that two years before had refused to hear the attorney general's request to charge Mundy with murder.

As soon as the case began in winter, 2000, the Privy Council's senior judge, Lord Johan Steyne, a strong advocate of human rights, born in South Africa during the apartheid, told media that the court found Meerabux' decision astounding. The judge was wrong to throw out the case before it went to the jury, Lord Steyne wrote. The case was not "within one thousand miles of abuse. The judge should never have discharged Justis Smith."

Evidence supported the case, the senior House of Lords judge agreed, the trial should have proceeded. A strong case, despite failures in gathering evidence. Steyne found it "surprising that the judge took the view that the circumstantial evidence was inconclusive." Not only was it "no doubt a surprising view for the judge to have taken," it was "perhaps an astonishing one."

When he heard Steyne's comments, Dave Middleton, in London with Rick Meens for the hearing, for the first time believed he was not "totally nuts, that I'm not the only guy in the world who thinks this way. It gives me hope for their decision being the way I'd like it to be."

Again, hopes slid to a halt. Although unlike Kirk Mundy's case, in which the Privy Council refused to hear the appeal, the court listened, but again cited double jeopardy because of the way Bermuda's appeals code read.

Until Becky's case reached the Privy Council in 1998, judges' rulings routinely had been appealed—erroneously it seemed. After the Privy Council's determination in Becky's case, only errors "in law" could be appealed. No appeals based on anything to do with facts of the case. What was the likelihood of identifying errors in "law only," with no connection to fact? Experts would suggest: a legal rarity.

On the twenty eighth of February, 2000, the court restored Justice Vincent Meerabux' decision. Already on bail while he awaited the Privy Council ruling, Justis Smith kept his freedom. Seemingly, a glitch in Bermuda law had sunk the case, and Justis Smith—as had Kirk Mundy--successfully facing an unencumbered jury in the murder of Rebecca Middleton.

Nonetheless, Bermuda had options, Steyne wrote. "The legislature may abolish or qualify this principle…after the widest possible consultation…only after the opinions and desires of all the disparate elements of the society are known…We so recommend."

No one hurried to do so.

Now international furor exploded, while Bermuda's 2000 tourist numbers dived. Governor Thorold Masefield relented to demands for an inquiry. At the governor's invitation Dave Middleton met with Masefield.

Dave told the media he was "delighted with the decision to hold a public investigation of Becky's murder and the subsequent investigation."

Masefield promptly corrected Becky's father—the inquiry wouldn't focus on Becky's murder, only serious crimes in general.

Moreover, with Attorney General Dame Lois Browne Evans at the helm in March, 2000, and the FCO watching from London, many could not help noticing signs of an impotent inquiry.

Browne Evans had little patience with what she viewed to be oppression to blacks and favor to whites. She saw no reason for an inquiry into Becky's failed case. If Rebecca Middleton had been black, more than a few black Bermudians publicly stated, her death and subsequent mistakes in the handling of her case would have gone unnoticed.

Rick Meens mailed Dave Middleton a tape of a Browne Evans' radio interview. "Why do we need an inquiry?" she asked. "What do we owe the Middleton family?"

At the same time, government created a new job—director of public prosecutions, established to be independent of government (which the attorney general is not), responsible for criminal prosecutions, an arrangement suggested by the 1977 Riots Commission.

Browne Evans' protégé' Khamisi Tokunbo, Crown counsel who prosecuted Kirk Mundy's accessory charge, would handle criminal prosecutions. Browne Evans held on to policy, administration.

The FCO quietly sent a representative to make sure the inquiry didn't get out of hand. Governor Thorold Masefield's order limited "terms of reference" to serious crimes in general. Although no one doubted the inquiry came as a result of Becky's failed murder investigation, Masefield's terms gave commissioners an excuse, if they chose, to stop speakers mid-sentence if subjects became too hot.

Canadian media suggested the commission was small consolation. "The fact the Bermuda government wouldn't hold a separate inquiry into the Middleton case, but rather lumped it in with other 'serious crimes' belittled the tragedy," Becky's hometown newspaper suggested. "That was the second insult to the girl's family--that's the third strike for the colony which promotes itself as a safe, scenic paradise getaway for tourists...."

There was the inquiry's type. Rather than a Royal Commission reporting to the FCO, this simple commission answered only to the premier and the governor, likely joining others sitting on shelves, collecting dust. With no subpoena power overseas, many doubted that the major players in Becky's investigation would attend.

Human rights activist LeYoni Junos requested, without success, an explanation for Governor Thorold Masefield's choice for chairman-- Stanley Moore, a judge in the Eastern Caribbean, who spent two years as attorney general of tiny Montserrat, a few miles off Puerto Rico, abandoned by most in the 1990s following a volcanic eruption.

No public mention of Moore's long association with fellow Guyana native Richard Hector, Mundy's bail lawyer. Neither did most recognize that Justice Vincent Meerabux and former Attorney General Elliott Mottley were by no means strangers to SCC Chairman Stanley Moore.

Some years later Richard Hector told Rick Meens during a private meeting that Stanley Moore had escaped from Guyana to avoid political arrest. Moore's 1979 appearance on television in Guyana, the film contained in files held by Vanderbilt University, discussing the case of Larry Layton, wasn't common knowledge around the world, certainly not in Bermuda.

Layton was the only man arrested in the mass murders of U.S. Congressman Leo Ryan and four others as they ended a 1978 fact finding mission in Guyana investigating the Jim Jones cult. Bullets cut down the five Americans as they boarded a small plane, while cult leader Jim Jones at the compound shouted his "premonition" of Ryan's death. Those notorious suicides and commune murders resulted in the deaths of more than nine hundred people.

A country with major problems and political complicity, Guyana's law and order, forensic, and judicial procedures to this day remain light years behind Bermuda's. Layton's first trial in Guyana ended in a not guilty verdict.

However, after Layton's acquittal in Guyana, the U.S. wasn't complacent. The state of California arrested Layton, trying him twice. First, a hung jury, then a conviction for aiding and abetting Ryan's assassination. He received a life sentence.

Vanderbilt files show Moore discussing Ryan's murder

Of course, like the appointment of Meerabux in the Smith trial, it wasn't difficult to discern who appointed SCC Commission Chairman Stanley Moore, despite the governor's refusal to say. During the SCC, Richard Hector, Mundy's bail lawyer, was president of the Bermuda Bar Association, with the authority to recommend his long time associate to the governor, who would make the final decision.

Neither was the rationale for the appointment of Bermuda defense attorney Shirley Simmons to the SCC difficult to understand. Simmons and Attorney General Lois Browne Evans were colleagues, with strong PLP ties. Nonetheless, Simmons, unlike Browne Evans, agreed there was reason for concern that the inquiry was not solely into Becky's death. "Somewhere, there was a change in the playing field," she told media. "I know initially…people were led to believe it would be on that case."

Representing police, Commissioner Don Dovaston had recently retired as deputy chief constable of Derbyshire, having developed a British program to rescue kidnapped children, established homicide databases and worked on DNA legislation. Bermuda has training ties with some U.K. communities.

Finally, no one appeared troubled by Richard Hector's appointment as SCC marshal. Not only had Hector obtained bail for Mundy, unusual in armed robbery cases, but he also was law partner of Mark Pettingill, who orchestrated Mundy's "confession." Moreover, Hector had helped Pettingill plan Mundy's defense, Pettingill would remind Hector during SCC testimony.

At about the same time the SCC got under way, Richard Hector was preparing to defend one of four American men arrested in the 2000 Tortola murder of American Lois McMillen—another high profile island murder which caused Tortola to fight to save its reputation for safe travel. This case, with its twisting island justice, also resulted in a fateful ruling from London.

Shortly before the inquiry began, Commissioner Don Dovaston told the *Bermuda Sun* that Dave Middleton could rest assured that his daughter's case would not be diluted. Chairman Stanley Moore rushed to respond, "I don't wish to disagree with anything (Dovaston) said," but the inquiry was to be on serious crime in general.

Then, whose invitation seemed welcoming—and whose did not.

For the next three weeks, LeYoni Junos and Rick Meens would attend every session while SCC Commission Chairman Stanley Moore diligently sought to assure that testimony didn't go too near the murder of Rebecca Middleton, the case that had brought about the inquiry.

Fortunately, for the occasions that Becky's case took center stage, which were often, Rick Meens brought his tape recorder.

EIGHTEEN

....What is emerging so far is a pattern of contact between a few members of the Black Beret Cadre and one Mr. Green (sic), a hardened criminal with a hatred for those in authority...If this sort of pattern continues, it could mean that the motive is not political alone, but that there is a criminal element also; and, if Green is involved, a personal motive, a compound of ambition and hatred for authority...

--Secret brief from Acting Governor Ian Kinnear to Sir Duncan Watson, Deputy Undersecretary, FCO-- March 20, 1973 (The National Archives, London)

Sex, Lies and a Tape Recorder

August 7, 2000

BERMUDA GOVERNMENT officials and media packed the patio of Government House this day, where bullets cut down Governor Richard Sharples and his ADC Capt. Hugh Sayers twenty seven years before, a fact that went unmentioned during the pageant-like swearing in of the inquiry that had been brought about by the murder of Rebecca Middleton.

Known generically as the Serious Crimes Commission (SCC), the inquiry took place under the watchful eyes of Attorney General Dame Lois Browne

Evans, publicly more concerned about the accused than victims. "I was always a defense attorney at heart," Browne Evans reminded Bermuda's Parliament in 2001.

LeYoni Junos glanced around the small courtroom. Likely, LeYoni thought, Attorney General Dame Lois Browne Evans would recognize the man who now approached the witness box as keeper of many of the secrets of the 1970s political murders.

Likely, too, with SCC Commissioner Shirley Simmons' experience in criminal defense, including assisting Browne Evans in the appeal to spare Larry Tacklyn's life, Simmons also would be able to identify the man offering evidence.

Chairman Stanley Moore, Marshal Richard Hector, and Commissioner Don Dovaston? Unlikely.

"Do you remember the Students for a Democratic Society (SDS), the Black Panthers?" the witness began. "There was a group formed here, the Black Beret Cadre (BBC). But, prior to their formation, I, along with a couple of others, put in motion the idea to assassinate every government official on this island—it's in the court records."

If commissioners were surprised, they didn't appear so.

The witness told commissioners he felt "trepidation" about the sincerity of the inquiry. He was among some fourteen Dennis Beans in Bermuda, he said— "the Dennis Bean who once worked with notorious Bobby Greene" at Greene's Court Street restaurant, where drug peddlers and other criminals gathered, a meeting site for the BBC.

"They called it armed robbery and kidnapping, because that's, in fact, what we did. But what they didn't say was that they could have counted it as treason, it was our intention to overthrow the government. A guy that got kidnapped—he just happened to be a guy that got in the way…We were going to buy arms and shoot every danged politician in this country."

Bean's voice escalated. "Are you listening to what I'm telling you? Justice was far from being served to our advantage in this country." He got fourteen years, he said, out on parole in less than half the time, "but it didn't take away from the fact that nothing's changed up to this very day."

"Youngsters don't know an arm from an elbow. That's why if you poke a guy in a nightclub, he'll stab you…That's why if you talk to a guy's girlfriend, the guy will get his gang and beat you up.…They just lash out, they're not justified, but I understand that their mothers and fathers were abused and misused...."

Chairman Stanley Moore asked Dennis Bean whether he had had any previous contact with police.

"Ya, as a young individual...Let me put this to you, you would be hard pressed to find guys in my age group at that time, black males particularly, without some sort of contact with police in their youth.

"Let me drop something on you," said Bean. He'd been falsely accused in a sexual assault of a young girl when he was young. "When we appeared in front of the panel, they told me not to say anything." His mother sat next to him, "all nervous and shaking. I asked, 'Mama, can I say something?' She was terrified and warned me, 'Keep quiet, don't say nothing,' and they ended up sending me...for corrective training."

The fact is, he said, he had been trying to "fight the guys off when this little girl was being poked around...but nobody wanted to hear my story."

Moore interrupted, asking Bean whether there existed at the time any system of record expunging, appropriate for protection of juveniles.

Dennis Bean, though, didn't perceive Stanley Moore's question as one of concern—rather, someone else who wasn't listening. "Just a minute, sir," Bean shouted. "Either you want me to answer my way or your way, and I'm here to tell you the truth now. If you're going to interrogate me--"

"No one is interrogating..."

"Don't lead me, but allow me to tell you the story, then you pick out the bones and eat the fish. That was the problem with the juvenile commission, nobody allowed me to tell the danged story...That's the problem on this island--nobody's allowed to tell their danged stories. That's why there's so much manipulation and deceit taking place. This is the reason for this danged commission. Nobody wants to be honest.

"...I got to tell my story to somebody. You can either accept it as truth or discard it in a danged rubbish heap...And I'm telling you...There's been a significant abuse of power on this island over the years.... Certain people in the police department take law unto themselves."

Becky's case was a perfect example, Dennis Bean told the SCC. "The case of the Middleton girl here, a prime case of manipulation, a case where certain people--lawyers in particular--get a case brought down to a certain level. People who are affected are people like me, because nobody wants to believe we're telling the truth. They're so used to telling lies that nobody would recognize the truth when they heard it.

"Let me touch on the Middleton case for just a second—a typical case of a lawyer exercising his righteous authority to have certain police officers minimize a charge against his client. Then the police officer showed up and said, after talking to certain people, 'Here it is, I gave you what you wanted.' The guys themselves manipulated the authorities…It's done all the time… The same rules used to suppress people have turned right around and come back to haunt them.

"The little girl gets hurt," Bean said, "because of something that happened down through the years, and it happened all the way from England down. It's a travesty of justice…that a white tourist or black person of privilege warranted an inquiry, but someone like me is allowed to wander for forty years."

Dennis Bean, for those who were listening, presented a clear picture of Bermuda's racial divide, police and judicial short cuts, perceptions of unfairness, conflicts of interest, and an ongoing problem with young people who act out their rage. In fact, with far fewer words and more clarity than did many of those who would follow.

More than a week into the inquiry, media queries as to whether invitations had gone out to former Attorney General Elliott Mottley or former Police Commissioner Colin Coxall went unanswered. Commission Chairman Stanley Moore suggested there was no need to invite Colin Coxall. "We will cross every hurdle when we reach it."

Attorney General Dame Lois Browne Evans told reporters she didn't believe the former police commissioner ever had any intention of attending. She didn't mention Colin Coxall's letter, reportedly sitting on her desk.

In fact, Governor Thorold Masefield had received Coxall's response in July to Deputy Governor Tim Gurney's letter detailing terms of reference, inviting former Police Commissioner Colin Coxall to testify.

Masefield forwarded Coxall's response to Attorney General Lois Browne Evans, who, as the SCC neared its close, the first week in September, still had not replied.

Publicly Browne Evans said, "It's obvious the man did not want to come; that's my feeling. I don't know why he thought he needed (indemnity) anyway.

Who is going to sue him in Bermuda—Mr. Middleton and Mr. Meens? We are not in America."

It would be several years before Bermuda would learn that Coxall immediately accepted on the condition that the indemnity he held as police commissioner was still in place—a request that some erroneously termed immunity. "My natural instinct is to do everything I reasonably can to assist the inquiry (and) the Middleton family to come to terms with the loss of their daughter, and to support my former officers," Coxall wrote to Gurney. Without assurance of indemnity, there was potential for civil liability. Moreover, Coxall requested independent counsel, usual in British inquiries and certainly not unjustified--particularly given his previous Bermuda experience. Gurney assured Coxall that the indemnity request was entirely reasonable, but didn't give the okay.

Bermuda's former police commissioner began to suspect, correctly it turned out, that he never would get an answer, so Coxall offered to give evidence by video link. Moore declined.

Bermuda media reported that Moore, who never made public several letters Coxall submitted to the SCC, offered to fly elsewhere to meet Coxall, but his attempts failed. Coxall recalled no such offer. It was nearly the inquiry's end before the public learned that Coxall would not attend.

"I'm very disappointed," Dave Middleton said. "They should have granted Mr. Coxall indemnity because he really is the last piece of the jigsaw."

As it turned out, while Stanley Moore was announcing that Coxall wouldn't attend, the FCO had sent Coxall on a mission to the home of Moore, Hector and Justice Vincent Meerabux—Guyana. Ironically, while Moore was pontificating about Bermuda's problems, Coxall was reporting Guyana's problematic police system to London. Murders went without investigation-- some of them allegedly by police.

Neither would former Senior Crown Counsel Brian Calhoun appear before the commission. Foreigners place themselves at great risk when they speak publicly, even the FCO agreed in its 2008 report. Calhoun had moved into private practice—not his greatest love, which was criminal law—but a choice that many agreed might have saved his life.

"I don't believe they wanted either Coxall or Calhoun there," Dave Middleton said. He wasn't alone in his opinion.

"I have read with increasing despair—the reports of the so-called "serious crimes" commission…It would appear that there are some supposedly eminent people involved in this whole sorry business who do not understand the difference between 'immunity' and 'indemnity,'" a letter to the *Royal Gazette* read. The first, said the writer, "is almost impossible to give (and was never requested). The ex-lamented (by some) commissioner of police sought indemnity, and why it should take the attorney general's chambers and the chairman of the commission two months not to make up their minds on so simple a matter is beyond comprehension.

"Once again, a man of considerable experience, expertise and complete integrity has been left out in the cold. Could it be that once more (former Police Commissioner Colin Coxall) could have made things too hot for someone?"

NINETEEN

A Constitution where responsibility for law and order is vested in the Governor...gives the impression of a colonial regime imposed from the outside...the Governor, therefore, is not only left with the not very pleasant task of maintaining law and order...but unjustifiably becomes the target of a frustrated minority....

-- 'The Implications of the Murders in Bermuda, Secret Memo Acting Governor Ian Kinnear to Secretary of State, FCO— May 1, 1973, (The National Archives, London)

Changes in Tune
August 12, 2000

AT FIRST, CHAIRMAN STANLEY MOORE seemed to resemble a kind cleric before his congregation, not a man tasked with investigating police and judicial failures in Bermuda. Nothing controversial had occurred, which suited him well--until five days into the inquiry when Detective Superintendent Vic Richmond, a quiet and disciplined Scotsman and veteran of more than three decades in the Bermuda police service, caught commissioners by surprise. It began with an innocent question from SCC Marshal Richard Hector and an offhand remark by SCC Chairman Stanley Moore.

"Do you refer to the director of public prosecutions for advice if needed?" Richard Hector asked.

"It seems to me that the decision whether to arrest or not to arrest is taken without any consultation with a legal advisor, entirely by police?" Stanley Moore interjected.

No, the detective answered, the director of public prosecutions office would be called after the arrest to consider charging decisions. Richmond got specific, referring to the July twelfth meeting between police and the attorney general's office regarding the murder of Rebecca Middleton.

"…That afternoon, I, together with others, arrived at the attorney general's chambers at seven minutes past five, Friday the twelfth of July--."

Richmond didn't get to finish his sentence. Stanley Moore announced lunch, dismissing Richmond and adjourning to a meeting behind the closed doors of Attorney General Dame Lois Browne Evans. When the lunch break was over, Vic Richmond was nowhere to be seen.

"There was a sudden and obvious halt in Richmond's testimony," Dave Middleton told the press, saying he feared that the truth never would be told.

A *Royal Gazette* editor voiced concern. "Just when the commission seemed to be getting to the bottom of the case, it decided that its terms of reference forbade it from delving too deeply. The fear seems to be that an individual will get blamed, and based on what the commission was able to find out before cutting itself off, there was plenty of blame to go around."

Would the commission do its job? "Surely we don't want them thinking and saying Bermuda not only botched a horrific murder case, which the police do not regard as an unsolved murder, but they could not even conduct a simple inquiry," said UBP minister John Barritt.

Clearly, someone had become uncomfortable.

The behaviors of SCC Chairman Stanley Moore and Commissioner Don Dovaston toward Scenes of Crime Inspector Howard Cutts confirmed for LeYoni Junos, watching with Rick Meens in the viewers' section, what some suspected was the inquiry's mission—to lay the blame for the botched case on police.

An inquisition, it seemed to LeYoni. Richard Hector began with department protocols. Procedures, Cutts replied, were consistent with international standards. "As far as my department is concerned, there is no difference wherever you go around the world, the procedures—"

Stanley Moore interposed a strident sigh. "Do you understand Mr.

Hector's question? Please do your best to answer Mr. Hector's question in the way he framed it. If you would like to say anything further you will be permitted to do so. Answer Mr. Hector's question as he put it."

Junos and Rick Meens noticed Cutts' face redden.

"I was wondering if there are any written protocols," Hector repeated.

"Yes, there are."

"Were they put together by you?"

"The manuals came from attending overseas training," Cutts said, offering copies to commissioners, "...training reviews, procedures and other guides, all put in place during recent months since I was put in charge of serious crimes."

What about DNA testing, not available in Bermuda? "Is there any particular place you'd send them?" asked Hector.

"Certainly not England," Cutts remarked, to Dovaston's obvious surprise. "The turnaround time for Scotland Yard was the reason we decided to go to the Royal Canadian Mounted Police. Since the early 1980s we've enjoyed excellent cooperation."

"Turn around time?"

"Greatly improved since PCR-DNA testing."

"Beg your pardon, what was that?" Moore asked.

A recent discovery, Cutts said, involving chain reaction, where DNA is synthetically tested. Recently turnaround time had been weeks, rather than months.

"We've heard evidence in a particular case the turnaround time was six months or more," Hector said.

"I think that's outside of the time frame. "

Moore's impatience escalated. "Mr. Cutts, let me assist you if I can. Mr. Hector has a reason for framing the questions in the way that he is framing them. He is seeking a specific response to the particular question to which he puts. Please do your best, first of all, to try and understand the question. If you do not understand, please ask him to rephrase. Answer directly or specifically."

Cutts started to speak, but Moore held the floor. "This is an inquiry, not an inquisition, but it certainly would help if you would do your best to answer the question put to you. Do you understand?"

"Yes, sir."

"We take it that you are unaware…We have received information of delays in excess of six months," Hector said. "You are unaware of any delays?"

"I don't agree that six months is the time frame that you are talking about…"

"Not the norm," Hector agreed. "But it has happened, do you know?"

Now Moore badgered. "Has it come to your personal knowledge that in any case whatsoever there has been a delay longer than six months?"

"No, sir."

Hector, too, seemed surprised that Cutts wasn't going along with the six-month time line.

Most explanations of why the Rebecca Middleton murder case had gone so awry focused upon DNA results, rumored to have taken six months, untrue.

"As a layman, what is DNA?" Stanley Moore asked, his tone condescending. "Is it something you grasp from the atmosphere, is it something that grown on trees, or is it a thing that has to relate to some part of the human anatomy…?"

Cutts started to answer.

"Just a minute, please…which has to be collected, and when collected submitted to an expert for analysis and identification and comparison. Is that not the case?"

"Roughly yes, sir."

"You must bear with us because we are not experts, and we are looking for your guidance." Hector's soothing voice contrasted with Moore's bristles.

"Well, I'm trying to, sir."

"…Can you point us to the instruction?"

"I don't have copy of the full document, but you're welcome to have this document."

"Count the pages," Moore demanded.

Sixty one pages, Hector reported.

Cutts tried to speak, Moore interrupted. "Is that the kind of book one can carry to a scene?"

"I—."

"Just a minute, Mr. Cutts. I try to speak slowly and deliberately, so that I can achieve clarity. Is that the kind of a document that an officer, hurrying off to a crime scene...or perhaps hurrying from the crime scene. Is that the kind of document?"

SCC Commissioner Don Dovaston took over. "You're relying on documents--called a home office document, which is not a home office document. You're suggesting that it is state of the art, and it isn't state of the art. It's a document that sounds to me to be well outdated, and you're still relying on it. What would you say to me about that?"

He wasn't suggesting it was state of the art, Cutts said.

"How is it reliable when so outdated?" Dovaston asked.

"Well, in Bermuda we're dealing with a criminal code of 1907, that's outdated as far as fingerprints are concerned," Cutts responded, his face scarlet.

"Well, I ask you this question. In law, lawyers like to say the law must be stable, but it cannot stay still." Moore's voice boomed. "I am told the principle of stability also exists in science, but in science the developments take place in far more rapid pace than in law."

It took sixty two words for the SCC chairman, who admitted he enjoyed his own voice so much that he once taped the Magna Carte to listen to himself speak, to advise Scenes of Crime Lead Inspector Howard Cutts to rely on a more recent document.

As Cutts attempted to speak, Stanley Moore delivered his next rant. "...When you've reached the tangent upon which you've embarked and gone down, give me an answer to the question which I asked. I'm not going to stop you from going down your tangent." Forty four words later, Moore had finished reiterating his belief that the document was outdated, asking Cutts to agree.

Cutts said nothing.

The sound of a crash, Cutts silent.

"Well, I take it you have declined to answer the question, and I return the microphone to Mr. Don Dovaston."

Dovaston continued the scolding.

Scenes of Crime Inspector Howard Cutts recognized the futility of responding. He remained mute.

Later, SCC Marshal Richard Hector apologized to Cutts, saying he had no idea that Moore and Dovaston would treat him as they had.

Hector, though, had not interrupted the inquisition.

TWENTY

Although the island has all the trappings of a colonial democracy and the undisguised air of easy wealthy contentment, there are subterranean rumblings. Black is their color, brown is their expression, and white prefers not to know...

The Guardian--March 13, 1973

'The Only Evidence'
August 15, 2000

"WAS IT NOT on the basis of Mundy's statement… that Justis Smith was charged?" SCC marshal Richard Hector asked Bermuda's first Director of Public Prosecutions Khamisi Tokunbo.

"Yes, eventually that would be it. We charged him on the basis of his caution statement in the hope that we would use him as a witness. That would be the only evidence that we had—his statement."

A statement that both Rick Meens and LeYoni Junos found odd, given all the evidence reported by media in Becky's murder.

Hector reminded, a "caution statement is not evidence." What was the evidence? A question to which Hector already knew the answer, having been consulted by Mark Pettingill, the lawyer who had maneuvered the accomplice charge for Mundy.

"Basically that Mundy said that he had consensual sex with her." In July,

1996, "there was no evidence to suggest that Mundy was involved in the murder," Tokunbo replied.

Hector asked if Mundy had been given any sort of immunity.

"Of course not. No document was written by Mundy's lawyer or anyone." To anyone's claim of a deal, Tokunbo added, "I can state categorically and unequivocally that this is absolutely incorrect and untrue."

Six days after he was interrupted mid-sentence, Detective Superintendent Vic Richmond returned to the SCC witness stand.

"When you were last here you asked to be allowed to return to clear up certain matters," Richard Hector said.

For the first time, Richmond publicly identified those present during the fateful, July twelfth, 1996, charging decisions meeting: himself, Lead Detective Inspector Carlton Adams, Inspectors Lee Gay Farley and Stuart Crockwell, from police; Attorney General Elliott Mottley, Solicitor General Barry Meade, and Crown Counsel Khamisi Tokunbo, from the attorney general's office.

Senior Crown Counsel Brian Calhoun's absence, Vic Richmond said, was "worthy of note. His advice and opinions would hold much weight…

"Now, I'm not saying that the decision that was reached by those that met that afternoon would have been any different if Mr. Calhoun had been there."

Richard Hector interjected. "You merely mention the fact."

"He is normally at these meetings," Richmond continued. "As I say, much weight is placed on his advice and his opinion…"

The meeting lasted for an hour and eighteen minutes, Richmond said. "Much was discussed, and we (police) informed the members of the attorney general's chambers of what evidence we had at that stage that connected Justis Smith, Mundy, or both, to this crime"--Mundy's statements, the knife, people who saw Mundy and Smith together, Dean Lottimore's lineup identification, the security guard's witness reports and those of the two men whose car had broken down, Smith's statements, and autopsy findings. Richmond listed eleven pieces of evidence.

What followed after he gave the information to the attorney general? Hector asked.

"A lot of discussion…There had been a very successful prosecution not long before of a brutal murder of an elderly gentleman in St. George where one person was charged with the murder, the other with accessory after the fact, and a conviction resulted."

But there was no deal, Richmond insisted. "…There was consensus that holding charges (would be laid). Smith would be charged with premeditated murder and Mundy with accessory after the fact."

"By holding charges?" Hector asked.

"They could be changed later on…You're under pressure because you've got the unwritten law in Bermuda of detention without charge of about seventy two hours. This was now about forty eight hours…"

"Do you remember whether you were given any instructions by the attorney general…how you should conduct yourselves thereafter?"

"No, as I say, we decided what the charge would be for each person, and the investigation would continue in a full tilt."

SCC Commissioner Don Dovaston spoke up. "We're grateful for your bringing to our attention this confusion—innocent or otherwise…Would there be any reason for you to be conveying any sort of deal?"

"I do not have the power or the authority…but I think it was my duty to convey to the attorney general what Mr. Pettingill had told me," Richmond said.

Dovaston helped Richmond along. "It is reasonable that you would be open with the attorney general. But in terms of you being an experienced detective, the purpose of that meeting was to progress as professionally as you could, faced with the evidence that had become available to you… nothing more than what would happen in many other cases…So if it was suggested by any person…that this was a process where a deal was constructed, would that be 'in folly'…?"

"Totally incorrect," Richmond said.

"And was any deal struck as far as you're concerned?"

"No, sir."

"Would you have known any other person who could have construed that there was a deal?"

"..No. The only way I think a person could have misconstrued it would have been Mr. Pettingill himself, based on the comment made by Inspector Crockwell when he handed the copy of the charge sheet to Mr. Pettingill at the court the next morning. I was not present that morning."

"You did not have in your mind in any way that this was part of any deal?"

"No, sir."

"Thank you very much, indeed." Don Dovaston sat back.

Chairman Stanley Moore finished wrapping the package. "Let me put a specific question to you. In the light of a written presentation that the deal was struck—listen to me carefully--Did anyone at that meeting to which you have made reference, where the attorney general was present, other legally qualified officers, you, other officers...Did anyone suggest the offering of a deal to anyone?"

"No, sir."

Moore enunciated each syllable. "Did the attorney general himself or any legally qualified officer of the attorney general's chambers in your presence at that meeting instruct you or any other police officer or anyone else in your presence to offer a deal to anyone?"

"No sir."

"Were you ever at any time between the afternoon of the twelfth when you had the conversation with Mr. Pettingill until now instructed by anyone to offer a deal to anyone?"

"No, sir."

"...You are a meticulous officer who keeps careful notes in the form of a journal which you complete at the end of each working day. Would that be correct?"

"I do keep a journal."

"Is there anywhere in your journal any reference to any instruction you may have received from anyone, or any instruction you were a witness to be given to anyone to offer a deal to be given to anyone?"

"Definitely not."

"Mr. Hector?"

"Just one question. We have evidence that at that meeting the attorney general told Detective Chief Inspector Carlton Adams to get a witness statement from Mundy. Did you hear that happen?"

Richmond appeared startled. Would police take a witness statement without concluding a deal? Richmond would know. "I doubt very much that that occurred at that meeting. In fact, I'm also sure that it didn't. I may be wrong, but I don't think...not at that stage..."

"Not sure that meeting," Richard Hector continued. "But he (Inspector Carlton Adams) was instructed--"

"Thank you very much," Moore brought the discussion to a full stop.

Not everyone would agree that no "deal" existed between Mundy and the attorney general's office, although LeYoni Junos and Rick Meens wondered whether SCC Chairman Stanley Moore seemed to be trying to steer the commissioners from that view, discouraging discussion of any deal.

Saul Froomkin, former Bermuda attorney general when the appeals law that prevented judges' rulings from being challenged was passed (1981-1991) and honorary Canadian consulate, and Mundy's most recent defense attorney, had been among first to testify at the SCC. But Tokunbo's testimony, Froomkin believed, made a second trip necessary. It was "abundantly clear that there was an agreement," Froomkin began.

Moore cut Froomkin short. "Were you a witness firsthand?"

"No, it's only hearsay, but I am aware of affidavits that were filed...."

Froomkin's colleague, former Kirk Mundy lawyer Mark Pettingill, supported Froomkin's stance. "I took very detailed instructions from Mr. Mundy…assisted by partners in my chambers--including yourself on the telephone, Mr. Hector."

He was "sewing the seeds," Mark Pettingill said, aware that police had no authority to make a deal. "I wasn't asking to make one, but I certainly was aware that it would be passed up, if you will. On the evening of July twelfth,… at the conclusion of that quite exhausting two days, I had occasion to speak with Mr. Vic Richmond"--

The chairman's protest halted Pettingill. "L-l-l-let's try and go in some sort of orderly sequence…I think it may help… if, first of all, we know what the proposal was, and emanating from whom, made to whom, in the presence of whom, where, and what time."

Outside of the incident room, Pettingill explained. "I indicated that Mr. Mundy was prepared to give evidence on the basis that he would be charged as accessory after the fact. It makes no sense otherwise, because as a co-defendant--"

Again, Moore interrupted. "If you propose to me now to swim across the harbor…I would decline the proposal, because I have not got the capacity to swim across the harbor… When you made this proposal to these two officers, you believed that these two officers had the capacity to respond to these proposals?"

He'd had experience with both Vic Richmond and Stuart Crockwell, Pettingill said, "who I respected in a professional and a personal manner, and Mr. Richmond indicated to me that they were on the way to discuss the—"

"Ah, ah, ah, I would like your answer to the specific question…"

Pettingill attempted to speak.

"Just a minute! Did officers have a right to make deals?"

"No, and I understand now what you're asking Mr. Chairman…My…request…was that they pass that on."

"Then you were using these officers as a mere conduit?"

"That's correct."

"Pass the proposal onto whom?"

"The attorney general."

Not the answer Moore sought. "Was there some--let's see--how I should put it--cocoon surrounding the attorney general which precluded you from approaching him directly?"

"Well, it would appear that there was, because certainly during the course of these very busy times, I did endeavor to contact the attorney general, and I failed to do that…"

"Attempted by what means?"

"Telephone."

Moore's tone became deriding. "In 1996 were there facsimile transmissions available? Were there email opportunities available? Was the old hand-delivered letter route available? …With a matter of this seriousness, would it not have, perhaps, been…that a written proposal be sent, and delivered, and signed for in the attorney general's chambers?

"Or are you asking this commission to accept that all channels of communication between yourself and the attorney general were cut off, sealed, and foreclosed?"

"No, sir, I wouldn't expect you to say that…..I clearly recall Inspector Crockwell handing me the pink form with the information on it, the comment, 'You got what you wanted.'"

"But with hindsight, do you think there should have been some recording, some writing, about these transactions, these exchanges…?" asked Hector.

"My personal view is no…A good barrister, if you're dealing with directly, he's as good as his word…."

By now LeYoni Junos, taking voracious notes, wondered whether there might be something else.

TWENTY ONE

...This British Colony, a ...speck in the Atlantic, is a symbol of imperialism hated by the Black Power leaders of America and the Caribbean...and for years outsiders have been agitating that they should rise up and drive the white population which holds the economic power back to America and Britain. In a part of the world where independence is the cry, the island...sticks out like a sore thumb.

Daily Express--March 12 1973

Clashing Recollections
August 21, 2000

"I THINK IT'S WIDELY SAID in this country that everybody's related to one another." SCC Chairman Stanley Moore grinned as the next witness approached the stand.

"There's no question about that." Richard Hector, who said privately that he'd been in Bermuda almost eighteen years but still felt like an outsider, smiled.

"Welcome back to Bermuda," Moore said to former Attorney General Elliott Mottley, approaching the witness box. This inquiry that officials insisted repeatedly had not been established to investigate Rebecca Middleton's murder clearly was attracting her key players.

"I'm grateful to have this opportunity to give evidence." Mottley smiled at Moore, no strangers among Caribbean colleagues.

Unlike others who reviewed their own credentials, Moore reviewed Mottley's for him. "..And while you were in Bermuda you acted as deputy governor on several occasions… Were you accountable to anyone?"

"No, not under the Constitution."

When he came to Bermuda in 1995, former Attorney General Elliott Mottley began, there had been "some concern about the prosecution of murder cases, and I intimated then during my interview that I personally would prosecute all murder cases, and I did that while I was in Bermuda, and I may add, successfully."

Marshal Richard Hector asked about plea bargaining. "Is there such a thing in Bermuda?"

"Not that I'm aware of."

Moore interjected, "Plea bargaining is an American practice…That system is unknown to English law and Bermudian law, as well. Prosecutors have no authority to make deals. Although the prosecution accepts conditions, a final decision would be… entirely in the hands of the judge."

A rubber stamp, most knew.

"We've been hearing a lot about a case which is called the Middleton case. Were you attorney general when that offense was committed?" Hector asked.

"I was. Police came to me, and after discussions, it was decided that I would charge Kirk Mundy with accessory after the fact and Justis Smith with premeditated murder. Suddenly, Mottley's voice quivered.

"Let me say this. This was based entirely—and I repeat entirely—on the nature of evidence that existed in July, 1997 (sic). It was not done with immunity granted to anybody. I understand, sir, that people have said there was an immunity agreement. What I've yet to hear is this, the date, time and place, and with whom the agreement was made."

"Do you mean 1996?" Moore suggested.

"Ninety six, yes, ninety six, ninety six. Oh, I'm so sorry. Ninety six. Ninety six." Mottley coughed twice. "July, 1996."

Mottley composed himself. "Let me say this. The other reason why it is a fallacy to say there was an agreement…not to prosecute Mundy for murder. No, sir, let's be realistic. The state of the evidence in July, 1996," Mottley insisted, "did not involve or implicate Mundy in the murder. So it would be stupid for anybody to enter an agreement, or even his counsel, and even more foolish of me."

No one had stated uncategorically that it took two men to kill Becky until eighteen months after her murder, Mottley insisted, when police sent evidence to Dr. Michael Baden, who put his opinion in writing. He admitted that Dr. Valerie Rao had suggested the same thing some nine months before that, but when he asked her to put this is writing, "Dr. Rao told me, 'no,' but if I asked her on the witness stand she would tell me (so)."

Not strong enough, he said. If police were going to prosecute Mundy for murder they would need other forensic evidence. "I am not a person, and anyone can tell you, as an attorney general, I did not hand down edicts. I like collegiate discussion. I invited even the most junior officer's input. In fact, I used to be annoyed if they didn't say anything. I draw that to your attention to assure you that it was at that meeting that, for the first time--one of the members of the attorney general's raised this theory, and called it no more than a theory—that it took two people."

Mottley turned toward listeners in the gallery, where Rick Meens and LeYoni Junos listened intently. "You see, this is not as easy as you might think it would be. I remember one meeting at Government House. I was told by someone there...that there is no way that a Bermudian jury was going to convict a Bermudian (Smith) for murder after a Jamaican (Mundy) had been convicted for the offense of accessory after the fact."

The former attorney general, in fact, hadn't been alone in hearing that attribution. Most who lived in Bermuda those years immediately after the murder of Rebecca Middleton likely would have heard: "A Bermudian wouldn't do that; it had to be the Jamaican." Said openly more than once on the tiny island where xenophobia, many complained, was all too common.

Had Mottley known that Mundy's attorney had approached Detective Superintendent Vic Richmond with Mundy's offer to testify against Smith in return for an accessory charge? Richard Hector asked.

Mottley's voice rose. "I'm aware that...I'm aware that..." Now a falsetto... "Mr. Pettingill had certain expectations...that it was in his interests—his client's interest...that it would be to his benefit when he came to be sentenced as accessory."

Along with Becky's case, Mottley said, "Mr. Pettingill was aware that his client faced far more serious charges (than accessory to Becky's murder) of robbery, or something like that. Mr. Pettingill hoped to have the courts go easy on his client, not only with this (case), but in regard to his other one, which I think he eventually got twenty years."

It was "malicious for people to say that the commissioner of police tried to get me not to accept a plea from Mundy. It never arose." His voice escalated.

"It suited a lot of people in Bermuda to put abroad a lot of malicious statements that the police were trying to get me not to plead (Mundy) guilty to a lesser charge of accomplice." Red-faced, the former attorney general shouted. "This is utterly untrue because the police were present when he was charged with accessory after the fact…"

Gently, Moore interceded. "Could you reflect on the twelfth of July and see whether you recall Messer's Richmond and Crockwell coming to your chambers?"

"Yes, along with Detective Inspector Farley, and others, I believe."

Did the attorney general then "dispatch those two officers with any message to anyone…that a deal had been done, and that the attorney general had accepted a deal, and you were authorizing them to convey the impression the deal was consummated and accepted by the attorney general?

"Absolutely not, sir," Mottley said.

"Did they bring with them any proposal concerning 'a deal?'"

Mottley's voice seemed to levitate. "They didn't bring any proposals that day. I think that they may have, in the course of discussions, stated what Mr. Pettingill was hoping for—that his client would be willing to give evidence. But that was only because he was the sole witness.

"Let me say this again to you, sir, for all this, after he pleaded guilty he was willing to assist the prosecution—But it was not a case of anyone granting immunity. He was charged entirely on the evidence that existed at the time, not based on any agreement."

What would you make of it, Moore asked, "if it was said to you that after Messrs. Richmond and Crockwell had gone to your chambers…that on the following morning, Mr. Crockwell said to Mr. Pettingill, 'You got what you wanted.'--What would you make of that?"

"Nothing, sir…not that there was any agreement." The choice not to charge them jointly was "deliberate. I wanted to separate both of them. Based on the evidence there was no way that Mundy could get out of pleading guilty....I have always maintained there was never any agreement, and it is disingenuous for people to come here and say that there was an agreement."

"The word used specifically in writing by Mr. Pettingill is 'deal,'" said Moore.

"There was no deal either, sir."

Was that decision to use Mundy against Justis Smith "dictated to you or contributed to by any previous experience in a murder trial in a similar situation?" Richard Hector asked. "We heard the evidence--"

Elliott Mottley no longer suppressed his irritation. "I know, I know. But when that other decision was made, I wasn't in Bermuda. Let me say this, the first time I knew about that other murder case was the day after—either the day after or the day before…I know that… this other gentleman pleaded guilty to accessory after the fact, and I know that there was hue and cry about Kirk Mundy's guilty plea.

"…Circumstances were the same. But there was no hue and cry. In fact, I think that person probably actually took part when the body was disposed of…the person had still been alive. But there was no hue and cry about that. I say no more about that."

Another comment that startled LeYoni Junos, who nudged Rick Meens. "An accomplice charge? Under a criminal code that holds both accused equally culpable?"

"Mr. Mottley, is there anything you'd like to suggest to improve relations between yourself and the police as they relate to prosecutorial decisions?" Richard Hector asked.

The former attorney general's voice approached a squeal, his face turned plum-colored. "I don't know that the relationship is bad!"

Stanley Moore soothed. "Not yourself… Mr. Mottley, seriously, with your vast experience, were there any difficulties that you experienced? What would be the way forward? That is what Mr. Hector seeks."

"I have views of the attorney general's chambers, not regarding the police," Mottley said.

He had prepared to prosecute the Middleton case, Mottley said. "Mr. Meens, who I see sitting there, would visit my office from time to time to be kept informed on behalf of Ms. Middleton's parents. On one occasion he asked if I was going to prosecute, and I told him, yes."

He traveled to a Barbados conference in August, "and to my surprise when I got back (Smith's) case was fixed for the twenty-third of November, (meaning that) I was taken out of the prosecution completely...because everybody knew that my contract was coming to an end in November." His situation changed when the PLP took power in October, and "I was asked to stay on for a short while."

Mottley reminded that he had recommended that Bill Pearce take Brian Calhoun with him to prosecute. "Mr. Pearce told me no, he wasn't doing it. I can't force counsel on anybody, so the case was started...What bothered me was the manner in which the prosecution was conducted... Junior prosecutors were coming into me, expressing concern... I believe that Mr. Pearce on one occasion wanted Mr. Tokunbo, who was not even involved in criminal matters at the time...."

Mottley's voice turned acerbic. "I think it is important to find out how many murder cases Mr. Pearce ever prosecuted...Nobody can walk straight in a prosecution of a murder case--not the Middleton murder case--not with the complexities that arose.

"And I must finish by saying this. One day before the close of the prosecution's case, I said, 'Bill have you closed the prosecution's case yet?' He said, 'No.' I said, 'Are you going to call Mundy?' Mr. Pearce said, 'I don't know. I don't think so.'

"I told him, 'You would have to prove who the two people were that went down to Ferry Reach. You don't have to prove what took place there.'"

It was imperative, Mottley insisted, "Pearce call Mundy... 'Do you know Justis Smith? Did you see him that night? You saw Rebecca Middleton? You went down to Ferry Reach? How many people went? Three. How many people left?' Two people. Done. Finished!"

But Pearce had argued with Mottley, claiming he had enough evidence without calling Mundy. Then, Mottley accused Pearce, "He told me 'And in any event, if I don't, and I lose the case, I can always blame you.'

"Me! That is what Mr. Pearce, the solicitor general, told me. That's exactly what happened. I have nothing more to say, sir."

"Mr. Mottley," said Stanley Moore, "I want to thank you sincerely for coming, first of all, and for being so forthcoming and candid in answering the questions put to you by Mr. Hector...Thank you so much, and I wish you a safe return to Barbados." Moore bowed.

Elliott Mottley returned the exaltations. "Thank you and the commission for affording me the opportunity to give evidence in this matter, sir. From the very beginning, sir, when I was informed by the deputy governor that the commission was going to take place, I knew that I could not be summoned to give evidence, because the writ does not go overseas. I volunteered to come and give evidence. Sir, I was always ready at all stages to answer any questions put to me."

"I think the last word must rest, rather, from Mr. Hector," Moore chimed.

"Yes, I'd like to thank you too, for coming. Good to see you."

Finally, the weekend. The inquiry chairman's adulation of Mottley was obvious, and the former attorney general's message transparent: Mottley had come, Coxall had not.

But few expected Monday's surprise guest.

Former Solicitor General Bill Pearce, who had prosecuted the Justis Smith case, hadn't planned to attend the SCC. Years later he recalled his discomfort when he entered chambers. His appearance took more than a few aback. He felt "unwelcomed." However, he decided he would not let former Attorney General Elliott Mottley's testimony go unchallenged.

Reminiscent of his trial demeanor, Pearce calmly addressed listeners. Rick Meens audio taped, LeYoni Junos took detailed notes, and television news director Bryan Darby filmed, with no idea then how important their records would become.

To Mottley's charge that Pearce had threatened to blame him if the case collapsed, "I say with the greatest respect to Mr. Mottley, I think he's mistaken. I never said those words. It is not something that I would say, even in jest. It saddens me because I thought we enjoyed a good relationship through the time that I worked with him."

Unlike Mottley, Pearce provided his own background-- "extensive experience with expert testimony, many complex cases...and I knew that this case was going to be won or lost on technical evidence...."

"If it were suggested that the Justis Smith case was the first in which you had appeared as a prosecutor in a murder case, what would you say to that?" SCC Chairman Stanley Moore began.

"I would agree. This is something that Mr. Mottley was well aware of."

Elliott Mottley hadn't expressed dissatisfaction or reservation about his taking the case. Pearce said. However, the attorney general had suggested Senior Crown Counsel Brian Calhoun work with him.

"Let me give you a brief background," said Pearce. "Before I left (for vacation in July, 1998) I expressed an interest in working with Mr. Mottley on the case"...Much to Pearce's surprise, when he returned he found himself lead counsel. Pearce quoted his former boss. "'Bill, the case has been set at a time when it's going to conflict with my departure. I might not be able to finish the case. I'd like you to assign it to someone.' Mr. Mottley gave me no direction as to whom.

"He just dumped it on my lap. I was a bit taken aback, to be perfectly honest. We were getting very close to the start of the case. The investigation wasn't complete, the file had been sitting around the office far too long. Even as late as August, 1998, there was a considerable amount of work still to be done...with forensic evidence in particular."

When he approached Senior Crown Counsel Brian Calhoun, Pearce remembered, "I said, 'Brian, you are the person to take this case...let us work together as co-counsel. I think we would make a good team...I think we could get this forensic evidence in order.'

"Mr. Calhoun told me he couldn't take the case 'for personal reasons.' I said, 'Brian, you have to tell me, why can't you take it?'"

Calhoun told him he couldn't tell him the reason, Pearce said. "He told me, 'You'll just have to take my word for it. I can't take the case.' I took Mr. Calhoun's word as a professional whose integrity I respect."

Now there was "the problem of finding someone on short notice to do one heck of a lot of work that still needed to be done," said Pearce. The suggestion that Crown Counsel Khamisi Tokunbo work with Pearce came from Senior Crown Counsel Brian Calhoun.

"The logical choice, he was Bermudian, and he would have a good understanding of the Bermudian jurors. I approached Mr. Tokunbo and told him I would be very pleased if he could join me on the case. He asked for time to think about it. Finally, he said he had other duties and could not accept my invitation." Sandra Bacchus, an experienced Canadian lawyer, accepted the case.

To Mottley's suggestion that Bill Pearce should have ordered Calhoun to serve, "I thought in actual fact that Elliott Mottley should have taken the case—because he had the best qualifications." He said he could never understand why Mottley did not.

Chairman Stanley Moore's thunderous complaint transformed the SCC's atmosphere from Bill Pearce's soothing tone. "Mr. Pearce, Mr. Pearce. When I ask a question I do for a specific purpose. I would be happy if some attempt were made to answer my question…I understand Mr. Mottley had passed the case over to you to deal with it yourself. Is a lawyer in chambers free to decline?...But I am not here to cross examine Mr. Pearce. If I were cross examining him, I would take a different approach."

Moore's dramatics failed to fluster Bill Pearce, who reminded that Dr. Michael Baden had insisted two people murdered Becky. "And in the course of the sentence, the Crown counsel (Khamisi Tokunbo) asked the judge to give (Mundy) a sentence of only three to four years, although he could have received seven, requesting a discount for Mundy's cooperation." Then Elliott Mottley laid the joint charges of "simple murder" against Kirk Mundy and Justis Smith, despite Mundy's guilty plea to accessory.

Pearce shook his head. "Never have I— either before or since—seen such. Normally if… the witness gives the testimony, if it comes up to proof, you go back to the Court of Appeal.…to determine if the sentence should be reduced."

If the Crown found evidence to discredit Mundy, Pearce said, then the Crown was entitled to void the agreement. Mundy had lied, thus "the Crown can't put the witness in the box as a witness of truth, then there's no obligation to do so."

Moreover, Bill Pearce disagreed with his former boss's claim that nothing other than Mundy's statement was available. "We also have the statement of Justis Smith that he was with Mundy from the time that he left St. George at three a.m. until he got home in the Hamilton area later that evening, he was with Mundy the entire time. Those statements place Mundy and Smith at the scene."

Additionally, the evidence of Jasmine Meens and Dean Lottimore "that immediately before the murder, Mundy and Smith departed…with Rebecca

Middleton between the two of them, heading toward the bridge." Shortly afterward, the men rode by on the same motorcycle "without Rebecca Middleton, and that point in time was immediately after the murder." Next, police saw them in Flatts.

"It shows in approximate terms that Mundy and Smith were with Rebecca Middleton from between ten and fifteen minutes at the end of Ferry Reach when this rape and murder occurred-- evidence which would indicate that those two, and only those two, would have had the opportunity to do what happened."

Then evidence of combination. "When you look at the photos, what you see is a lack of defense wounds. There are no cuts to the hands. One of the reports does describe one scratch, but not enough to draw blood." Also, the bruising of Becky's upper arms. "Those photographs indicate that she was restrained, evidence of two people acting in concert."

Given the evidence, Pearce suggested, "If Elliott Mottley made a decision simply on the basis of a statement and nothing else, I think that's highly irresponsible. I mean, any prosecutor approving a charge of that magnitude has to look at all the evidence—all the witness statements, all the reports, what was the rush to judgment? Why did he have to make the decision then? Why not look at the scene…and do an analysis of the case, like you would in any other one before making charging decisions?

"That was not done, Mr. Hector. The charging decisions were highly irregular, in fact, something I've never been able to understand."

Bill Pearce ignored the commission chairman's attempt to interrupt. "May I say this, Mr. Chairman, the evidence to you that I am summarizing now is the same evidence the Court of Appeal considered, the same evidence that the Privy Council considered…(and) both said that this was sufficient evidence to prove the Crown's case. In fact," he reminded, "the Privy Council said it was astonishing that the trial judge made the decision that he did on the evidence."

Chairman Stanley Moore sniffed. "I observed that I was ignored."

"I don't think you were ignored." Richard Hector attempted to keep peace. "I think he was trying to finish what he was saying."

"Yes. Well, anyhow, let's pass onto matters of substance," said Moore. "What was the reference?"

"I think it's important to look at the position Kirk Mundy found himself in on July tenth, which is two days before the charging decisions were made—and before he made the statement..." Pearce said.

"Here you have the physical evidence of the most violent rape and murder that you could possibly imagine...her clothes...punched in the face..., evidence a bra was cut. In the area of the shoulder where the bra was cut, there's evidence of superficial knife wounds. The skirt, the panties were cut, bruising in the vaginal and anal regions. This was all evidence of a violent rape and murder.

"Mundy knew his semen was there. He knew samples had been taken from him for DNA purposes. He knew when the report came back, it would show he had sexual intercourse... he would also probably know the DNA would not identify Smith—that he was the only person. He was hung out to dry. He knew that he was going down for the count on a murder wrap.

"That's what I think was in the mind of Kirk Mundy...on July tenth--and that's why I think he made this preposterous, implausible statement that he had consensual sex...and then wandered down to wash...and came back and knew absolutely nothing about what had transpired. I find that totally implausible."

Then, onto the scene came Mark Pettingill, said Pearce. "And as any good defense lawyer, he dangled before the prosecution this prospect of 'I'll plead my client guilty to accessory after the fact, and my client will agree to testify against Smith....' To his and everybody's amazement, they bought it...hook, line, and sinker."

Adding to the incredulity, Pearce said, was that "Kirk Mundy was on bail facing a serious robbery charge for which he received sixteen years. Here's a man who had a prior record of theft and who had given two alibi statements which conflicted completely with this July tenth statement, and here is a man who had an obvious motive to lie to get out of a murder wrap. That's the situation that happened."

As for the deal controversy, Bill Pearce told the SCC the issue was nothing more than "... a red herring....The courts have found there was a deal. Whether it's implicit or explicit is irrelevant. There was a deal, and that's a fact. Therefore, when the attorney general files the new murder charges against both Mundy and Smith, you are calling Mundy a liar, all deals are off."

Pearce's voice maintained its calm. "When Mr. Mottley suggests that I should have called Mundy to place Smith at the scene, on the inference that

I had made a gross mistake—that if I had called Mundy, all would have been well, and the case would have been different...I find that incredible. I do not believe that Elliott Mottley would have, in all seriousness, called Mundy as a witness when he had sworn to the effect that Mundy was a liar.

"No one knew what he might have said if he had been called. There were the clearest of reasons not to call Mundy. He could even have theoretically said he did it. The Privy Council's ruling prevented him from being charged with murder."

The initial charging decisions, Pearce said, became "the albatross which we had throughout the case," made even worse when joint charges were filed. "If we'd had a joint trial (initially), I can assure you we wouldn't have had those difficulties that we had in the case.

"But we made our case...and we made our case in spades." Mottley's attack on his experience, "just another red herring."

Moreover, Pearce found Mottley's refusal to take the case incredulous. "He's already been granted several extensions in this particular year. I think it's only fair to say with his experience and the fact that he's highly valued as a prosecutor, especially for a murder, if he wanted an extension for two to three weeks, it would have been there for the asking. The statement is preposterous."

Finally, Pearce told commissioners, two questions continued to baffle him. "I think they are deserving of answers if closure is going to be brought to this case--

"Why on July twelfth, 1996--nine days after the murder--did the prosecution believe the Mundy story that there was consensual sex, when all of the evidence indicated to the contrary?

"Why did he (Mottley) not do what any normal prosecutor would do... assess the evidence, see what deficiencies there are, and if further reports are required, suggest that further reports be taken before making charging decisions...If he had done his job, and those forensic scientists had been brought into the picture, I think there is a very good prospect that we would now, as we are sitting here, have two people behind bars serving time for the murder of Rebecca Middleton.

"That's the tragedy of this case. Now that's all I have to say."

Rick Meens' tape recorder clicked in the hushed room.

Stanley Moore interrupted the silence. "Based on everything that you've said so far, it follows, therefore, that the officers from the local crime scene management department would be required when they arrive at any given scene to make...a very critical determination as to whether what they observe is within the range of their own competence and experience...or whether this is the kind of situation where they need to call in immediate expert forensic scientists from above."

Rick Meens crossed his arms and whispered to LeYoni Junos. "How did he get back onto the police? Bill Pearce was talking about the attorney general's office."

LeYoni Junos had her own theory, which she whispered to Rick Meens.

SCC Commissioner Shirley Simmons took the floor. "Mr. Pearce, what I was just wanting cleared up--prior to coming to Bermuda in January, 1998, when was the last time you actually defended a criminal case...?"

He prosecuted, Pearce reminded.

"Prosecuted? Within six months?"

Again, the inference that the failure was Bill Pearce's.

"Now once you had the case...it was your decision...not to call Kirk Mundy. In hindsight, do you think your decision not to call Mundy was the best decision?"

"Absolutely, no question..."

"You have no question?"

"No question," Pearce said. "I think it would have been an absolute disaster. First of all, how can the Crown call a witness who the Crown has already discredited? You're calling someone who is not a witness of truth to begin with, and you're calling somebody you hope will give evidence in the way that will support you. But you've already made him a hostile witness, so you have no control over what he's going to say."

Mundy could do "an incredible amount of damage," Pearce said. "If Mundy were on the stand, he would have had a field day. Mundy would have been an absolute disaster."

Simmons wasn't convinced. "Well, would you agree with me, Mr. Pearce, that if Mr. Mundy were in the stand and would have lived up to this...Would there have been a better chance of going to jury?"

"It should have gone to the jury without that," Pearce said. "In honesty, I have spoken with other senior members of the profession in this country after the fact, because immediately after you do naturally question your judgment, you know, did I do the right thing? In each case when I've sought that counsel, I've gotten a resounding approval for the decision I made."

"Why do you believe that the prosecution team believed Mundy in July of 1996?" Don Dovaston asked.

"I think Mr. Mottley said that there wasn't any evidence to implicate the two at the time," Pearce said. "I think he was mistaken in that view, maybe he didn't have all the facts before him...Maybe he thought that was the best he could get in the whole case and that he had to grab it at the time."

Dovaston's second question, "Why did Mr. Mottley not look at all the evidence before charging?..The evidence is, and I would support it, that they should have waited for the forensic results. Why would you think those decisions were made in the light of that professional knowledge?"

"I don't have the answer," Pearce said. "Rather, it has remained a total mystery, to be honest with you....I just don't understand that...."

Years later Bill Pearce recounted another meeting, one that suggested he understood more than he was willing to tell the SCC. He listed attendees: himself, Senior Crown Counsel Brian Calhoun, Solicitor General Barry Meade, and Crown Counsel Khamisi Tokunbo. Pearce called the meeting immediately after the Privy Council refused to hear murder charges against Mundy. The discussion: filing other charges against Mundy, particularly sexually-related crimes.

But not everyone in the meeting discounted Mundy's consensual sex claim, Pearce recalled. He was appalled by such a world view, he said.

"If the attorney general had laid a charge of aggravated sexual assault instead of murder, double jeopardy would not be the case," Pearce said. "Moreover, the Crown had ample evidence for that...."

Without consensus, Pearce didn't pursue those charges.

"Was there an over reliance on (Kirk Mundy's) confession statement?" SCC Chairman Stanley Moore asked the former Solicitor General, Bill Pearce.

"After charging decisions on July twelfth," Pearce said, "police almost dropped their investigation altogether. They thought, 'Oh well we've got our man. We've got our swabs. DNA is going to come back, and we've got the case...End of story....'"

Moore sighed. "I was thinking of the timing of the availability of legal advice.....Suppose the evidence was that someone threw a shoe at the chairman, which missed, fortunately."

The chairman appeared to be enjoying himself.

"The question of an attempted assault, maybe, the evidence was also that Mr. Dovaston was on my left, Ms. Simmons was on my right...

"There was some uncertainty as to who was the person who hurled the missile...No statements from Mr. Dovaston or Ms. Simmons...an oversimplification, but it clearly illustrates the point that if that went forward to a law officer, and he said to the police investigator, that's the evidence which I have..."

"Exactly what I was stating when I made my earlier remarks," Pearce answered.

"Oh." Moore said no more.

"I know you have a busy schedule. I would now ask you to return to it," Richard Hector instructed Bill Pearce.

Rick Meens hurried from the courtroom, although he had hoped to thank Bill Pearce personally. "I went to Air Canada to try to extend Dave's ticket a few days. I was informed by Air Canada that the governor (Masefield) had telephoned and said absolutely that this ticket is not to be changed. He felt that if Mr. Middleton wishes to come here for a holiday, he can pay for his own ticket."

TWENTY TWO

Returning to the events which led to the outbreak of rioting on the evening of the first of December, 1977,....the Royal Commission should ask what, if anything, Mrs. Browne Evans was overheard to say to susceptible and angry young blacks hovering nearby as she emerged from the Sessions House...when the decision of the Court of Appeal was announced?

--Report of The Royal Commission into the 1977 Disturbances

Human Wrongs
August 30, 2000

DAVE MIDDLETON PLACED Becky's photos next to him on the podium, the same album that Judge Meerabux had refused to allow. By now, there was little question that this inquiry was about Dave and Cindy's beautiful teenage daughter, murdered during the vacation that might have been the highlight of her life, and the indignities that followed—even if the SCC still refused to acknowledge that fact.

"The Middleton family lost everything...the day Becky died," Dave told the silent audience. "Becky's trip to Bermuda with a friend was not unusual—although grand, not like a week of camping." Dave read Becky's letter from Bermuda telling her dad of her fun.

"Both boys were absolutely devastated by Becky's death...and the way it was handled by the legal system in Bermuda has forever changed their lives--obviously in a negative way."

Governor Thorold Masefield's "terms of reference" added to Bermuda's refusal to address victim impact, said Middleton, handing Richard Hector a copy of Canada's Victims' Bill of Rights. That he learned the details of Becky's murder from Belleville newsman John Ferguson added to the travesty. Again, Bermuda failed in its obligations, as had the taxi services the night Becky died.

The girls would have been desperate to get home, said Dave, and "Becky would have trusted Kirk Mundy and Justis Smith to get her home…She would have booted one of them, fought to the end. Neither Smith nor Mundy were big people, but there were two of them against Becky, and they had a knife. When it came down to it, she didn't stand a chance.

"We have a situation here where we know what happened to Becky, and we know who did it. But the judicial system failed Becky, the family, and the people of Bermuda. From the start," he said, "I thought there were two people involved in this murder, and they should be charged jointly."

Then Mundy's absurd plea and light sentence. "I will never understand why Khamisi Tokunbo recommended a three or four-year sentence for Mundy when the maximum was seven years, and then the judge set only five years—after describing Becky's murder as 'gruesome.'"

Then, during the murder trial of Justis Smith, Justice Vincent Meerabux summarized the case "very well," but suddenly ruled there was no case to answer. "Why did this happen? It makes no sense."

Middleton told commissioners he considered Justis Smith "pint-sized" and "weasel-like," another reason he had no doubt that two were involved.

From the start, he said, Elliot Mottley "assured us he would handle this case himself…We let him know that this was a family and something needed to be done…When we left we were very assured that things were going to go well. But, everything seemed to fall apart--and no one was made to pay…."

Moreover, Crown Counsel Khamisi Tokunbo, Middleton alleged, had been inappropriately friendly with Justis Smith's father. Middleton claimed to have seen him pat Richard Smith's shoulder in the courtroom.

If Bermuda didn't make changes in its judicial system, he warned, other families would endure the same torture. Dave Middleton's predictions would turn out to be on the mark—with murders reaching closer to home.

Rick Meens followed, telling the SCC that he wouldn't be bowing to court rulings. "Not only must we understand what happened and why, but also why the tragedy was handled as it was." Without honesty the case would not go away.

"How did Bermuda's justice system let rapists and murders off? One thing that has always been clear to me is that Rebecca was raped before she was murdered. Physical evidence was available in July, 1996, to prove that she had been punched in the face, tortured, and her skirt, bra, and panties were cut off with a knife.

"As a matter of pure common sense, that physical evidence would not exist if she was consenting. It appalls me that anyone could believe a consensual sex story, and I will not stop until I find out why. There is absolute proof that she was raped, and somebody calls it consensual sex.

"Why (didn't) Elliott Mottley and Khamisi Tokunbo at least charge Kirk Mundy with rape in July, 1996, when all the physical evidence clearly proved that Rebecca was raped?

"Why has Mr. Tokunbo, who is DPP now, still not charged Mr. Mundy with rape when he must know by now at least that Mundy's consensual sex story is a lie; all of the physical evidence still exists; he has Dr. Baden's report, as well as all the other evidence that Rebecca was raped.

"When all appeals courts have said that Kirk Mundy can't be prosecuted for murder now because of the way Elliott Mottley laid the original charges and the deal he made, why is Mr. Mottley now trying to shift the commission's attention to Bill Pearce?" No one is owning up, Meens said. "But the answer is there. And we will find it."

Rick Meens would remain true to his words.

Director of Public Prosecutions Khamisi Tokunbo didn't appreciate Dave Middleton's charge that he'd been inappropriately friendly with Justis Smith's father, Richard Smith, in the courtroom. As the inquiry neared its close, Tokunbo reappeared.

"I do not know Justis Smith, Justis Smith's father, or any of Justis Smith's family. I did not know them then and still don't know them now." Allegations DPP Khamisi Tokunbo termed "disturbing and unfortunate." Moreover, he charged, there had been a campaign led by Rick Meens to stop him from becoming Bermuda's lead criminal prosecutor.

Meens, in fact, admitted showing the front page of the December sixteenth *Royal Gazette*, charging erroneously that one of the young men photographed celebrating the verdict was Tokunbo's son. Meens, Tokunbo said, showed the paper "to anyone who would listen, asking, 'Is this the man you want" as top prosecutor?' The Middleton case is probably the worst case example how this community has been polarized along racial lines," Tokunbo told the *Royal Gazette*.

Being a father, Tokunbo said, he found Rebecca's murder to be a "tragic and brutal killing," and he sympathized with the Middletons.

"Unfortunately, like everything in the country, race became involved."

A point on which few would disagree.

LeYoni Junos had taped Lois Browne Evans comparing Becky's case to a murder on a beach many years ago, when a skeleton washed ashore. "What more do the Middletons want?" That family got only a bag of bones.

Now testifying before the SCC, Browne Evans made no mention of the case that had brought international furor and the inquiry. The PLP was leading Bermuda's judiciary toward "democratization," she told listeners. She was "most annoyed" that it took so long to physically separate her office and that of the director of public prosecutions, "thereby removing any hint of interference." The budgets, she said, still weren't separate. "I wish we could hurry up so we could get this country into the Twentieth Century," she said.

SCC Richard Hector interrupted. "The year 2000 is the Twenty First Century."

"No, no!" Browne Evans pursed her lips. "I do mean the Twentieth Century."

As for victim's rights, Browne advocated psychiatrists and social workers for the accused. However, she told the inquiry, psychological and grievance counseling shouldn't be the purview of prosecutors."

Frankly, she said, she found appalling those U.S.-style victims' impact statements. She was grateful that nothing like this existed in Bermuda.

"Don't be too long," SCC Chairman Stanley Moore warned LeYoni

Junos when she notified him she planned to follow Attorney General Dame Lois Browne Evans the next day. She'd take as long as she needed, LeYoni replied.

Strong evidence placed Kirk Mundy and Justis Smith with Rebecca Middleton at the time of her murder, LeYoni began. Yet, "Mr. Tokunbo and Mr. Mottley—senior prosecutors involved with the case from the beginning—maintain, under oath, that there was 'no evidence' in existence in July, 1996, except a caution statement by Kirk Mundy claiming to have had consensual sex with Miss Middleton." She asked how Bermuda's former Attorney General Elliott Mottley and current DPP Khamisi Tokunbo could support that sworn claim.

From the SCC testimony, LeYoni believed that ample evidence of sexual crimes existed in July and August of 1996, *before* Kirk Mundy went to court. Taken against her will, aggravated sexual assault, sodomy, torture, murder. "Yet the attorney general and crown counsel persisted in their belief and acceptance of Mundy's statement of consensual sex…in direct conflict with all other evidence."

Junos could arrive at only one explanation: To reach such a decision, LeYoni told the SCC, "they would have to have endorsed some judgment as to the sexual behavior or character of Miss Middleton. This, in my opinion, is unethical, highly irresponsible and discriminatory behavior on behalf of the prosecution; and it can be the only rationale behind such a decision." Horrific, fatal wounds, Junos said, yet Rebecca Middleton faced prejudice.

Bermuda, she reminded, has an international legal obligation "to investigate, prosecute and punish rapists. In any environment in which a woman has to prove that she did not consent, a woman will face enormous difficulty--"

Chairman Stanley Moore interrupted. "What I would like Miss Junos to know is that…(there has been) serious revisiting of the offense of rape… For example, in some jurisdictions, rape has now been widened to include unlawful forceful sexual contact against men, the old offense of buggery had gone…Do proceed."

LeYoni glared at Moore, halted, ignored his comment.

"Elliott Mottley was adamant that the charges laid against Mundy were based on the evidence that was available to him at the time—that Mundy had said he had consensual sex with Becky," LeYoni said. "How much injury does a victim have to show?"

Moreover, LeYoni Junos asked, how could Mundy's statement be the sole evidence, as both Elliott Mottley and Khamisi Tokunbo had told the inquiry? Detective Superintendent Vic Richardson had listed eleven pieces of evidence discussed during the July twelfth meeting--Mundy's statements, the knife, several witness statements, Smith's statement, the autopsy, the government analyst's reports, and more...

"This was enough evidence to charge both of them or to lay holding charges on both of them, then let the jury decide whether the sex was consensual, which of the two or both murdered Miss Middleton, in the light of incoming forensic evidence.

"It is highly irresponsible of Mr. Mottley to come before this inquiry and to make those statements," she charged. "He said, and I quote, 'You did not have to prove what took place down there. You had to prove who the two people were there, how many people went to Ferry Reach, how many people left Ferry Reach. Two people. Finished. No one could get anything else from it, because it would have proved who the two people were.'

"Why didn't (the former attorney general) think the same thing back in July 1996 when Kirk Mundy was charged only as an accomplice to murder—when the same evidence was not enough to place holding charges (for murder) against both of them?"

The decisions ignored the most important evidence, LeYoni said, "--Rebecca Middleton's body, and clothing cut away from her body. This was her silent, yet horribly graphic, witness statement...(that) fell on the deaf ears of those who had the authority and duty to prosecute.

"...Which brings me to the first question which Mr. Pearce asked and which Mr. Dovaston agreed—'Why on July twelfth, 1996, nine days after the murder, did the prosecution team believe the story of Mundy that there was consensual sex, when all the evidence indicated to the contrary?' Until that question is answered, there will be no closure."

LeYoni took a deep breath. Commissioners Moore, Dovaston and Simmons all stayed silent. She referred to the former attorney general's statement that juniors in his office had complained about the handling of the case. "I think it highly unprofessional that if he were so concerned with the...prosecution... of such a high profile and horrendous murder case, he would discuss it with junior members of his chambers. Yet Mr. Mottley did not exert his authority to take over and continue with the proceeding of this case."

The former attorney general's criticism of Bill Pearce, hired from ninety applicants, was arrogant, LeYoni charged. "If he had truly wanted to prosecute the case, Elliott Mottley could have done so. He had a moral responsibility. He had promised the Middletons over and over…, and he was on the island when the case was going on. He could have explained to the Middletons personally why he did not prosecute it. But he chose to come here, at the expense of the public, and make these statements before this commission."

The former attorney general left Bermuda in a hurry, said LeYoni, "because he didn't want to be in the attorney general's seat when the hue and cry came for a probe into the attorney general's chambers.…highly irresponsible, arrogant…I believe that Mr. Mottley simply did not want to be on the losing side…"

LeYoni stepped toward the bench. "Why didn't the SCC commissioners question Elliott Mottley more forcefully? I do think that when it comes to cases, the buck does stop with the attorney general, and I think that he should have been far more vigorously examined, especially in light of the evidence…In all seriousness, answers to those questions must be sought, and commissioners should make that recommendation."

Still silence from the commissioners.

Perhaps, however, LeYoni suggested, the Privy Council was not the last option. "I want the SCC to consider that this document. *The Legal Status of British Dependent Territories* actually states that Bermuda is bound under the European Convention on Human Rights.

"Now, what I am simply asking is, does Bermuda have the right of further petition past the Privy Council to the European Court of Human Rights? I am just wondering if the commission could explore this with legal persons, because I think that if that is the case, then we can look at how, if at all, this could benefit the Bermudian community."

The handling of Rebecca Middleton's murder was by no means the only example of Bermuda's judicial failures, Junos added. "Most of the time these light sentences are indicative of a mindset of how our culture views assaults against women, and sexual assault, itself. Until we can address that, until we can raise public awareness, and make some things in the system mandatory, then it will continue to happen."

Junos cited a European Convention of Human Rights report on violence, handing a copy to Richard Hector. "Even where crimes of violence against women are recognized in the law, they are rarely prosecuted with vigor.

"What I am trying to stress is that regardless of whether the evidence is collected in the most professional and pristine manner; regardless if all the procedures are followed accurately and professionally—if ideas about women and their sexuality…whether they consent or not—come into play in the decision-making as to whether a case should be prosecuted or not, then this commission and the recommendations that it makes will be useless to the treatment of sexual assaults and rape of women; I feel that this is an extremely serious issue, one that needs to be dealt with, with the most sincerity, transparency and seriousness.

"A state that does not act against crimes of violence against women is as guilty as the perpetrators. States are under a positive duty to prevent, investigate and punish crimes associated with violence against women."

Much to Commission Chairman Stanley Moore's surprise, LeYoni Junos' testimony forced the commission to "pay attention," the *Royal Gazette* suggested.

However, events to follow would suggest otherwise.

Artist Peter Woolcock's *Royal Gazette* cartoon on the day the SCC closed its doors showed black fingers, white fingers, pointing at each other from the Magistrate's Court windows, with a helmeted tourist couple perched together on a motorbike peering at a map, speculating that they must be on Point Finger Road (named for its geography).

Police thrust blame at the attorney general (who returned the favor), the attorney general impugned the solicitor general. A silent governor, a mute FCO. Woolcock's artwork captured the circular blame and underlying racial conflicts that have long threatened to override Bermuda's lush radiance.

"I believe they tried to shove Becky's death under the carpet, and I think they are probably trying to do the same now," said Dave Middleton. "What on earth was the point of having an inquiry? I don't think we got any answers. It was deliberately set up so that nobody would delve too closely into Becky's death. What am I supposed to think? I still believe we should have had an inquiry just into this one case. I will always think that."

Appalling charging decisions, a bizarre plea and its accompanying consensual sex allegations, an "astonishing" judicial decision, a glitch in Bermuda's appeals law, a white washed inquiry.

LeYoni's query about European Court options made no media reports, and commissioners did not reply. The SCC's written summary made no mention of LeYoni's conclusions or recommendations. "…A very impressive oral presentation before us (in which Ms. Junos) drew attention to the international movement against domestic violence."

Did the SCC misunderstand? Or were its members, as Dave Middleton suggested, sweeping his daughter's murder under the rug? With the SCC over, and a six-month limit for filing European Court applications after final court decisions, the option to pursue the human rights failures seemed to have passed—or had it?

The answer would surprise Kirk Mundy and Justis Smith.

Courtesy of Peter Woolcock
First Appeared in Royal Gazette on September 1, 2000

PART SEVEN

Truths, Consequences, or Neither of These?

TWENTY THREE

In a small tight-knit community, there is a natural tendency to avoid getting involved...But I must ask anyone who knows anything about this crime to think seriously about the implications for themselves and the community as a whole...

Personal Statement, Acting Governor, Ian Kinnear, March, 12, 1973

Mundy's Tale
September 15, 2000

PERHAPS A FIRST in Bermuda—access to a criminal file for someone outside of police or the attorney general's office; no freedom of information legislation existed here. Normally secretive, the Supreme Court registrar allowed LeYoni Junos and Rick Meens to spend a week tucked away in a cluttered back room, ignoring confidential files of other cases strewn across tables, piled on the floor, and upon dust-covered shelves, determined to find out why Kirk Mundy had escaped murder charges. Whatever tale he'd told, they thought, the story must have been either clever or believable.

His story, LeYoni Junos found as she read, turned out to be neither.

"I would like to start by saying that I am not responsible for this girl's death, but in any case, I am truly sorry that it happened," police records quoted Mundy, who promised to tell police exactly what had gone down.

He claimed he first saw Becky at Moonglow, he'd danced with her, she'd disappeared when he left to get another beer. When he couldn't find her, "I just continued dancing in the club by myself, finished the two beers, went back to the bar, and ordered another round… So it didn't bother me none. I just kept drinking and dancing." (Police confirmed Becky and Jasmine had been nowhere near Moonglow).

Just after three a.m., he left Moonglow with Justis Smith, heading toward town. "On our way out of St. George, I noticed the girl that I was dancing with inside the club was on the sidewalk talking with this guy on a bike, with another girl." Becky was interested in him, Mundy claimed, when she got on the bike "she was becoming affectionate…While I was riding she started reaching her hands all around my waist and started playing with my private areas, then whispering in my ear, saying that 'I want some of this, big boy.' So I turned off the main road and headed towards Ferry Reach.

"She told me to pull over." He asked Becky why. "She told me, 'I want some of this now'…expressing the *now*. So I pulled over down by Ferry Reach, parked the bike and started playing with the girl, touching her rear end and all of that. I was also playing with her chest. She started kissing on my neck then pushed her tongue down my throat. So I kept caressing her while Justis was on the bike watching, an' it seems as if that didn't bother her."

They had consensual sex, Mundy told police. "After I finished, I got up and told her put her clothes on. After I done that I walked down by the waterside. I took my condom off and threw it in the trees. I went down to the waterside to wash my genitals off."

He returned about five minutes later, he said. "I heard a little scream, like a 'no' scream. 'No, no, no, no.' I got closer, and it looked like he was punching her in her face. I saw red coming from her neck area, but I wasn't sure what it was. So I told him, 'stop hitting the girl,' and pulled him off her. When I looked he had a knife in his hand, covered with blood. I told him, 'Get on the bike, let's go.'"

Mundy chain smoked as he told police how Justis Smith pulled up his pants and jumped on the bike. "When I looked back at the girl, the neck to her chest region was covered with blood. To my knowledge he was just punching her until I saw the knife in his hand after pulling him off of her. The reason why I told him, 'Get on the bike and let's go,' is because I was shocked and frightened." They sped back toward town. When they crossed the bridge leaving St. George, Mundy told police, Smith threw something into the water. "I assumed it was the knife he used. I never touched the knife, and if you was to recover the knife, you would notice that my fingerprints are not on it. But I am sure Justis' fingerprints will be on the knife."

Police, LeYoni Junos noticed while she read court records, didn't appear to be taking Mundy's story at face value, questioning his claim that Becky could have whispered to him while, according to Mundy, they'd been traveling at about "fifty kilometers, maybe more."

"Would you agree, at that speed, and, as you said, the girl was whispering, it would have been difficult for you to understand what she was saying?" asked Detective Constable Peter Clarke.

"I had a helmet on. She could have been shouting, so it sounded like you know, she was whispering."

"You said that the girl was telling you to pull over."

"She was telling me, 'pull over, 'I want some now.'"

"Could it be she was telling you to pull over because she realized you were traveling too fast on the bike and going the wrong way?"

"It's not the impression that I had."

"Why did you stop the bike in that particular location?"

"No particular reason."

"You also said in your statement that you were playing with the girl's chest. What were you doing?"

"Playing with her breast. On the outside of her shirt."

"What were you using to play with her breast?"

"My hands."

"When you were doing this did Justis say anything, or did he participate?"

"No, I was with her myself."

"In the statement you admitted that you had sex with the girl. What kind of sex did you have with her?"

Mundy requested a bathroom break.

Clarke continued, "It is my information that people have sex via the vagina, the anus, or oral sex, maybe other ways. Which way did you use?"

"Normal sex, meaning by the vagina."

"Was that the only way you had sex with her?"

"To my knowledge, yes."

Mark Pettingill interrupted, requesting to be alone with his client.

When they returned, Inspector Peter Clarke continued. "You have admitted having sex with the girl…You have stated you used a condom. What type?"

"Maybe a 'Rough Rider,' might have broken."

"Did Justis have sex with the girl?"

"I don't know."

"How would you describe the sex, for instance, was it rough?"

Normal, he said, without force.

"Did Justis hold the young girl down to the ground while you had sex with her?"

"No."

Oral or anal sex?

Mundy again qualified his answer, "To my knowledge, no."

"So would it be correct to say that no semen or body fluids belonging to you should--" Mundy's attorney requested another private meeting.

Inspector Peter Clarke resumed. "So would it be correct to say that no semen or body fluids belonging to you should have been found in the girl's anus or mouth?"

"To my knowledge, no." In the vagina, if the condom broke.

A consistent pattern, LeYoni thought.

Vague responses to questions about oral and anal sex.

"Did the girl protest your having sex with her?"

"No."

"In your statement you said, 'After I finished, I got up and told her put her clothes on.' Did she make any attempts to do so?"

"Only her panties were off. That's what I meant by putting her clothes on."

"Did she make any attempts to put on her panties?"

"I'm not sure. I walked away to the waterside."

"Why did you just walk off and leave the girl?"

"'Cause I wanted to freshen up."

"You stated that the area you had sex was in the dark. Weren't you concerned for the girl's safety when you walked off and left her?"

"We were alone as far as I knew."

Police asked Mundy if police possessed the clothing that he wore the night of July third. Mundy said they did. He admitted removing a bag of clothing, but claimed it included only a jacket that he was taking to Keasha's house. Those clothes, Kirk Mundy insisted, remained with his mother or father.

Could he find that particular jacket? "Sure."

"Did you tell Marjorie (a friend of Kirk Mundy) about the circumstances surrounding the murder of Rebecca Middleton?"

"I believe I did. I'm not too sure."

"If you did, did you tell her the truth?"

"Of course."

"Did you tell your aunt, Sharon Mundy, about the circumstances surrounding the murder of Rebecca Middleton?"

"I believe I did."

"If you did, did you tell her the truth?"

"Yeah."

"Did you tell Sharon that while enroute to Ferry Reach with Rebecca Middleton and Justis Smith that you dropped Justis off somewhere?"

"No."

LeYoni turned to a third interview. Without doubt, police questioned Mundy's account, even suggesting, as prosecutors in the Smith trial had asserted, two men were responsible for Becky's murder.

"I am putting it to you that you were the person who caused the injuries to the girl with the knife and then gave it to Justis to throw away so that your fingerprints would not be on it," Inspector Stuart Crockwell challenged. "What do you have to say about that?"

"Absolutely not."

"So who stabbed the girl to death?"

"I have no idea. I assume it was Justis. It most definitely wasn't me. And again, I will like to say, I am truly sorry that this happened."

"Was the girl still alive when you left her at Ferry Reach?"

"I'm not too sure. I was just too scared when I saw the blood and fled the scene."

"Did Justis say anything to you about having sex with the girl and stabbing her with the knife?"

"No."

"I'm putting it to you that both you and Justis had sex with the girl forcibly and at the same time administered wounds to her body with a knife which caused her death. What do you have to say about this?"

"I did not have sex with her at the same time as Justis, nor do I know of him having sex with her, and I myself had no part in her death."

"When did you become aware the girl was dead?"

"When I heard it on the news the following day."

"Why didn't you come voluntarily to the police to assist in the investigation?"

"I was frighten' (sic) 'cause I thought they would lock me up. But I was more frighten' to hear that she was dead and to know that if I had said anything, Lord knows what Justis might have done to me."

"We have received information that several items of jewelry are missing from the body of the deceased girl. Did you take this jewelry?"

"No, I did not."

Did Justis take that jewelry?

"Not to my knowledge." Coincidence? Again, LeYoni noticed Mundy hedging.

"It is our information that when you and Justis stopped to talk to Seon Smith and Tajmal Webb, you were asked by (Seon) Smith why the license plate of the cycle was covered with a piece of cloth, and you replied the bike is unlicensed. Did you tell him that?"

"No."

"Is the bike unlicensed?"

"No."

"Did you have a piece of cloth covering the license plate?"

"Not that I know of." No definite answer.

"On your journey back to town did you stop and speak with two men at the Swizzle Inn car park?"

"No."

"During your journey back to town you stated that you saw the police dealing with a man at Flatts, and this man later rode town (sic) with you and Justis. Do you know this man?"

"Yes, by sight."

"In your first statement you told police that on the night of Tuesday July second, you were at your girlfriend's house from eight at night to the next morning on Wednesday, July third. Was that a lie?"

"No comment on the advice of my attorney."

As Pettingill signaled the meeting's end, police asked if Mundy had anything else to say.

Mundy did. "Yes, that I'm very, very shocked of this sort of thing happening, especially around me. And I would like to send my gratitude and sympathy out to Rebecca Middleton, the late, and her family. I'm deeply sorry. Such things should not happen to no one. I'm even sorry that it happened to her. May God bless her life. With love."

"Anything else?"

"Again, I'll like to apologize for such things happening to Rebecca, and I will send out my deepest sympathies and thoughts to her family. May God bless you all."

LeYoni read Keasha Smith's statement in which she asked Mundy what happened "with the girl who was killed." Mundy told Keasha the same story. He didn't kill Becky, Justis Smith did.

"He was crying and just told me that he was sorry for what he had done to me. He was crying and said he did not kill the girl. Justis did it. I asked him why he had sex with the girl, and he said that it was just something that happened. The girl came onto him, and it just happened. I asked him if he wore a condom, and he said yes. I asked him, why did Justis have to kill the girl? He said he didn't know." Keasha claimed she never again saw the clothes that Kirk Mundy was wearing on July third.

Then Justis Smith's statement. Unlike Mundy, LeYoni noticed, Justis Smith didn't lie.

"How were you and 'Fly' dressed on that Tuesday night?"

Smith stayed tight-lipped. "No comment."

"I will be even more specific with this allegation. The allegation is that you and 'Fly,' who actually is Kirk Mundy, murdered Rebecca Middleton on Ferry Road, St. George, on Wednesday morning the third of July, 1996. What do you have to say to that?"

"No comment."

"Can you give me any reason why you and Kirk Mundy murdered Rebecca Middleton?"

"No comment."

"Kirk Mundy has implicated you solely in the murder of Rebecca Middleton; is there any reason you can think of to indicate why Kirk Mundy would say these things if they were not true?"

This time Justis Smith answered. "No."

"Is there anything you would like to comment on?"

"No."

"Do you wish to read over this record?"

He didn't. Police read the record, Justis Smith refused to sign.

LeYoni Junos nudged Rick Meens. "Look at this, more than once—all three doctors say she was raped." Dr. Keith Cunningham reported diffuse genital bruising, cuts and bruises on Becky's inner thighs, and bruising on both upper arms, even anal bruising, Becky had been sodomized.

Dr. Henry Pearse, police and prisons medical officer's report: "There was evidence suggesting forceful vaginal and possibly anal intercourse…shortly before death." Her body was so blood covered that Pearse found it difficult to identify all stab wounds.

Blunt force injuries and stabs showed beating and torture, Dr. James Johnston wrote. Semen and sexual injury, battering, multiple stabs to her body, both front and back. Her attackers even stabbed Becky's skull, causing severe hemorrhage. Her right lung collapsed, her jugular spat blood, stabs to the right ventricle of her heart, and to her abdomen.

Only a "fine laceration" on each of Becky's palms—not multiple cuts that one would expect if she could have held up her hands to defend herself, an automatic response. Johnston returned the following day to recheck Becky's body, finding darkened bruises, now all over her body. "A vicious murder," he wrote.

Overkill, sexual motivation. Missing jewelry, obvious souvenirs. A blitz attack on Becky, who had been missing only thirty to forty minutes.

LeYoni reviewed each page, drawing Rick Meens' attention to the statement of someone whose name she'd never heard mentioned before she saw these reports—a police report dated after Mundy's plea acceptance. Police identified Marjorie Hewey as a friend of Kirk Mundy's.

As often happened in Bermuda, with no freedom of information, Hewey's story never had been made public.

Marjorie Hewey had known Kirk Mundy for about two years, LeYoni Junos learned. Thirty-one-year-old Hewey told police she lived on the western end of Bermuda, in Somerset, not far from where Mundy and two friends had robbed a bank security truck. Kirk's uncle from Jamaica had married Marjorie's sister, Sharon Mundy, so they were related, sort of.

"I'd heard of him having a number of problems, he was constantly getting into trouble," Hewey told police. "As a matter of fact, I used to see Kirk every evening."

For Hewey the second of July, stood out. Why? Hewey refused to tell police.

Mundy had stopped by her job at a Somerset boutique to invite her to Moonglow that night. Hewey declined. Mundy told her he'd go anyway and would take his friend, Justis Smith. Marjorie Hewey met Smith once when Mundy brought him to the boutique. "There was something about Justis that I didn't like, and I mentioned this to Kirk, who never brought him back here."

At about 11:30 a.m. July third, while pathologists were examining Becky's body, Marjorie Hewey visited Kirk Mundy at his house. On the way over, Hewey heard about Rebecca Middleton's murder on a car radio. She asked Mundy if he'd heard about it.

"I was there," she quoted Mundy.

Hewey said she told Mundy, "You're lying. You don't know what's happening."

Mundy told her, "I'm not in any trouble. I didn't do anything, it was Justis," Hewey said.

"I asked him what Justis had done, and he told me that he'd let me know later."

Mundy was in a hurry to get out of the house, she said. He returned from his room with a small blue and white plastic bag. "I asked Kirk what he had in the plastic bag, and he showed me the black sweat suit I had seen him wearing on Tuesday evening." A few hours later, Mundy turned up at her job asking for a yellow meshed tee shirt. She gave him one, and he put it on beneath the shirt he wore.

Mundy hung with her until the boutique closed at 6:30 p.m., she said, when they headed together to the home of his aunt, Sharon Mundy. There, Kirk Mundy went outside to clean Keasha's bike. When they left about an hour later, Hewey watched Kirk Mundy, with his new yellow mesh shirt and Keasha's scoured bike, drive away.

Hewey's concerns didn't keep her from meeting Mundy later that night at Swinging Doors. She found him inside the Court Street bar with Justis Smith. When it closed at three a.m., less than 24 hours after the kidnapping, rape, torture, and murder of Rebecca Middleton, they loitered outside. "We talked, but not about the murder," Hewey later told police.

As local and foreign media broadcast details of Becky's murder, Hewey said, "I began to realize that Kirk was telling the truth about being there." She saw Mundy daily, but when she asked about the murder, "he would get upset with me and say that I shouldn't ask him any questions. He said he hadn't done anything and didn't want to talk to me about it."

Later police learned that Mundy crashed Keasha's bike on Sunday, the weekend after Becky's murder. Marjorie Hewey said Mundy spent Sunday night with her. The next morning, Monday July eighth, Hewey brought up the murder. Mundy "ran to the bathroom and started vomiting," Hewey told police. When he came out, he insisted that he had done nothing wrong. "He maintained this all along, telling me 'she sat between them, and Justis was feeling her up.' He said that Justis raped the girl and killed her. Kirk told me that he didn't rape the girl, and I believe him."

Later Monday night, Hewey and Mundy went to Moonglow. They spent time together again on Tuesday the ninth. When he was ready to leave, Mundy told her he was heading to Moonglow.

Perhaps he shouldn't, Hewey warned Mundy.

He had nothing to hide, he said.

"He told me the next day (July tenth) that the cops had stopped him when he was leaving St. George that morning. He said that if he was guilty they would have locked him up there and then. I told him that if he is involved, the cops will come and get him in time."

That Dean Lottimore immediately had gone to the scene at Ferry Reach, moments after Becky died, and that he had not come clean when police first interviewed him on July third, alarmed LeYoni as she read the reports.

"She (Jasmine) told me that I was a nice guy, but she had to panic because she is in a foreign country and that that was her ace girl." Despite the park being almost a mile down a dark road that heads away from St. George, Lottimore claimed Ferry Reach was on his way home.

He veered to Ferry Reach, he said, because "I started really thinking about Jasmine's ace girl…There were towels and blood over her, so I couldn't get a good look… Me, myself, personally, I believe she is the same girl."

After he left Ferry Reach, "I still came to St. George's police station. I explained what had happened, and he said, 'Alright, alright.' He asked me my name and address. I gave it to him, and then I went home."

Once home, Lottimore told police, "I still couldn't rest off my head, so I told my girlfriend. She jumped on the bike with me and told me to go back to the police station and explain everything properly to the police officer. That's when the police officer told me that the girl was dead."

Dean Lottimore denied he knew either man. "I believe if I saw them again I'd recognize them."

But in another interview room, Jasmine Meens told police about Lottimore's "high five," saying she believed Lottimore knew the men who took Becky.

Lottimore again denied he knew the men who took Becky. "Just a greeting people use if they don't know your name," Lottimore told police. "I raised my hand and said 'Yeah, cool bum.'" Lottimore repeated that he didn't know the men.

Also not forthcoming were Sean Smith and Tajmal Webb, the two men police saw standing beside the broken down orange Toyota. "…Only a woman in a white car, two men who offered help, and a police woman--no men on a motorcycle," Sean Smith said. Tajmal Webb told the same story.

Police never charged any of the witnesses with obstructing justice, although it became obvious that their silence had helped suspects get their business in order.

Closing the file, LeYoni Junos wondered how Mundy had lucked out, despite the obvious. The pieces didn't fit. Lines of questioning suggested that more than one police officer hadn't bought Mundy's story. So who did?

Meticulously, LeYoni Junos prepared her findings.

TWENTY FOUR

Bermuda business prospectuses and tourist pamphlets continue to proclaim that the island is a political rock, a haven of tranquility. But as days go by, it is becoming increasingly difficult to ignore the tension and strains that threaten to ruin this holiday paradise.

Daily Express-- March 12, 1973

A Shocking Allegation
Fall, 2000

BERMUDA'S MIDSUMMER SUN now dimmed by sprinkles and wind gusts that hint of brisk, soggy days to come, now October, 2000. LeYoni Junos huddled in a dark corner booth of a small Front Street café. Content with her own company, she intended to read a book in the cozy spot before she headed home.

LeYoni glanced across the room. Senior Crown Counsel Brian Calhoun looked like he was leaving, but he moved to the seat next to her. They'd never met, but to her surprise Calhoun thanked her for her testimony before the inquiry. "He couldn't understand how anyone believed Mundy's story, given the evidence that was there from the start, on day one," LeYoni recalled.

Junos listened intently as Calhoun explained that one of the junior staff members, who had been assigned to help with the Smith trial preparation, asked him why the case had been prosecuted as it had been. Not for him to say,

Calhoun recounted, telling LeYoni he suggested the young lawyer approach persons who had worked on the case.

Shortly afterward, the young lawyer returned to Calhoun's office with a shocking allegation. LeYoni scribbled the accusation on an envelope on which she already had written Dave Middleton's telephone number. She kept the envelope with its words in her script: "Little white Canadian girls come to Bermuda to have sex with little black Bermudian boys."

Who had said that? Who knew about the alleged attribution? More than a few, it would seem.

Later LeYoni would hear that some police officers, reportedly at least two assigned to Becky's case, allegedly echoed those racist, sexist comments while discussing the case at a used book store near the Hamilton Police Headquarters. Junior attorneys in the AG's office, she said, confirmed that they believed that racism and sexism had influenced the case.

LeYoni always had supported strong protections for people accused of crime. Freedom for everyone is compromised when the accused don't receive due process, she said. "But liberty also suffers when playing the race card or the gender card is acceptable."

Moreover," LeYoni said, "gender abuses can become so pervasive and so passively accepted in rape cases that using sexism isn't even seen as playing a card, much less an offensive bigoted one."

The sad picture, for LeYoni Junos, seemed all too plausible. What else would cause someone to buy a story of consensual sex—despite evidence of rape, sodomy, torture?

Race and gender—twice the bang for the buck.

The SCC's report, released three months after the inquiry's close, not only suggested the commissioners hadn't heard much, at all, of what LeYoni Junos had said, but writers of the document seemed to infer that Becky had some personal responsibility in her own death.

"First and foremost, be aware of your surroundings," the SCC report warned. "Trust your instincts and take sensible precautions…stick to well traveled, well lit roads and avoid deserted areas… Do not thumb or accept rides from strangers, particularly late at night…."

The report recalled another mid-summer Bermuda murder. "One evening in July, 1941, the same month of the Middleton murder, Miss Stapleton (a

British censorette) was last seen pushing her pedal cycle along a moonlit railway track…Like Miss Middleton, she too was attempting to get home late at night. She too was seeking transportation home. Her half-naked body was found near Prospect Railway… She had been raped and beaten to death."

The end of this tale differed from Becky's. Her killer, a convicted rapist, was sentenced to death and executed two years later. That hanging was the last until Buck Burrows and Larry Tacklyn met their fates thirty four years later.

The Serious Crimes Commission document, with its forty six recommendations to police and five to the attorney general, appeared in the *Mid Ocean News*, with many complaining that it did nothing to address the Rebecca Middleton case. The report took its place on a shelf, languishing.

Seven months later, in April, 2001, the *Royal Gazette* complained there had been silence regarding whether SCC recommendations had been implemented.

In Belleville, Becky's hometown newspaper asked, "What value is placed on life in Bermuda?…The British colony's charade continues…a third strike for a colony that promotes itself as a safe, scenic paradise… Individuals may want to consider whether they want to spend their money in a place that appears to put so little value on justice and human life."

A month after the SCC released its report, LeYoni Junos publicly called for another inquiry—independent this time, not political, and on Becky's case alone, a human rights violation, she charged, that Bermuda and Britain needed to address.

Each Wednesday evening, LeYoni Junos joined vendors on Front Street where tourists and local shoppers jammed Hamilton's horse and carriage-filled streets at Harbor Nights. By September, 2001, more than ten percent of the island's thirty thousand-plus voters had signed her *Appeal for Accountability*.

Among exceptions was an editor of Bermuda's union newspaper, who had long complained that Becky's case had received favoritism she believed that a black female victim in Bermuda would not. "She talked with me about other things," LeYoni recalled, "then walked away, and really loudly shouted, 'And I'm not going to sign your petition.'"

LeYoni Junos would not carry the petition to London, as she had hoped to do. Circumstances would make her far too uncomfortable for that to happen.

TWENTY FIVE

Sir Richard made a start at playing things in a lower key, to the distress of the older expatriate element but to the delight of the more politically sensitive...The quiet approach could have the disadvantage of encouraging Bermudians to slip back into their traditional lethargic attitude toward political change, for a governor who is very much in evidence is an irritant,,, not only to the colored youth but to the politicians...

--Secret Memo Acting Governor Ian Kinnear to Secretary of State, FCO—May 1, 1973 (The National Archives, London)

Retribution
July 12, 2001

EXACTLY FIVE YEARS TO THE DAY of charging decisions in the murder of Rebecca Middleton, July twelfth, 2001, LeYoni Junos did the unthinkable on an island where lying in the tide is a way of life.

She personally delivered her *Appeal for Accountability* to Governor Thorold Masefield. In spite of two years of public uproar, LeYoni wrote, the governor had set up "terms of reference designed to ***prevent*** (sic) the specific, transparent and thorough examination of the prosecution of the Middleton murder...

"From the start, there were racist and sexist influences," LeYoni Junos charged. "Rebecca Middleton was white; the two suspects were black....Police were publicly accused of 'racism' because they (questioned) young black men who fit the description of suspects."

She told how junior Crown counsel had made comments in her presence that racism and sexism had influenced the prosecution. "It has come to my attention that a former and most senior and experienced member of the attorney general's chambers...has information regarding (alleged) racist and sexist comments made about Rebecca Middleton...(alleged) comments which may indicate an influence behind the prosecution and sentencing of Kirk Mundy as an *accessory* to murder.

"Racism and/or sexism have no place influencing the prosecution of serious crime," LeYoni Junos wrote. "Racist and/or sexist comments (allegedly) made...about a victim of serious sexual assault are unconscionable and border on criminal conduct."

Junos called for thorough questioning of key witnesses. Unlike the Serious Crimes Commission's political appointments, the tribunal should be independent, protect witnesses from reprisal, and be held "without delay."

Two weeks after she hand delivered her materials to the governor's office, Deputy Governor Tim Gurney met with LeYoni, promising to contact her after considering her submission.

Two more weeks passed, silence. When LeYoni contacted Gurney's office, he had "misplaced" her report. She hand-carried a duplicate.

"I find the claimed loss of this report—and the lack of response to its contents—suspicious and very disturbing," LeYoni wrote to Baroness Valerie Amos at the FCO, calling for an independent inquiry with subpoena powers to "examine testimonies...under oath" during the SCC, a matter that "needs to be dealt with, with the most sincerity, transparency and seriousness."

No response.

Finally, in October, eleven months after the SCC closed its doors, Parliamentarian Wayne Perinchief, a former Bermuda assistant police commissioner, brought the commission's report to Parliament for discussion, telling the *Royal Gazette* that he hoped that new legal precedents allowing a second trial if compelling new evidence were found--a decision approved in Britain--would lead to justice in Becky's murder.

Immediate dispute. Former SCC marshal and Mundy's bail lawyer Richard Hector contended there should be no rush to change the law. Attorney

General Dame Lois Browne Evans told Parliament, "I like the law the way it is right now."

Justis Smith's lawyer, Elizabeth Christopher reminded prosecutors should investigate properly in the first place. Another high profile Bermuda defense attorney, Tim Marshall, objected to changing the Constitution." What happened in the Rebecca Middleton case is a rare unfortunate circumstance that happens in all jurisdictions...."

NEWSMAKER

LeYoni champions women's rights

LeYoni's failure to "lie in the tide" would cost her dearly

Minister Wayne Perinchief told Parliament he disagreed. "A blight on our record should be removed... We should try to redeem ourselves." The way the case had been handled and Parliament's refusal to act, Perinchief said, turned out to be his biggest disappointment and regret so far as a politician.

"I normally don't listen to the House of Assembly, but finally they were debating the Commission of Inquiry Report they had delayed, and UBP Minister John Barritt mentioned the petition that was going around," LeYoni recalled not long ago. "He and another lawyer who has made a lot of noise –positive noise—about it—Trevor Moniz…He was so angry about the whole thing…I transcribed that…It's public record in The House of Assembly."

John Barritt, LeYoni remembered, asked, "'Why do you think the people are not happy?…Why do you think this lady (he called my name) could be circulating a petition and getting signatures?'

"I couldn't believe what (Attorney General Dame Lois Brown Evans) said. She actually called my name--She said something about 'back in the days,' you know, with the racial things, we needed petitions, but we don't need petitions now…Then she said, 'Don't tell me that LeYoni Junos is doing us a great service.' I couldn't believe it…"

LeYoni Junos' *Appeal for Accountability* sat in the offices of Governor Thorold Masefield and Baroness Valerie Amos, virtually ignored.

But Amnesty International hadn't been oblivious to LeYoni's message. Despite her public statement that she was speaking for herself, not Amnesty International, Amnesty officials from London sent a scathing letter, most annoyed by LeYoni's having termed former Attorney General Elliott Mottley's behaviors "arrogant." They were short of funds, Bermuda's Amnesty board members claimed when, not long afterward, they ended LeYoni Junos' contract. The human rights commission also removed her.

Desperate for work, doing odd jobs, LeYoni felt renewed hope when she discovered an advertisement for a Bermuda Police Service victim's advocate. Successful on her police service written examination, LeYoni was waiting for her scheduled physical tests when she received a telephone call telling her not to show up. At first, police refused to give her reasons. Eventually, officers directed her to Police Commissioner Jonathan Smith.

When he granted a meeting, LeYoni arrived to find the commissioner, with another officer, holding newspaper articles about her testimony to the SCC and copies of her appeal. Smith told her, and confirmed in 2004 during a meeting with Rick Meens and this author, he had pulled her job application owing to her testimony at the SCC and her subsequent appeal to the governor, which he termed illegal for police department employees. (Bermuda law states that appeals cannot be made to Bermuda's government, but appeals to Britain are not prohibited).

In desperation to pay her mortgage, LeYoni spent four years driving a bus.

Fearing more repercussions, LeYoni Junos spoke up no more for the memory of Rebecca Middleton--until the arrival in 2007 of a visitor who would revitalize the Rebecca Middleton murder case—British human rights lawyer Cherie Booth.

TWENTY SIX

. . . . What is emerging so far is a pattern of contact between a few members of the Black Beret Cadre and one Mr. Green (sic), a hardened criminal with a hatred for those in authority…If this sort of pattern continues, it could mean that the motive is not political alone, but that there is a criminal element also; and, if Green is involved, a personal motive, a compound of ambition and hatred for authority…
--Secret brief from Acting Governor Ian Kinnear to
Sir Duncan Watson, Deputy Undersecretary, FCO
-- March 20, 1973 (The National Archives, London)

Daily Express-- March 12, 1973

Another Attack... Another Deal?

February 2, 2002

SHE THOUGHT SHE HAD BEEN PUNCHED, but when Shanae Outerbridge grabbed her stomach, she discovered gushing blood with Justis Raham Smith's knife tearing into her flesh.

Only a few months after LeYoni Junos gave up on her effort to seek justice for Becky, Justis Smith did it again, stabbing Outerbridge and beating her friend, Hanifah Taalibdin. Just six months before, Justis Smith had admitted in court to being involved in a gang-related brawl. A Bermuda judge discharged him with only a warning to "behave."

Again at three a.m., when bars were closing, Justis Smith left a club, this time on the opposite side of the island from where Rebecca Middleton was murdered six years before. The Dockyard night club stands not far from where the body of murdered German tourist, Antje Herkommer, had been found ten years before.

Armed with a Swiss army knife, Smith sneaked into the back of a filled taxi. His friends had left him; he was frantic to get home. Passengers demanded that he get out. Smith refused.

"All hell broke loose," said a security guard who rushed to help. Some twenty others joined the fight. Smith punched Hanifah Taalibdin so hard her knees buckled, then stabbed Shanae Outerbridge.

This time, police never found Smith's weapon, which a police officer's son claimed he pulled from Smith's hands, throwing it into nearby bushes.

With a bloodied lip and broken nose, Smith fled on a friend's bike, but not before the two women smacked him with punches that Smith described as like blows "thrown by a guy."

When he came to trial in 2003, Smith told the Supreme Court he was an easy going guy who had to "be really provoked to hit someone."

Again, there were "deal" accusations. Inspector Stuart Crockwell, the same officer who told Mark Pettingill, "You got what you wanted," in Mundy's case seven years before, denied the charge of Justis Smith's once-again lawyer, Elizabeth Christopher, that one man had been released in exchange for giving evidence against Smith. Police again lost evidence—a blue headscarf and earrings. Dave Middleton said he would have expected better.

It took a jury only a little more than two hours to convict Smith of unlawfully wounding, possessing a knife, and assault.

Two months later, Supreme Court Justice Charles Etta Simmons released Smith, crediting him for "time served," chiding the women for their returned aggression.

Rick Meens barreled out of Supreme Court Number One, on his way out slamming his fist against the empty seat in front of him. "Getting on with his life? Becky doesn't get to do that. No high school graduation, no college, no kids, no grandkids. And this guy's lawyer worries about this his GED?"

After a quick trip to police headquarters, Justis Smith was free again. Immediately, the Crown appealed the "manifestly inadequate" sentence.

Six months later before the three-judge Court of Appeals, Prosecutor Lloyd Rayney reminded that Justis Smith committed a crime of violence, he was armed with a weapon, and the attack occurred in a public place. Rayney reminded that Smith had been convicted of violence twice before--against a police officer in 1996 and fighting in a public place in 2001.

"At the time of this sentence," said Rayney, "crimes of violence in Bermuda are prevalent, and especially those in which young men are armed with a weapon in the public places." The community "should have showed condemnation, and eleven months in prison doesn't do that."

Elizabeth Christopher argued, instead, that the jury's guilty ruling should be thrown out. Smith, now twenty five, needed to "get on with his life." He was working on his high school equivalency exam, Christopher repeated. Besides, the women had fought back.

Also, Christopher insisted, Rick Meens, who was sitting in the gallery watching the appeal, should be barred from the court. Already Meens' presence had prejudiced the jury in its guilty decision, Christopher charged. Judges ignored that request, giving Smith eighteen months: a year on the stabbing charge and six more months for fighting, to be served consecutively. Still, significantly less than Bermuda law allows—five years.

Smith continued to deny guilt. He was convicted only because of his association with Becky's murder, he complained.

Said prosecutor Lloyd Rayney, "That assertion by Mr. Smith is entirely fallacious."

Bermuda often excuses prisoners who serve two thirds of their sentence. Thus, police escorted him to Westgate Correctional Facility for what Justis Smith correctly assumed would be only a two-week stay.

"Smith came in laughing," a prison guard reported. "He spent his two weeks, and when the time was up, he called his 'daddy.'

"The family came right away and picked him up, the guard said. "He had money. I'd have let him call a cab."

TWENTY SEVEN

"If Bermuda is to remain prosperous, it must be peaceful... Bermudians cannot afford to forget or to ignore the issues which have hitherto divided them. They need to face these and, in particular to take stock of race relations."

Governor Sir Peter Ramsbotham,
(successor to murdered Governor Sharples)

1978 Memo to FCO (The National Archives, London)

A Wake Up Call?
2004-2006

A QUEST, on the basis of LeYoni Junos' findings, by Dave Middleton, Rick Meens and the author, would take more than three years—the goal: get Becky's case back to court. First needed—something official, a recent decision by Bermuda's director of public prosecutions.

We decided to be upfront, no secrets. We set up meetings with those we believed could and should make a difference. Attorney General Larry Mussendon, Police Commissioner Jonathan Smith, Acting DPP Kulandra Ratneser, and newly appointed DPP Vinette Graham-Allen each lamenting during our meetings about the injustices of the murder of Rebecca Middleton and its judicial handling.

Supreme Court Chief Justice Richard Ground, who twice had ruled in favor of attempts to seek justice for Becky, responsible for deciding whether to allow a judicial review of the DPP's refusal, expressed his sadness to Dave Middleton and Rick Meens.

Governor Sir John Vereker, while he expressed sympathy, refused to meet with Dave and Rick, referring them to the government of Bermuda. His deputy Nick Carter, according to Rick Meens, told him during a telephone call that "I needed to put the matter behind me—'We at Government House have.'" In an email to Meens, Carter claimed he was hurried, and perhaps his words were misconstrued.

When he returned to Belleville, Dave Middleton again appealed to the Canadian government. The Canadian consulate general in New York City, Pamela Wallin, pledged to write a letter of concern to the Bermuda government. However, her replacement arrived, and no letter.

Repeatedly, Rick Meens wrote to the Bermuda government, reminding that he had been Becky's guardian when she was murdered, he had a right to be heard, justice had not prevailed. Although murder charges were off the table, others weren't.

Experts had suggested that evidence in Becky's murder, still held by police and at King Edward VII Hospital, should be re-examined using current scientific technique, by now a common procedure in modern jurisdictions.

Now the murder of Rebecca Middleton fell into the lap of newly-hired Director of Public Prosecutions Vinette Graham-Allen of Jamaica. A small woman with a warm smile, her hair neatly tied in place, and fashionable business suit, Graham-Allen, unlike many foreigners working in Bermuda, and even more so in government jobs, made it clear she was not concerned by potential threats to her work permit—Wherever she served, her goal was to make a significant difference. "Not just a difference, a significant one," she said.

Graham-Allen did exactly that. In March, 2004, DPP Vinette Graham-Allen became the first Bermuda official to agree that the handling of the murder of Rebecca Middleton deserved reinvestigation.

Even with Kulandra Ratneser, the former acting DPP who had refused to review Becky's case, as her consultant, Graham-Allen had more than a few challenges—court cases crowding the dockets, a march by her own staff nitpicking about her assertive management style, with crime mounting.

Delays, a busy schedule, the case was under review, she said. Internationally, media repeatedly addressed her silence.

Two years after those first meetings, Graham-Allen made her decision. Like the Privy Council, she cited double jeopardy. However, Mrs. Vinette Graham-Allen spoke loudly and firmly--Becky was sexually assaulted before she was murdered—the evidence was present from the day of her murder.

Evidence that would suggest doubts regarding Mundy's veracity were available to the Crown *prior* to Mundy's commitment to trial, she ruled. Charges could have been added or changed up until Mundy's plea, just two and one half months after Becky's murder.

Because there had been evidence of sexual crimes from the outset, the DPP would not file kidnapping, rape, or other related charges alleged before Becky's death. "It is a well established rule of law that a man should not be punished twice for an offence arising out of the same or substantially the same set of facts."

Neither would she allow the evidence to be revisited.

Graham-Allen's refusal saturated front pages in Bermuda and Canada, seemingly an end to the Rebecca Middleton matter. But that decision in March, 2006, resulted in the exact opposite—exactly as Becky's family and friends hoped.

In the U.S., FOX network's Greta Van Susteren and four attorney commentators by no means missed the failures in Becky's case. Forensic pathologist Dr. Michael Baden termed its handling "unconscionable," while photos of Becky and her family streamed across the television screen, only days after Graham-Allen's ruling. Bermuda television news director Bryan Darby expressed the shock of his fellow Bermudians, Dave Middleton talked of Becky, and Rick Meens described the horrors of the night Becky died.

Also, for the first time, the murder of Rebecca Middleton caught the attention of Britain's media, for the most part not in the habit of publicly scrutinizing the behaviors of its occasionally rebellious children thousands of miles away.

In July, 2006, the tenth anniversary of Becky's murder, the *Royal Gazette* quoted former Police Commissioner Colin Coxall's call for renewed investigation using current technique, a procedure applicable to all murder cases in Britain where there is no conviction. The handling of Becky's case, said Coxall from London, was "the most disgraceful miscarriage of justice" in his forty-year career.

Criminalist Dr. Henry Lee, who had reviewed blood spatter evidence during the Smith trial, concurred, saying evidence retesting was basic to good police work. In 2005 a re-investigation of a rock held in evidence had resulted in a conviction for an eighteen-year-old Bermuda murder.

Attorney General Larry Mussendon, who had replaced retiring Attorney General Lois Browne Evans in 2003, disagreed, claiming the system "worked," even if some people didn't like the results.

Nonetheless, Rick Meens and Dave Middleton had achieved their hope: Although they would have preferred that Graham-Allen had agreed with their application to recharge and reinvestigate, they hadn't expected that she would.

But they had achieved a recent official decision--capable of court challenge. Applying Bermuda appeals law, they had six months from the DPP's decision to get a judicial review—if the courts agreed.

Meanwhile, only few outside of the Middleton family knew that on the first day of March, 2006—nearly a month before Graham-Allen faxed her decision to Bermuda's newspapers, radio, and television stations--human rights lawyer Cherie Booth, QC, wife of U.K. Prime Minister Tony Blair, had agreed to represent Becky's case.

LeYoni Junos' research, Booth said, "most certainly caught my attention."

In late September, 2006, lawyers filed affidavits challenging the DPP's decision, claiming she had been wrong in law—that kidnapping, sexual crimes, which happened before Becky's murder, were not the same as murder, could be done independently of murder, and were not on an "ascending" scale of gravity, as DPP Vinette Graham-Allen had written.

Chief Justice Ground agreed the claim, brought by Becky's father, Dave Middleton, should be reviewed, promising a quick process.

Bermudian lawyer John Riihiluoma, a Bermudian senior partner of internationally respected Appleby Global's Bermuda offices, proactive and aggressive, and Kelvin Hastings-Smith, an energetic, silver-haired Englishman who had been in Bermuda twelve years, joined Cherie Booth, QC, who required Bermuda's immigration's permission to appear in Bermuda's courts.

Graham-Allen rallied her defense, and the government retained British Queen's Counsel James Guthrie, experienced with Privy Council level appeals and constitutional law, who had recently defended a decision not to prosecute three police officers for murder in Jamaica, where Amnesty International has reported numerous failings in the investigative system for police killings. In 2005, with the level of police killings among the highest per capita in the world, there were reportedly 168 fatal shootings by police, according to Amnesty. Guthrie had appeared before the United Nations and Inter-American Commissions, having worked in death penalty appeals and human rights cases.

Ground also sent notice to Kirk Mundy, who refused to leave his cell to accept court documents. Another server, notifying Mundy several months later of the date Ground set for the judicial review, found that first document in a guard's office.

Justis Smith wasted no time heading for Jamaica via the U.K., the only route out of Bermuda for a convicted felon. Officials reported he left in early December, 2006, with a return ticket for March, 2007.

A ticket that would go unused.

TWENTY EIGHT

...Murder or mayhem is as unlikely a happening on Bermuda as one of the island's cricketers throwing a Bowie knife instead of a ball at a batsman. But it's an image that will never be the same after yesterday's bloody killings.

Daily Express--March 12, 1973

Sinister Seas
April 16, 2007

EARLY THIS DAY, skies had turned oddly dark for mid-April in Bermuda. Gale force winds and rain deluged the island, reminiscent of storms on that 1977 winter night that judges in this same building refused to spare Larry Tacklyn and Buck Burrows from the gallows.

Almost eleven years after Becky's murder, international media again swarmed the island. This morning, reporters and photographers filled the gallery of Supreme Court, where Kirk Mundy had escaped murder charges and where Judge Meerabux eight years ago had opened the case that set Justis Smith free.

LeYoni Junos quietly took her seat in the back, watching as a parade of lawyers, along with Dave Middleton and Rick Meens, escorted Queen's Counsel Cherie Booth into the courtroom. Booth, Junos knew, faced an uphill battle.

According to Bermuda's Constitution, the director of public prosecutions is independent and has the authority to exercise discretion on whether to prosecute—if nothing irregular has occurred, like a mistake in law. If the DPP made an error in law or a decision that a court deemed unreasonable, then the court could ask the DPP to reconsider the decision.

Rebecca Middleton's mother, Cindy Bennett was first to arrive almost two hours before hearing time. She found the front doors unlocked to the empty Supreme Court building, also open to the courtroom. An hour later, four Bermuda police officers rushed in to sweep under benches, above blinds, beneath lawyers' tables and behind the judge's bench, in preparation for Booth, whose husband still served as U.K. prime minister.

Bermudian Marsha Jones, wearing a jacket stitched with her murdered son's name, sat down next to Cindy. Like many others cases in Bermuda during recent years, no one had been charged with murder in Shaundae Jones' 2003 killing. Marsha Jones knew the outcome of the judicial review in the handling of Becky's murder might impact the management of her son's case.

Marsha Jones handed Cindy a paper. Just months before he was shot to death at Dockyard, Shaundae Jones had written about injustices in Becky's murder case for a class assignment. Becky's mom read the words written by Marsha Jones' now dead son, whose murder investigation, like Becky's, appeared to be ending in limbo. In Shaundae's case, like Becky's, prosecutors complained of lack of evidence of murder, saying they had enough proof to charge only with possessing a weapon, not murder. Just hours before the trial of a man extradited from Jamaica by private jet on gun possession was to start, the only witness who police could find (of the dozens who witnessed the shooting) refused to testify, afraid of consequences. Judge Archie Warner, Justis Smith's former defense lawyer, ruled "no case to answer."

Again, because of Bermuda appeals law, the judge's ruling could not be challenged.

She had met privately with DPP Vinette Graham-Allen, Marsha Jones said. "She told me she didn't want to abuse the powers of her good office" to file murder charges, despite a reported police admission to Shaundae's mother that a bullet found in her son's body matched others given to them, reportedly by the witness who refused to testify.

For Cindy, Supreme Court Chief Justice Richard Ground's presence at the bench contrasted starkly with that scene almost a decade ago when Justice Vincent Meerabux deferred to John Perry, and both made jokes during the testimony. "They thought they were being funny. I lost my daughter."

Few locals, though, had forgotten the 2003 ruckus that accompanied the appointment of Richard Ground to be Bermuda's new Supreme Court chief justice. Ground, who had ruled that Kirk Mundy could be charged with murder, even though sentenced as an accessory after the fact, and ruled that Smith should be retried, would replace Austin Ward, who had given Mundy only five years as "accomplice," then sentenced him to 16 years for armed robbery.

Richard Ground had left Bermuda in the late 90s, highly respected.

The PLP was incensed, another white foreigner, when, in their opinion, a Bermudian was available. Premier Alex Scott insisted that if Jamaican lawyer turned Bermudian Norma Wade Miller didn't get the post, the PLP would increase its moves toward independence.

Governor Sir John Vereker, in an unusually assertive move for any governor since Lord David Waddington, announced that "Mr. Richard Ground OBE, QC, currently chief justice of Turks and Caicos Island, will be the new chief justice."

Union organizer Edward Ball urged Bermudians to kick up a storm. If Mrs. Wade Miller didn't get the job, it would fly in the face of the message that qualified Bermudians would eventually get top posts. The governor hastily referred the appointment to the foreign secretary, who confirmed the governor's position.

Former Westgate Prison resident, now attorney, Charles Richardson, who had studied law while serving time for shooting two men in a Court Street bar, hurriedly took his seat at the defense table to represent Kirk Mundy. Richardson hastily presented his documents to the judge, apologizing for his tardiness. Smith's consistent supporter Elizabeth Christopher sat next to Richardson.

Director of Public Prosecutions Vinette Graham-Allen and her lawyer, James Guthrie, QC, at the same table, flipped pages of documents in thick black leather-bound binders, preparing to defend Graham-Allen's decision.

"If the court agrees, it doesn't mean there will be fresh charges," Bermuda lawyer Kelvin Hastings-Smith explained publicly. "If with us, then the court can order that the decision be quashed, and it goes back to the DPP, who will have to reconsider her position...An individual cannot be tried a second time on a charge arising out of the same facts as the first...(but) a review of evidence using current forensic technique could provide new data for inspection."

Bermuda's lawyers wandered in and out of the courtroom, intrigued. Judicial reviews were common in Bermuda. But the presence of human rights lawyer Cherie Booth, QC, for a case that had caused international angst for more than a decade, was not.

Furthermore, for the first time the Supreme Court was reviewing a decision not to prosecute, along with another matter not often argued in Bermuda Supreme Court--human rights.

Cherie Booth, QC, covered her navy blue suit and white blouse with her black robe, comfortably topping her shining brown hair with a bristling silver wig. On their heads, Booth's appeared soft, Ground's lionesque.

"Rebecca Middleton's killers showed no remorse for having dehumanized and killed" her. Bermuda operates in a "culture of impunity" when it comes to sexual assault, Booth charged. Furthermore, until the way in which the country pursues such crimes is brought into the Twenty First Century, "it is actually repugnant to justice."

Becky's mom loosened her grip on the bench, relieved that her daughter's case was in good hands, those of a woman with soft blue eyes, also a mother, whose presence was palpable.

"Deliberate acts...Rebecca's life has gone; her parents know that only too well. There's no chance of the redemption Mr. Mundy has had by being allowed to take his exams in jail. There's no second chance for Rebecca.

"Abduction, torture, rape, sodomy—all violation of European Union human rights laws...There is absolutely no doubt that any of these things took place."

Bermuda has the capability to open the door to justice, Booth argued. First, the Privy Council had in 1979 ruled that Bermuda's constitution had to be interpreted more broadly than any other statutes. "A constitution is a legal instrument that assures the individual certain rights capable of enforcement in a court of law."

Therefore, suggested Booth, that appeals law that prosecutors had misinterpreted frequently before the Privy Council's ruling in the Rebecca

Middleton murder case, would take second place to Bermuda's constitution and its fundamental promise.

Bermuda failed Rebecca Middleton and her family when it neglected to guarantee "every person in Bermuda fundamental rights, especially the right to life," Booth charged. The DPP's decision failed to balance Justis Smith's and Kirk Mundy's trial rights to Rebecca Middleton's right to life--"A fundamental right, a supreme right… a right 'basic to all human rights.'"

That right to life "enshrines one of the basic values of the democratic societies making up the Council of Europe…The Inter-American Commission on Human Rights … the United Nations, both view the right to life to be "supreme…a right basic to all human rights."

Booth's words sounded reminiscent of those arguments that British Parliament failed to heed in 1977, when its leader refused to allow discussion of the impending hangings of Larry Tacklyn and Buck Burrows, moving the men toward the gallows.

These rights, Booth reminded, regularly are applied by the U.K., upholding priorities set by international standards. "The individual's right to life is the most fundamental of all human rights. Thus, when right to life is engaged, the options available to the reasonable decision maker are curtailed."

That courts believed Rebecca had consented, Booth charged, highlighted Bermuda's lenient stand on sexual-assault cases. "She is assaulted, she is threatened with a knife, she is restrained, she is sodomized, and she is raped. All of that and we're asked to believe it was consensual," she told the hushed courtroom. "That is, indeed, repugnant." In fact, "it is actually repugnant to justice to say that the decision is set and that it cannot be changed or put right. . . Once your life is gone, as Rebecca's parents know all too well, there is no putting that right."

When the DPP made her choice—placing Kirk Mundy's and Justis Smith's rights above Becky's fundamental right to life—Vinette Graham-Allen erred in law, Booth charged.

Kirk Mundy should not be allowed to hide behind the 1996 "deal" which only related to the murder charges and were "wrong in law." The Privy Council itself had termed Justice Vincent Meerabux' decision to stop the Justis Smith murder trial "astonishing," questioning the competence of the court.

Carol Shuman

Security officers accompany Cherie Booth, QC, walking with Kelvin Hastings-Smith of Appleby Global.
Photo Courtesy of the Royal Gazette

Becky's dad leads the way for the judicial review of the handling of Becky's case.
Photo Courtesy of the Royal Gazette

Kill Me Once...

Marsha Jones and Cindy Bennett, both mothers of children murdered in Bermuda, remind that no one was charged in either murder, not unusual on this tiny island where silence often is golden.
Photo Courtesy of the Royal Gazette

Governor John Vereker administers oath of office to DPP Vinette Graham Allen--who now faced the Rebecca Middleton matter.
Photo Courtesy of the Royal Gazette

Chief Justice Richard Ground, QC, hears Booth's human rights arguments.
Photo Courtesy of the Royal Gazette

"...The state has duties under the ECHR to see rape cases prosecuted, but that doesn't seem to have crossed the DPP's mind. The state has been remiss to the victim...and the family stands in her shoes for this purpose."

For Bermuda to say there was nothing that could be done "is wrong," said Booth. "There is something you can do. Not murder; that is concluded. But sexual assault would not break the double jeopardy rule on repeat prosecutions."

The original charge against Smith was murder. Mundy was charged as accessory after the fact to Justis Smith's charge of premeditated murder. Never did any attorney general place charges related to the torture, kidnapping, imprisonment, theft, rape, or sodomy of Rebecca Middleton included in an indictment against either Mundy or Smith. There was no doubt that police and prosecutors weren't blind to what happened to Becky. So why did they not lay those charges?

The answer to that question, Booth charged: sexist expectations of Rebecca Middleton's behavior. Those charges "never saw the light of day, owing to the acceptance of an absurd tale of consensual sex," a human rights failure that should be considered "special circumstances," requiring the court to correct the judicial wrongs done to Becky and her family.

A new case would deal with alleged acts before Rebecca's death, said Booth.

"The issue at hand is whether the court can correct a grave wrong--and now provide justice for Rebecca and her family, and for the integrity of Bermuda."

The DPP's argument that "the only choice now would be to apologize and do nothing" would suggest a 'council of hopelessness' and a 'culture of impunity' regarding sexual offenses.

"Bermuda has obligations to its citizens and to visitors to protect life and provide a safe environment." Bermuda failed in its responsibility to "use criminal law provisions to deter commission of offenses."

In the U.K., Booth reminded, courts have held states legally responsible for failing "to put in place an adequate and effective investigation to protect the right to life."

The DPP's refusal to retest forensic samples using the latest DNA and other techniques, and her failure to pursue the charges of rape, unlawful sexual assault and kidnapping against both Smith and Mundy amounted to such a failing.

Bermuda, she said, "allowed a climate of impunity to prevail in respect of the offenses committed against Rebecca Middleton. Not only in her case, but the reputation of Bermuda internationally has been adversely affected."

Especially, "when it may be suggested that an attack was racially motivated, it is particularly important that the investigation should be pursued with vigor and impartiality."

Booth cited a landmark British case (*Connelly vs. The Queen, 1964*) in which the court ruled that a man acquitted of murder could be retried for armed robbery from the same event. In that case, the court cited "special circumstances" because British law at that time prohibited adding charges along with murder. The complicated ruling dissected conditions that would allow exceptions to the double jeopardy rule.

"We say, if this isn't such a case—one is at a loss to consider what such a case would be."

Booth named:

--New evidence: Although the DPP argued that sufficient proof already existed, the issue becomes one of principle--of human rights-- that an investigation into the murder be complete. "No one can be proud of the way this case was investigated," she reminded.

--Bermuda's obligation to victims: "The DPP has the responsibility to the victim, but she made only a bleak reference... We say that she has not properly addressed matters that are fundamental..."

--Mundy's mendacity: "His dishonesty, deceit, lies, falsehoods, and fabrication." There was sufficient evidence to go to a jury "to decide whether a seventeen-year-old virgin consented---an idea that flies in the face of belief. What could Mundy (or those who accepted his tale) have been thinking?"

--The competence of the court: "Judicial conduct was questionable. Direction to the jury in the Smith case was plainly wrong...Higher courts have agreed repeatedly that Justice Vincent Meerabux erred."

--No real serious grappling with the judicial handling of the case: "Two individuals, the balance of evidence shows a heinous sexual assault on a girl who had just turned seventeen, a young virgin, in the middle of night, without transportation...of huge concern in Bermuda and other parts of the world, not the least of which is Canada."

The DPP was not obligated to provide reasons for her decisions, Booth agreed, but by doing so she provided evidence "she had infected her mind with error...Where the offense is different (rape is not murder and can be accomplished without murder) the case could be made."

Graham-Allen, she argued, should have filed the charges and let a court determine if there had been abuse of process. "An imprecise regret that (the accused) might have to face another charge is not sufficient for abuse of process."

Bermuda has territorial obligations to the UK and to the European Court, said Booth. "There is an obligation of the state to investigate...to punish and apply prosecution...The evidence in Becky's case was overwhelming...The prosecution fell short of obligations set by modern standards of international law...."

Based upon Bermuda's human rights obligations, Booth challenged, Justice Ground and the Supreme Court of Bermuda, she said, "must quash the DPP's decision not to prosecute, order the DPP to reinvestigate, including obtaining up-to-date forensic evaluation of the evidence. Finally, the DPP must reconsider her decision on the basis of any new evidence."

In 2008, FCO official Hugo Frost provided unequivocal confirmation that Bermuda has full treaty obligations under the human rights act, contradicting some attorneys in Bermuda who have insisted that Bermuda's Human Rights Law limits the island's responsibilities. "The ECHR does apply in Bermuda…ratified by the U.K. in 1951 and extended to Bermuda in 1953. Persons in Bermuda also have the right of individual petition…This was most recently accepted by the U.K. for Bermuda on 14 January 2006 for a period of five years. This means that once a person has exhausted their domestic legal remedies in Bermuda…they may then submit an application to the court in Strasbourg.

"The United Kingdom expects Bermuda to comply with all its obligations under the Convention and indeed any other international instrument that has been extended to it." Any case, he wrote, would be brought against the U.K. as "the State party to the ECHR. But we would look to the government of Bermuda to remedy any violation…."

Cindy Bennett and Marsha Jones dashed through the blustery downpour to a restaurant nearby, joining LeYoni Junos and several reporters for the lunch break. She'd hesitated to return to Bermuda, Cindy told *Bermuda Sun* reporter Nigel Regan. Now, hearing Cherie Booth, meeting and thanking Booth, as well as LeYoni Junos, she was optimistic, despite Booth's warning to her, "I don't know how this (the judicial review) will work out."

"I've kept myself level headed. It hurts to hear what happened to Becky, and it's been almost eleven years, my emotions are pretty consistent now," Cindy told the reporter.

"When I think of Bermuda, the hairs go up on the back of my neck. I have always said that I would never go back again because the trial was such a fiasco and all the faults in the legal system. Just sitting through three and a half weeks…and having that result….I felt so bad for the jury because they never got to do the job they were called to do. So I said I would never go back. But I want to be here for this, to hear firsthand, to see the outcome. I want to see if they will try and do the right thing. I'm hoping for the best outcome that Bermuda can give.

"The worst has happened," she told Regan. "If they can get some kind of resolve on this, or recharges, that would be a good thing. I just wanted a good lawyer, and that's what she is. I feel bad for her when I hear people say she is the wife of the British prime minister. She should be seen in her own right."

Cindy said she accepted that some people just wished Becky's family would simply move on. "They don't say it to my face, but all I say to them is, 'If this was your child, you would be doing exactly the same thing.'"

Marsha Jones agreed. "The average Bermudian does show remorse to me," she told Regan. "But there are a few who wish I would just go away. Some people don't want to deal with it. We have some serious crimes going on in Bermuda, but nobody wants to deal with them."

Had Cindy been able to find peace since Becky's murder? "Yes, I can enjoy life. In the short seventeen years she was here with us, we have so many good memories of Becky. We have our sad times, but it is overwhelmed by the good times."

A sentiment with which Dave Middleton agreed. The murderers, ultimately, no matter what the court's judgment, he said, would get what they deserved, whether it be in their lifetimes on earth or afterward.

Cindy smiled when Bermuda police officer Terry Maxwell, who had supported her and Wayne during the horrifying verdict in the case of Justis Smith, sat down next to her after the lunch break.

The DPP's attorney, James Guthrie, QC, turned toward Dave sitting with lawyers in the jury box and then peered into the crowd, finding Cindy. "No doubt," Guthrie said, "there has been great injustice to Becky and her family." Guthrie, speaking for DPP Vinette Graham-Allen, for the first time, publicly admitted there had been a miscarriage of justice and offered an apology.

"The director of public prosecutions accepts that the applicant, and indeed Rebecca, suffered great injustice, and it's a matter of very sincere regret on her part. The applicant is entitled to say that his daughter has been badly served by what has happened."

Contrition, repentance, regret, but not accountability. That remained the chattel of no one.

"We repeat, it's a matter of profound regret, but it's sadly the case that the only way justice could be served is if we could turn the clock back to Smith and Mundy's arrest and take proceedings on a different course."

Director of Public Prosecutions Vinette Graham-Allen had made a mistake in law, Guthrie admitted, when she ruled that new charges could not be filed on an "ascending scale of gravity." Rape is not a more serious crime than murder, Guthrie agreed. However, a "wider" rule prevented a second trial on the same facts, simply to correct errors made in the past, he argued. Double jeopardy. Period.

Further investigation, Guthrie argued, would be irrelevant. The DPP already had agreed "there was evidence of sexual assault against both men from the outset. Her objection was to allowing the prosecution a further opportunity, based on the same or similar facts, to proceed until they get a decision to their liking."

Cherie Booth's notion that the issue of "abuse of process" should be left to the courts, Guthrie argued, was misconceived. "Prosecutors routinely consider the likelihood of conviction by a jury." Also, he suggested, "Bermuda is a relatively small place, and the history of the matter is very well known."

As for right to life's taking precedence--mentioning the rights of Rebecca Middleton simply wasn't necessary, James Guthrie maintained. "She did not need to do so."

A remark that LeYoni found disconcerting.

Several years before, LeYoni Junos, sitting on Bermuda's Prerogative of Mercy Committee, had agreed with the group to allow early release for Kirk Mundy's current attorney, Charles Richardson, long before he completed his sentence for the 1994 Court Street bar shooting of two men. Now LeYoni bristled as Richardson spoke for Mundy.

There was "no substance to the claim that authorities in Bermuda don't take offences of sexual assault seriously," Richardson argued, citing a case in which an accused man received "twenty years for sexual assault."

There was no way Mundy could get a fair trial now, he added. "Newspapers have spilled gallons of ink in pursuit of this story...The pulse of public opinion in this country already has my client convicted of murdering Rebecca." The deal remained in place. Kirk Mundy admitted to no more than being an accomplice to murder, Richardson reminded.

On her way to report the afternoon's events, *Royal Gazette* reporter Liz Roberts recognized LeYoni Junos. With her advocacy experience, what did LeYoni think about Bermuda's response to sexual crimes?

Despite her job at Bermuda's Department of Tourism, which frowns on release of information that might make tourists nervous, LeYoni Junos spoke out. "Scores of rapes every year in Bermuda are never investigated, let alone brought to justice." Becky's case was "fundamental, not only for Becky, but for Bermudian women," LeYoni told Roberts.

Although there were two hundred four reports of rape reaching Bermuda police from 2000 to 2004, "convictions occurred in only sixteen of these cases, eight percent," she said, citing statistics from Bermuda's Women's Resource Center. "And when you allow a suspect to plead guilty to accessory after the fact based on consensual sex--when you have all of that evidence that indicates sex could not have been consensual--what message have you sent to the community about crimes against women?"

Day one over, despite the downpour, Cindy Bennett and Marsha Jones stood on the courthouse steps telling reporters they hoped for justice in their children's cases. As long as Bermuda failed to act, Marsha Jones said, some believed they could get away with murder, with some success.

Riding home together, Marsha pointed to a church graveyard on Middle Road, less than a block from her home. They could see her son Shaundae's gravestone from the road.

Parents who have lost children share something that, sadly, only they can experience, they agreed.

Another day of rain and gusty winds greeted the second day of the judicial review. Again first to arrive, Cindy found the scene from the day before repeated-- unlocked doors to an empty courtroom, police scurrying into the courtroom an hour later.

To Cindy's surprise, the government's defense files—judicial documents related to her daughter's murder--sat unguarded on the tables a few feet in front of her. The files had been left there all night.

Like the knife Dave Middleton found unattended when he returned to Supreme Court early from lunch during the Justis Smith trial, confidential documents, accessible to the public.

"An apology--while appreciated--does not meet the standards of international law," Cherie Booth, QC, reminded the court. Four decades had passed since the Connelly ruling in which the House of Lords had attempted to define special circumstances. "Human rights in developed countries have matured, and Bermuda needs to consider this carefully."

The failure of an overseas territory to provide "good governance, to fail to implement human rights, is a matter for grave concern. If they aren't addressed, as well as for the citizens of Bermuda, they could give rise to significant contingent liabilities for the United Kingdom."

Britain, Booth reminded, "has a right to expect the highest standards of probity, law and order, good governance and observance of Britain's international commitments." For as long as the island chooses to remain a territory, said Booth, Bermuda is obliged to honor its human rights obligations. "Fundamental freedoms…are the foundation of justice and peace…the right to life, protection from 'inhuman or degrading treatment… the right to liberty and security.'"

At noon, Justice Richard Ground declared the review complete; he would rule in three weeks.

"I thought we got the point across. It is a special case," Dave Middleton told reporters. "They say it's a complete bungle, but it's tough bananas, that's the law, and get on with it. I'm very hopeful that the judge will rule in favor of us," he said. "It's been such a long time coming, I feel relieved it's over."

That afternoon, two days of rain and wind gusts that hadn't slowed since the case began, stopped. Sunshine broke through the springtime clouds.

"After waiting nearly eleven years, three weeks is a drop in the bucket," Cindy said. The experience had been "heart-wrenching, the sharp edge has gone, but you still feel the pain. I feel very confident, though. I'm glad I came to hear this."

For three weeks, deafening silence, until Appleby attorney Kelvin Hastings-Smith's telephone call to Dave Middleton.

TWENTY NINE

...Independence would not necessarily, by itself, be a cure for the cancer. Nevertheless when the time is ripe, I believe we must actively encourage Bermudians to think seriously about their present relationship with Britain and to consider whether colonial status is now more of a burden than an asset...The colonial relationship is an unnatural one...and the more so in an island as prosperous and well-endowed with human resources as Bermuda...

--Secret Memo Acting Governor Ian Kinnear to Secretary of State, FCO—May 1, 1973 (The National Archives, London)

'Like Nailing Jelly to a Tree'

May 5, 2007

"THE DOOR WAS OPEN...Chief Justice Ground chose not to walk through it. And so a family is left at a dead end on a long, agonizing road to find justice for their murdered child. And a judicial system is left... tied in knots...," Canada's *Globe and Mail* wrote. "A dark day for Bermudian justice."

Sympathetic, said Supreme Court Chief Justice Richard Ground, but bound by law. Human rights arguments? A distraction.

"I appreciate that that will be a bitter disappointment to the applicant and other members of Rebecca's family, for whom I feel great personal sympathy, but I have to declare the law as it is," Ground asserted. Human rights arguments did not amount to special circumstances, in his opinion, rather a distortion of the Connelly ruling.

LeYoni Junos' *Appeal for Accountability*, alleging racism and sexism, had been included among documents for the court to consider, including identities of those alleged to have made such statements. The same document seemingly overlooked by Governor Thorold Masefield, Baroness Amos of the Foreign and Commonwealth Office, and the SCC. Again, LeYoni's human rights concerns appeared not to warrant even curiosity. No further investigation.

Double jeopardy, no more, no less...a "well established rule of law that a man should not be punished twice for an offense arising of the same or substantially the same set of facts."

The director of public prosecutions, Vinette Graham-Allen, had been wrong in some areas, Ground agreed, but said the DPP understood the heart of the matter—"there is a common law against double jeopardy...save in exceptional circumstances"...Once the double jeopardy issue is accepted, said Ground, "all the other points fall away."

But Booth already had agreed that the issue of murder had been completed. At issue now were the matters of kidnapping, rape, sodomy, and other points not charged owing to the acceptance of Mundy's statement, human rights issues, "special circumstances" that required out of the ordinary deliberation.

The crux of the case, agreed Ground, was whether "there are special circumstances here." But there were none, he ruled.

Ground found Cherie Booth's human rights arguments "a distortion of the Connelly rule...open(ing) the door to precisely the sort of broad ranging discretion that the whole court was at pains to avoid and disavow."

Ground was "satisfied that the prosecution do not desire to be oppressive, but I have to look at the matter in the light of the results...It seems to me that I would be granting here a complete retrial....(on the same facts)." To support his decision, Ground referred to a House of Lords decision that halted a manslaughter prosecution of a landlord who previously admitted breach of duty in the carbon monoxide death of his female tenant. "Albeit without the human rights argument," Ground admitted.

"The rule is well-established and straightforward," said Ground. Another decision would require legislation or "possibly the intervention of a higher court to change it...."

Ground referred to Kirk Mundy's deceit. "Had (the Crown) thought about it for a moment, it would have realized its extreme improbability." Additionally, "no explanation is put forward for why the prosecutors in this case failed to join charges of sexual assault at the outset. I can only assume it was oversight or error, neither of which is a good reason...."

An oversight or error? Or a human rights violation based upon racial and gender profiling?

Would further investigation find new "facts" and clarify that question? Not unusual, according to both Dr. Henry Lee and former Bermuda Police Commissioner Colin Coxall.

Booth's arguments "eloquent." Nothing more.

"I think Ground has gone wrong here," an Appleby attorney not involved in the case wrote in an email to Brian Calhoun. "Surely 'any other offense' in the Constitution means 'any other included offense *only*' (like manslaughter, which would be a lesser offense with ingredients of the specific larger crime) --not 'any other offense *at all*? Sexual crimes and kidnapping would not fall under that list, he argued.

Calhoun agreed. "In that 'special circumstances' have at least some scope of wider interpretation than Ground's more restricted...interpretation—it is no small wonder that the public, particularly the younger ones, are increasingly resorting to self-help remedies."

Calhoun reminded, "If you both recall Mottley twice threatened to try to have me fired for 'too vigorously' arguing with him that; 1) they should both be tried together for murder—and sexual assault (given Mundy's consensual sex was ridiculous)..., and 2) the AG should not accept Mundy's plea to accessory after the fact charge as it had a minor penalty and was only offered to forever preclude a prosecution on the more serious offenses, and 3) if they proceeded their way, it would eventually embarrass them, and the Chambers and Bermuda internationally.

"Both the current DPP (or the QC acting on her behalf) and now Ground have confirmed the accuracy of my position," Calhoun wrote. "However, it is a vindication that certainly gives me no pleasure in the circumstances."

"I share your frustration that the 'right to life' issue that should have been the predominant factor...received no standing or acknowledgement in Richard Ground's judgment," a retired member of the attorney general's office privately wrote from England. "...It is almost as if he considered it unworthy of notice."

Ground's refusal to retest evidence, "a screaming error," the former Bermuda prosecutor contended. "It is up to attorneys to educate the courts. Scientific transformation of the legal system doesn't occur easily. Trial judges, governed by precedent setting decisions, are naturally slow to react to changes in the real world. But it's time that Bermuda traveled to the Twenty First Century," he wrote. "We must not fail in our responsibilities."

Meanwhile, former Police Commissioner Colin Coxall insisted, "A total reinvestigation by internationally respected and qualified investigators teamed with forensic pathologists would almost certainly produce overwhelming evidence that Becky had been brutally murdered and raped by more than one man and that those men are 'known to police.'

"Ground assumed in his judgment that a reinvestigation would consist of DNA examination. This is wrong. The DNA element of a total reinvestigation would be about ten percent, in my opinion," said Coxall.

For Supreme Court Chief Justice Richard Ground, "the deal" offered to Mundy appeared obvious--sexual assault would never even have been considered.

"...No other arrangement makes sense." Ground wrote. There was "little doubt what Mundy's response would have been if told that he would not be prosecuted for murder, but that he could be prosecuted for serious sexual assault, for which he could go to prison for thirty years."

Did Supreme Court Chief Justice Richard Ground believe that Mundy wouldn't have cooperated if the sexual crimes had been on the table? Thus, no other potential arrangement was possible?

Perhaps true? But one must remember that 1996, when Becky was murdered, the death penalty was still in effect in Bermuda. Perhaps in Kirk Mundy's mind, thirty years in prison for sexual crimes might not be as objectionable, if he had been found guilty of murder, as the possibility of the gallows?

"I'm disappointed. We were hoping that we could move ahead with this," Dave Middleton told media from Belleville. "We feel that this is a problem that needs to be resolved in Bermuda. Bermuda created the problem, and we think they should correct the problem. It's very disappointing, but we figured all along that we are going to have to go to a higher court to get some justice. It's like trying to nail jelly to a tree, but we are confident that sooner or later it will stick."

"I'm disappointed...but not at all surprised," said Cindy.

The Middletons, led by Becky's father, Dave Middleton, would appeal, Appleby Global lawyer Kelvin Hastings-Smith announced. Behind the scenes, lawyers held little hope for a different verdict at the Caribbean Court of Appeals. More likely, the Privy Council in London, or the European Court of Human Rights would recognize the injustices in the handling of the murder of Rebecca Middleton. In the ECHR, said Hastings-Smith, "fresh proceedings could be commenced against the State of Bermuda (and thereby the United Kingdom) requiring the state to properly investigate a crime committed within that state."

"The original criminal investigation, prosecution, and trial" all were "mismanaged and flawed," Hastings Smith reminded. The effort had been left to the family, alone, "to seek whatever justice and remedies they can on their own without the assistance of the state prosecutors." Those responsible, he said, should "take responsibility for the decisions...made previously...to pursue and secure a criminal conviction, the gravity and severity of which should reflect the savage attack upon an innocent seventeen year old."

But the price tag hit home. After Ground's ruling, a group helping to fund the case in Bermuda withdrew its efforts, its members fearing they would be individually responsible for outstanding bills that now amounted to nearly $100,000. Thus, Dave Middleton, afraid that he would lose everything, including the appeal, withdrew the case.

Along with the issue of money, Becky's father said, "there is so little to be gained...because the Bermuda government just doesn't want to participate in this at all. They just want it to go away. We'd make them be interested if we had a million dollars. But we don't have it. The thing is, do you want to give your house away to be able to have the Bermuda government pay attention to you? The answer is no."

In the end, Dave Middleton told the media, "Although we didn't get to where we wanted, a lot of good things have been accomplished. We made people aware…What's really failed here is the government of Bermuda. They've failed the people and not allowed it to come to an end that would help the people of Bermuda."

Hastings-Smith agreed that the legal team felt confident of a successful outcome eventually, but the costs were a major consideration. "If lessons can be learned in the investigation and prosecution of similar cases, then the efforts will have a lasting impact."

Rick Meens continued privately to seek funds, and ultimately, with the help of reports in the *Royal Gazette,* Bermuda private sources and businesses offered donations. Hastings-Smith's law firm wrote off a significant amount.

From England, former Police Commissioner Colin Coxall repeated his appeal that Bermuda not allow Becky's case to grow cold, but to keep it under continuous review, a proper practice standard in the U.K. and other advanced countries. "In the U.K., all such cases are reviewed every two or three years and potential forensic evidence is re-examined using the most advanced DNA and forensic examination techniques available at the time. Many unresolved murder cases have been successfully resolved following this review process.

"The most common reason jurisdictions fail to conduct regular reviews," Coxall reminded, "is fear that the review will show errors in the initial investigation and prosecution, likely the factor that has prevented Bermuda from following best practice and allowing an external review of the Middleton case."

Legal fees, the former Bermuda police commissioner added, should not be the deciding factor. In fact, said Coxall, the family should never have been required to take over the fight for justice.

Coxall cited the notorious unsolved 1993 murder case in Britain, in which an eighteen-year-old black youth, Stephen Lawrence, had been stabbed to death by a gang of white youths in a race-hate killing. Police in Britain were conducting fresh forensic tests on the evidence, with lawyers aiding the family by donating their skills for free. "The Bermuda Bar Association could help the Middleton family in a similar way."

Meanwhile, Coxall added, that forensic evidence gathered during the murder investigation presumably still exists. Permission for destruction, if that happened, would have to be obtained from Becky's family, never sought.

Becky's clothes, sputum, other body fluids, tissues, particles, threads, discarded condom wrappers, the blanket over Becky's body—DNA cells from these items can be "amplified." What starts out as fifty cells, bloodstains barely perceptible to the eye, a single hair root, samples in poor condition, even samples exposed to rain, sunshine, dirt, the size of the head of a pin, can become millions, even billions.

Is a deal is a deal, even if both parties don't hold up each end?

When Becky's family allowed her travel to Bermuda, they'd believed Bermuda to be a safe island for which Britain was responsible. However, as Britain's Shadow Foreign Secretary William Hague said some years later, things were happening in Bermuda without "a ripple reaching Whitehall."

Was the FCO paying sufficient attention to the conduct of the UK's overseas territories? Events in the not too distant future, especially a secret move by Bermuda's Premier Dr. Ewart F. Brown, would shock not only Britain, but Bermuda's Parliament, annoying more than a few internationally--even as far away as China.

*His fist raised, Dr. Ewart F. Brown leads the PLP to its third victory.
Photo Courtesy of Royal Gazette.*

THIRTY

On an island famous for long shorts and natty knee-high socks, Ewart Brown cuts an unusual figure in his tan double-breasted suit with wide lapels and turn-ups that sweep the floor. The suit has a distinct early-Seventies feel – and so do his politics.

The pro-independence Bermudian Premier rocked this offshore financial centre this week by threatening to break ties with the Governor of Britain's oldest colony. He came close to blaming Sir John Vereker, an associate of Tony Blair, for the leak of a document linking the Premier to a corruption scandal involving $8 million (£4 million) destined for a social housing body. A member of his Government called for Sir John to be stripped of responsibility for the island's police force. It is the second time Dr Brown, 60 – a former Commonwealth Games sprinter and a student activist at America's leading black university – has clashed with the Governor since taking office eight months ago. Although the Governor and the Premier issued a joint statement declaring a truce, relations between the sides remain under strain.

The Times Online: (James Bone) Black power makes waves on island colony--June 9, 2007

Carol Shuman

'Strong Support, Silent Support'
2007-2008

THE TWELFTH CHRISTMAS without Becky, neither Dave Middleton nor Cindy Bennett were willing to give their daughter's murderers, or those who had let their daughter and her family down, the power to take over their lives. They hugged their three young granddaughters, all beauties with grins that sparkled like Becky's once did. They dug themselves out from record high Belleville snowfalls that Becky would have loved.

In November, 2007, six months after Chief Justice Richard Ground's ruling, the Court of Appeals required nearly nine thousand dollars to guarantee the appeal on the docket for March, 2008. With no payment, the appeal stopped.

In the back of her mind, Becky's mother wondered if Bermuda and the U.K., with the case halted, had exonerated themselves from responsibility. Cindy Bennett wrote to Bermuda's new director of public prosecutions, Rory Field, recruited from Britain to replace DPP Vinette Graham-Allen, whose contract had ended.

"We formally request that you review the process of prosecution that has taken place in Bermuda relating to this case and with the aim in mind of further prosecuting those responsible for the many offenses against our daughter," Cindy wrote.

The public announcement of Field's appointment had referenced his expertise in human rights. "We ask that you make it your highest priority to consider this prosecutorial failure, "she wrote. Cindy asked the DPP to consider seriously "the facts presented by Ms. Cherie Booth, QC, in April, 2007, that 'right to life' has been ruled…to be the most 'fundamental' of human rights…."

A month later, no response.

Cindy followed up with letters to the FCO Foreign Secretary David

Miliband, three ministers of a Parliamentary committee that conducted a territorial inspection of Bermuda in March, 2008 (tasked with, among other matters, assessing human rights compliance), and to Territories Minister Meg Munn.

Miliband had launched the FCO's Human Rights report in 2007, citing the sixtieth anniversary of the Universal Declaration of Human Rights, commending the passions of activists and "brave journalists," which, he said, "I want…to be matched by the government: where people are working to achieve human rights around the world, we should be on their side."

Not until several weeks after she mailed the letters to Britain did she receive confirmation from DPP Rory Field that he would consider her request.

Then, in late July, 2008, with FCO Territories Minister Meg Munn's written response from Britain already in her hands, Cindy received Field's decision via regular mail. "I extend to you my sympathy concerning the awful crime of which your daughter was the innocent victim." He, too, was bound by law, he reminded.

Field listed only Cindy's letter, the Graham-Allen decision, and Justice Ground's ruling for his review. No mention of her request that he examine human rights, the handling of the evidence of her daughter's murder case, the basis for the charging decisions, or other documents, as she had requested.

FCO Territories Minister Munn, too, expressed her sympathy. She was speaking for Foreign Secretary David Miliband as well, Munn said, when she expressed "my deep sympathy for your loss. I share your frustration that justice has not been yet fully served, so many years after these horrifying crimes were committed against your daughter."

However, the FCO could not intervene, Munn insisted. The matter would require a change in law. "I can tell you that the Acting Governor (no name given) wrote recently to the Attorney General of Bermuda to ask if there appeared to be 'any prospect of the law being amended,' given that the Privy Council had suggested that Bermuda might look at this point of law again, and noting that the debate in England came down on the side of changing the law to allow an appeal," Munn wrote.

The answer was no. Again, no reference to human rights. "I am sorry this is not the reply you would have wished for."

"More of the same," Cindy said.

One month later, the murder of a young Bermudian man, eighteen-year-old Kellon Hill, set to leave Bermuda for college the next day, rocked the community.

Not the first to hit home. The body of a fourteen-year-old Bermudian girl, Rhianna Moore, had washed up at Blue Hole a few months before. But stress, they say, is cumulative.

Another week passed before a drive by shooting by a gunman riding pillion, likely gang related, injured a 22-year-old man. Gang shootings in 2009, two years later, killed five and wounded 17. By July, 2010, murders, robberies and sexual assaults had doubled since the same time the previous year.

"For some reason, maybe the apparent senselessness of it all, Kellon's death and the manner of his dying is about as tragic as it can get," the controversial lawyer who had helped Dame Lois Browne Evans try to save Larry Tacklyn from the gallows, Julian Hall, told the *Royal Gazette*.

Hall reminded that he had long advocated an end to capital punishment. "But I have to say that this incident has severely dented my commitment even to that cause. Maybe we need to put everything, and I mean everything, back on the table...."

A former tourism minister called for curfews, prevention of underage alcohol use. "The local and overseas drug barons are only happy to serve the demand and ruin so many lives...The violent action of some of our young people...is a result of the world they live in, in Bermuda being sadly out of control."

"We must stem this tide," Premier Dr. Ewart F. Brown told a special session of the cabinet, called because of the violence. Brown promised increased police presence, another war against drugs, and a review of laws –"If the nature of our crimes has changed then the laws will need to follow suit." He warned "those who choose gunfire to settle their disputes" to be on alert, a SWAT team was being considered.

Governor Sir Richard Gozney, photographed by the *Royal Gazette* next to Brown, said Britain offered "strong support, silent support."

Said Mundy's former attorney, Mark Pettingill, now a senator, "If Britain is going to have any say, then for God's sake have a sensible say." Pettingill reminded Bermuda already has an armed emergency response team. "If

Government House wants to stick its oar in and be sensible, they should be suggesting we have a commission or review."

A year later, four of the five accused of killing Kellon Hill walked free—again "no case to answer," released by the same judge who had freed Justis Smith after "time served" in the Dockyard stabbing. The trial of the remaining youth ended, first, in a hung jury, then a conviction for manslaughter, a reduced charge.

Two weeks later, this time under the direction of Chief Justice Richard Ground, another jury found the 33-year-old man accused of killing young Rhianna and dumping her body in the sound, stabbed eighteen times, guilty, sentencing him to life.

However, prosecutors never filed statutory rape charges or charges related to the death of Rhianna's seven-month fetus, citing Bermuda law and fetal viability issues. Bermuda's criminal code reads:

"Any person who, when a woman or girl is about to be delivered of a child, prevents the child from being born alive by any act or omission of such a nature that, if the child had been born alive and then died, he would be deemed to have unlawfully killed the child, is guilty of a felony, and is liable to imprisonment for ten years."

The lower limit of viability, according to the journal *The Developing Human: Clinically Oriented Embryology,* can be approximately five months. Sexually related charges, related to Rhianna's age, a prosecutor claimed, could have interfered with murder prosecution.

"Did no one hear anything that this family or Cherie Booth, QC, a human rights attorney, said?" Rick Meens wondered. When Meens learned of Cindy's futile communications with the DPP and FCO, he telephoned the director of public prosecutions for an appointment. After two weeks, with no meeting scheduled, he wrote to DPP Rory Field.

Becky had been under his care, Meens reminded. "As you know, she was raped, tortured sodomized and eventually stabbed more than thirty times by two men whose identity is well known and who have never been brought to justice owing to the incompetence of the entire Bermudian criminal justice process."

The DPP's response to Cindy had not been sufficient, Meens argued. "I ask that you refer to all related judicial review documents and original investigation documents and indictments that are held in Supreme Court, including *An Appeal for Accountability* submitted in 2001 by then Bermuda Amnesty International Director LeYoni Junos to both the governor and the FCO. It is by no means a mystery why the case was handled as it was."

To FCO Territories Minister Meg Munn, Meens wrote that he was "appalled that the (FCO), who have a responsibility for good governance of Bermuda, have treated Cindy and her family in such a cavalier manner." He suggested that she review what had happened "with the aim of holding those responsible—for her murder and the prejudicial handling of her case.

"Furthermore," Meens added, "I formally request a Royal Commission of Enquiry into the bungled handling of the entire Rebecca Middleton case by the Police, Attorney General, the Director of Public Prosecutions, and the Judiciary."

A short response from Munn's department, signed by Desk Officer Hugo Frost, apologizing if Meens had interpreted the territory's minister as "cavalier." However, Bermuda, he wrote, was responsible for legislating and applying Bermuda's law.

In April, 2008, Meg Munn's replacement, Territories Minister Gillian Merron responded to another letter from Meens. There was nothing more to do, she said. Then a third, from Merron's replacement.

Just like the deafening silence in 1977 when Bermudians begged its Parliament and Britain to spare the lives of Larry Tacklyn and Buck Burrows, heads were turned when it came to the Rebecca Middleton affair. Responsibility owned by no one, not by Bermuda's government, a parade of British governors, the FCO, or ultimately Great Britain.

Now even in the Twenty First Century, St. Peter's graveyard in St. George hints that not everything has changed on this island where lying in the tide is the norm—and there are serious repercussions for doing otherwise—where more than a few people still advocate amnesia regarding those violent political murders, the gory hangings, and the brutal rape, torture, and murder of that young tourist, for which no one, to this day, has been held responsible.

"Where did those Forty Thieves go?" Julian Hall asked in 2009, during the four hundredth anniversary of Bermuda's colonization. Instead, "…those nameless faces in the international business world (who could leave at any time) have become the masters," Hall told a *Mid Ocean News* reporter.

"The colonial system under which we are socially, politically and constitutionally organized," he suggested, "is designed to fail us and subordinate our best interests to those who colonize and control us…no one actually either 'runs the government' or is 'in charge'"…

Perhaps, unless something changes, Bermuda will lie like an infant in limbo, somewhere between salvation and damnation?

EPILOGUE

ON THE TENTH ANNIVERSARY of Becky's murder, July third, 2006, Matthew Taylor, chief reporter for the *Royal Gazette*, asked: "What Price Becky's Life? $2,840.63…

"While the Middleton family was enveloped in an outpouring of support from a shocked Bermudian public following the tragedy, Bermudian officialdom has piled on one insult after another, from day one.

"An inquiry launched partly to find out who was to blame for the legal fiasco failed to find who was responsible for the plea bargain at the heart of it. Meanwhile a senior Government figure publicly said Bermuda owed the Middleton family nothing.

"After years of campaigning by the family the Department of Public Prosecutions finally agreed to re-examine the case this year – only to rule out reopening it under fresh charges.

"A scholarship set up in Becky's memory at Bermuda College from funds raised by well-wishers was left unused for years until prompting from the family finally got it going again.

"This summer a tree which had become a shrine to Becky's memory was removed without warning by the Parks Department…

"And then, just a few weeks ago, the Criminal Injuries Compensation Board put a figure on Becky's life…after the family put in a claim for the maximum of $100,000 for pain and suffering. That figure? Just $2,840.63.

"After a decade of hurt all the Bermuda Government was prepared to pay for (was) the cost of Becky's ticket, the cost of flying her corpse home and sundry expenses such as the flight ticket to watch the failed trial."

BERMUDA MARKED THIRTY YEARS, December third, 2007, since the hangings of Larry Winfield Tacklyn and Erskine "Buck" Burrows and resulting riots--seven months after the collapse of the judicial review in the matter of Rebecca Middleton's murder. Bermuda's violence by now had reached a record high.

"When Hamilton burned," the *Royal Gazette* headline reminded Bermuda.

"Some say it (the rioting) was a catalyst for change, which brought the island's racial inequalities and the polarization of the white and black communities into sharp focus."

Still queasy from the executions, locals were more likely to recall the riots than they were the political murders four years before.

Had the island learned important lessons? Or did actors simply change roles?

"Bermuda has buried it," Parliamentarian Dale Butler told the *Royal Gazette*. "In other countries, five or six books would have been made and a big movie. It would be an important part of our history classes. Many young people don't even know about the riots."

DAME LOIS BROWNE EVANS suffered a stroke in June, 2007, and died, only two days before her eightieth birthday. A year later, on October thirteenth, 2008, its first Heroes Day, Bermuda honored the woman who succeeded in a shocking environment of racial and gender discrimination. This holiday replaces Bermuda's observance of the Queen's Birthday, perhaps one more step toward independence?

"I miss her quick wit and sarcasm during Cabinet or Caucus meetings," Premier Dr. Ewart F. Brown said. "I think her most important contribution was her persistence against the odds. It was contagious and led others, unseen, to join the fight for justice."

Former Premier Alex Scott told *Royal Gazette* chief reporter Matthew Taylor, "You might disagree with her, but you knew she had experienced firsthand just about every Bermudian political theme....She had become almost a mother to the country, black and white, young and old respected her ...."

Lawyer Julian Hall recalled his mentor's "sense of history and her insistence on constantly reminding us of where we come from, how we got here, and what principles we are supposed to represent. As tedious as (seemed) some of her 'walks down memory lane' ... I miss her counsel and her admonitions.... May she rest perpetually in peace."

Voters had returned Dame Lois Browne Evans to her Devonshire seat during every election until she retired in 2003, a year after she made headlines with slurs directed at colleagues, such as "black buffoon" and "Uncle Tom." Not long afterward, she took to the floor of the House of Assembly, accusing Canadian lawyers formerly in the attorney general's office of bad attitudes. "Don't bend over backwards and insist you're not a good prosecutor until you win every case--and strut about the street of Bermuda like you're the best prosecutor that ever came here," the *Royal Gazette* quoted Browne Evans.

"Leaving aside the xenophobia of the remarks," editors suggested, a number of high profile acquittals...might suggest that the current roster of prosecutors is not as experienced as some of their predecessors."

Browne could have been referring to any of the Canadian prosecutors—Brian Calhoun, Saul Froomkin, Barry Meade, Bill Pearce, or others, none of whom ever expressed surprise at words emitting from the lips of Dame Lois Browne Evans. However, no one doubted that in a shocking environment of racial and gender discrimination, Dame Lois had not only survived, but she had thrived--and helped others do the same.

LAWYER JULIAN HALL, who had given the "thumbs down" signal hours before the 1977 hangings, died in summer, 2009, at the age of 59. Thirty years after the hangings Hall told media, "I am appalled at the lack of care with which we have handled Bermuda's history...I am scared for Bermuda, that the level of ignorance is so high. Then there are those that do not want history to be discussed."

THE SHARPLES FAMILY, said the *Royal Gazette*, "declined to comment on the events and how they feel being so intimately linked to an important section of Bermuda's history."

LEYONI JUNOS' DAYS of bus driving are over. After four years, "I just threw everything to the wind. I quit the job and headed to a wonderful genealogy conference in New England." She still dislikes politics, she admits.

"But if I'm going to change anything, I'm going to have to become a part of them."

She has kept not only her own fiery spirit alive, but that of executed slave Sally Bassett, in 2005 dedicating the Sally Bassett Foundation for Independent Research and Education (SAFIRE). To raise funds for her foundation, LeYoni recently recorded an album using tracks with her late father, Leon Jones. "Just like Nat and Natalie," she said, with her usual huge grin. She'd cut her dread locks when she drove the bus, but now they framed her gentle face.

LeYoni studied overseas to learn calligraphy to transcribe the Bermuda Slave Registers, four volumes spanning 1821-1834, with an exhaustive index by slave name, profession and country of origin. As she's longed to do, she's writing books about Bermuda slavery including *150 Black Men Named Joe*, and *The Historical Mary Prince*.

For LeYoni, the natural Bermuda, the one that she remembered before seeming quests for power overtook the small island, remains her first love. In 2005, she was contracted by the Bermuda Department of Tourism to organize Bermuda's conference of the African Diaspora Heritage Trail (ADHT), an international event that ranged from museums to cuisine, ecology to music, history to architecture, and conflict resolution to community development. Chaired by actor Danny Glover, the trail is a UNESCO Slave Route Project.

However, in 2008, with public charges of cronyism circulating, LeYoni questioned some contracts by the Department of Tourism--seriously annoying Premier Dr. Ewart F. Brown, who, along with being premier and transport minister, headed tourism. She lost her job.

"The very thing that I was trying to save—my home and my right to live in my house, my mortgage—again was being taken from me."

To the shock of many, a judge ruled in May, 2009, that she'd been fired illegally, although the court exonerated the premier from responsibility.

She would stand on principle, said LeYoni. "I realized I've stood up for others, and now it's time to stand up for myself."

KIRK MUNDY, STILL lodged at Westgate, passed the GED on his second try. He was "sorry," a reporter quoted him in 2005. Without public access to information in Bermuda, few realized these were the same words Mundy used just days after Becky's murder--when he lied to police. Criminal justice rules one and two: rapists claim sex was consensual; murderers blame the other guy.

Meanwhile, Mundy looked forward to his transfer to the prison farm on Ferry Road, not far from Becky's murder. And to the day, probably not far away, when he, like Justis Smith, would walk free.

But a bit of bad luck. In summer, 2009, guards found drugs in his cell. A judge tacked another 18 months (likely translated: a year) onto his sentence.

JUSTIS SMITH, WHO RETURNED to Bermuda when Middleton judicial proceedings ended, again made headlines, photographed in May, 2008, wearing viper sunglasses like those once worn by his friend "Fly." This time the court found Justis Smith, accompanied by his long time attorney Elizabeth Christopher, guilty of possessing five foil packets of heroin, recovered from his mouth while resisting police.

A judge fined Smith one thousand dollars and released him.

"He understands that this is a serious matter," Christopher told the court. "He is tackling issues in his life and is taking steps to deal with them."

BERMUDA POLICE COMMISSIONER Colin Coxall continues to advocate for Becky, saying the case had been "shamefully abandoned" after the botched prosecutions of Kirk Mundy and Justis Smith.

In late 2009, Coxall expressed public concern over the news that a new "cold case" team in Bermuda announced it would not review the Middleton case. Coxall said he believed police would be happy to do it, "but I think the people in authority might be trying to hide that case. I feel the people in Bermuda were trying to sweep that case under the carpet. They should not be doing that." A year later, when Bermuda's attorney general watched crime accelerate and prosecutions deteriorate, agreeing that double jeopardy needed to be changed, Coxall suggested Bermuda should "just get on with" reviewing Becky's case. To do otherwise was inexplicable and unacceptable.

Coxall cited a similar case in Britain, the murder of a young mother of two, Vikki Thompson, in 1995. While she was walking her dog, an attacker hit her on the head with a rock, dragged her across a field and dumped her near a railway line, then attacked her again. Mark Weston, a local gardener and maintenance man, twenty at the time, was charged with murder but acquitted the following year.

In August 2005, the tenth anniversary of Vikki Thompson's death, her mother, Margaret Simpson, issued a fresh appeal for information, saying that she would never rest until her daughter's killer was caught. "It's never too late," she said.

That family was given hope a year and a half later when Thames Valley Police sent items from the Thompson murder scene for analysis in the light of advances in technology.

Coxall, who served as Deputy Chief Constable of Thames Valley Police, said the startling parallels between the Vikki Thompson and Rebecca Middleton cases demonstrate why detectives should never stop reviewing the Middleton files regardless of the issue of double jeopardy.

Meanwhile, when Coxall moved back to his London home in 1997, he landed on his feet. Exactly a year later, on July ninth, 1998, with Bermuda's drug businesses back in full swing, the U.S. bestowed the Drug Enforcement Administration's top award to Coxall.

Invited to the American Embassy in London's Grosvenor Square, he was commended by both the Washington DEA chief and the New Jersey office, which had supplied officers for *Operation Cleansweep*. U.S. officials reminded that the second phase of the assault on drug dealers--chemical analysis to pinpoint the signature and origin of drugs brought to Bermuda, along with freezing the drug barons' assets—had not happened owing to Coxall's forced resignation. Also departing with Coxall were international contracts to provide first rate forensic services to Bermuda. The government cancelled all of them.

The *Royal Gazette* reported not long afterward, "Coxall's advice is eagerly being sought in the troubled border areas of the Middle East and in areas of South America hardest hit by the powerful drug cartels." In July, 2005, just three weeks before London terrorist bombings, now a strategic security adviser, Colin Coxall testified on terrorism in Washington D.C. before a U.S. Congressional Committee on security. Some of those U.S. legislators he addressed thought Coxall's assignment in Bermuda would have been like a day at the beach. Coxall assured it wasn't.

With his wife, Shirley, well known for her dedication to Bermuda's community programs during their two years in Bermuda, the Coxalls travel internationally, relieved to return to their London home, where they have no need for armed guards.

CAYMAN NET NEWS reported in April, 2006, "On his arrival in the Cayman Islands, the new judge of the Court of Appeal, Hon. Justice Elliott D. Mottley, QC, received a warm welcome from the Cayman Bar...."

A Bermuda attorney privately commented, "Yes, and one of his most notorious 'challenging and interesting experiences' was as the attorney general of Bermuda, directly responsible for the prosecution fiasco in the Rebecca Middleton case—both points the Cayman Net News nicely overlooked."

The former Bermuda attorney general did not respond to several requests by this author to comment on Rebecca's case.

JUSTICE VINCENT MEERABUX died in London, England, in 2003. Reportedly Meerabux never got over the criticism of the Privy Council.

FORMER SCC MARSHAL, Bermuda Bar president, and Mundy attorney Richard Hector, during a 2005 meeting with Rick Meens and the author, predicted that Becky's murder case would neither return to court, nor would injustices be corrected. He died in 2006, before Cherie Booth, QC, appeared in Bermuda's Supreme Court for Becky.

RUMORS CIRCULATED in 2006 alleging offers to buy out Director of Public Prosecutions Vinette Graham-Allen's contract before its end and bid her goodbye. Unlike others, Graham-Allen didn't budge. She left the island late in 2007, her contract complete.

SMITH PROSECUTOR BILL PEARCE and his wife, Julie, returned to Victoria, B.C. Pearce retired from his private practice. Pearce said recently that it took several years for them to recover from the trauma of the experience in Bermuda with the Rebecca Middleton case.

Pearce's colleague, Sandra Bacchus, practices law in Toronto.

SENIOR PROSECUTOR BRIAN CALHOUN left the attorney general's chambers in 2000, remaining in Bermuda private practice. To date, he has suffered no more heart attacks.

WITH BERMUDA'S CRIME on the rise and several failed prosecutions, the island's first Director of Public Prosecutions Khamisi Tokunbo, former Kirk Mundy prosecutor, did not receive a second contract as DPP. He challenged the decision, but lost.

Tokunbo later became a magistrate judge, in whose court Kirk Mundy attorney Charles Richardson appeared in 2010 to answer charges of cannabis possession. Tokunbo gave Richardson, who pleaded guilty, saying the drug belonged to a houseguest, a "three-year conditional discharge." Richardson later appeared in court where his sentence was changed to a fine. Richardson reportedly requested the change, saying the conditions of the discharge had prevented him from traveling to the UK.

TOKUNBO'S REPLACEMENT, Acting Director of Public Prosecutions Kulandra Ratneser, arrived in Bermuda just in time to rule that an investigation of public housing funds deals that included Dr. Brown, among others, activities were "unethical," but "not illegal." Ratneser cited Bermuda's out of date public finance laws in his decision.

GOVERNOR THOROLD MASEFIELD returned to the United Kingdom. His successor, Sir John Vereker, refused requests to meet with Dave Middleton or Rick Meens.

While at Government House doing installation work recently, Rick Meens called Governor Sir Richard Gozney aside and introduced himself. Gozney told Meens he remembered Becky's case. The matter was in Bermuda's hands, Gozney told Meens.

FORMER DEPUTY GOVERNOR Tim Gurney, who allegedly lost, then failed to respond to LeYoni Junos' *Appeal for Accountability*, left Bermuda to reside in one-half of a transport container in his new assignment--Afghanistan.

BERMUDA POLICE CONSTABLE Stephen Symons, one of the first police officers to the scene of Becky's murder, was among four people, three of them officers who died, washed away on the Causeway in 2003, during Hurricane Fabian. Bermuda government turned away a British ship laden with supplies for isolated residents battered by the Category Four storm. Bermuda did, however, welcome supplies from Caribbean neighbors to the south.

UNKNOWN TO MOST TRAVELERS to Bermuda, the taxi controversy continues to trouble the island. Shortly before Jasmine and Becky's trip to Bermuda, the government ruled that taxi drivers no longer would be required to have radios in their cars. Drivers complained that radios were too expensive; they'd been "stretched to their limits."

One cabbie allegedly refused to pick up a rain-soaked passenger because he was wet, the *Bermuda Sun* observed. Drivers "actually blamed St. George for being too boring to work in at night." In 2002 many New Year's Eve revelers found themselves stranded because taxi drivers reminded they, too, were on holiday.

By 2005, government tabled a bill requiring GPS dispatching after a long fight by taxi drivers. More than one hundred and fifty taxi drivers still hadn't complied six months after the deadline, and one told the daily newspaper he'd go to jail before he would do so. Many simply refused to turn on their systems. Three years later, Parliament imposed a $1400 fine for each offense and brought in five limousines. Two of the three taxi companies halted GPS use, drivers ignoring unenforced laws. Bermuda's fishhook-like shape sent drivers miles out of their way, some complained. Lack of compliance continues.

POLICE COMMISSIONER JONATHAN Smith left his post in 2005, amid complaints of escalating crime. Smith, who had gained significant experience under the leadership of former Commissioner Colin Coxall, had developed a detailed policing strategy during his leadership, between 2001-05, which he reviewed during a 2004 meeting with the author and Rick Meens. Also, he reported a successful external inspection of the Police by the UK in 2003.

"One key recommendation of the Serious Crime Commission was that there needed to be more involvement in the investigation of serious crime at the senior level," Smith said recently. "Thus, I created and chaired the very first Serious Crime Group in the BPS. We met twice a month and reviewed ALL major investigations so as to ensure that forensic evidence was exploited, barriers reduced between investigators and the DPP or witnesses and so that I could also tap into my key contacts in the FBI and UK policing services."

Smith said recently. ...I took this role extremely seriously (as a former investigator) and by chairing this Serious Crime Group was directly responsible for bringing experts in from the USA and UK to assist with murder investigations and ensuring that a baby death case was reopened and investigated which resulted in a case before the Courts.

Smith's replacement, Commissioner George Jackson, fared even less well, with gang wars, drugs, road deaths, and assaults increasing. Police Commissioner George DeSilva, who took over for Jackson, termed gang warfare and gunfire "viral" at time of publication of this book.

"THE BUCK STOPS with me," said the governor, who suggested that Bermuda's Parliament should have more responsibility for policing, despite his own mandate. Meanwhile, a *Mid Ocean News* writer suggested the situation between Bermuda and Britain was "becoming a game of political hot potato."

PREMIER DR. EWART F. BROWN danced on Court Street in late 2006 when he led the PLP to its third victory. His predecessor, Alex Scott, assured that a plan to feature Court Street as a tourist cultural center wouldn't be halted by the April, 2006, late night gunshot wounding of three people at the Swinging Doors nightclub. That summer, during a four-month period five people had been shot on the island that is supposed to be gun-free. By 2010, gang warfare was in full swing, making international headlines.

"BLACKS MAY HAVE TO get back to the streets, boycott businesses, and make some noise...(It is) "the white man's burden," U.S. activist, Duke University sociology professor Eduardo Bonilla-Silva told a Bermuda Race Relations Initiative (BRRI) in summer, 2008.

Several thousand people did just that. Police, who are not permitted to march on government, joined a protest over pay, some wearing their uniforms, bringing Hamilton to a standstill.

Premier Dr. Ewart F. Brown, who did not appear until the protest was nearly over, said he had not been afraid to meet dissenters, reminding, "I grew up in a protest era, I grew up marching."

BRITAIN'S 2007 ANNOUNCEMENT of renewed interest in its territories left some in Bermuda concerned. "A vehicle for attacking international business rivals or a timely review of its responsibilities?" the *Royal Gazette* asked. Edward Leigh, chairman of the Committee of Public Accounts, a few months before the announcement that the FCO would be reviewing Bermuda, had questioned why Britain was subsiding Bermuda, describing the island as a "fabulously rich place...the highest in the world at $76,000 per head." Some at the FCO, he charged, were "asleep at the wheel," failing to "manage the risks arising from the U.K.'s liability for the fourteen Overseas Territories choosing to remain under British sovereignty."

With the exception of Gibraltar, there had been no territories reports for more than a decade. In 1999, the U.K. government published a White Paper setting out a "new partnership" between Britain and its overseas territories. Britain agreed it would willingly grant independence (Bermuda was the only territory to make its interest known), defend territories' interests...assure "the greatest possible autonomy" and financial help..."in return, expecting the highest standards of probity, law and order, good government and observance of Britain's international commitments."

In March, 2008, the Foreign Affairs Committee (FAC) split its members to visit four of its fourteen territories. Territories Minister Meg Munn joined Foreign Affairs MPs Andrew MacKinlay, John Horam and Malcolm Moss, tasked with examining standards of governance, the role of governors, transparency, financial regulation, treaties and constitutions, and human rights.

Citing Bermuda's lack of transparency, irregularities in financial management, and fears of ramifications for speaking up, the FAC report to the FCO made it clear that Bermuda wasn't alone in contributing to Britain's headaches:In the Turks and Caicos Island (TCI), the committee found allegations of corruption, "damaging TCI's reputation...tourism...(and) also a great risk they will damage the U.K.'s own reputation for promoting good governance." Finally, in 2009, Britain rescinded TCI's constitution and dissolved TCI's government, a move Bermuda Premier Dr. Ewart F. Brown, with close ties to the former TCI premier, termed "heavy handed."

In Anguilla, the FCO was dealing with charges that ministers accepted bribes. In the Falkland Islands, the matter of Argentine restriction of air space. Resignation of six of seven Ascension Island councilors, Spain's refusal to recognize Gibraltar's territorial waters, an illness outbreak on Tristan da Cunha, a successful legal challenge by refugees of The Chagos—and the question of whether the U.S. was routing detainees through U.K. airspace—which ultimately turned out to be true.

In Bermuda, it appeared that the FCO came and went, without much impact.

RUMORS THAT INDEPENDENCE was imminent circulated in 2009, despite polls suggesting the majority in Bermuda preferred to remain a territory. The PLP argued that its election gave it a popular mandate to take the island to independence when it judged the time to be right, and no referendum would be necessary.

Territories Minister Meg Munn said in 2008 that it would not stand in Bermuda's way of independence, but Britain must be assured that it is a "clear and constitutionally expressed wish" of Bermudians before the matter goes to Parliament for approval. Such a move would not be appropriate now, given a lack of voter mandate to the PLP, she suggested.

However, controversies seemingly killed such a plan, if there had been one. While black Bermudians seemed to unite under the PLP banner, they didn't seem to share the party's quest for independence. Perhaps because of so many controversies?

Brown's government in 2007 had already held the auditor general in jail overnight when documents alleging Cabinet-level corruption leaked into the media. Premier Dr. Ewart F. Brown threatened to suspend relations with the UK, and Scotland Yard leaped into a probe into the leak. A potential constitutional crisis appeared to be averted, for the moment, when the premier backed down.

Subsequently Brown, who led the way for government-owned media, announced that he would discontinue the government's relationship with the *Royal Gazette* and *Mid Ocean News*. A few weeks later, postal delivery personnel filled Bermuda mailboxes with newly-printed cards announcing "out with the old, in with the new...Get government news when you want it...Embrace new media...be the first to know what's going on," the card read- -*You Tube, Facebook,* and the government-owned and controlled television station. If one wanted to "befriend Government officials—even the premier," the card suggested, *Facebook* was the place to go.

THE *MID OCEAN NEWS* folded in 2009. "One down, one to go," the media attributed to Premier Dr. Ewart F. Brown.

BERMUDA GREETED THE U.S. ELECTION of its first black president in 2008 with approval. However, Obama's pledge to deal with U.S. laws that allowed overseas tax havens concerned some in government and off-shore business. Soon, a new Bermuda office appeared in Washington, D.C. Then, meetings with U.S. Congressional finance and tax law committees, all intended to "educate" the Obama Administration regarding the benefits of off-shore competition.

Then, not long after those 2009 meetings with U.S. officials about tax-haven issues, a blooper that would incite international anger.

FOUR FORMER GUANTANAMO detainees arrived in Bermuda by private jet, in the dark of night, escorted by U.S. officials. Neither the governor nor the FCO had been warned in advance—a deal by Premier Dr. Ewart F. Brown with the U.S. State Department. Britain, responsible for the foreign affairs of its territories, appeared to raise more than just an eyebrow when the controversial resettlement hit international news.

The agreement to give haven to four Chinese Muslims, known as Uyghurs, became an acute embarrassment for the British government, with angry telephone exchanges reported between the U.K. and Bermuda's premier, with Brown summoned to Government House.

"The proper authority here is the British government and the U.S. should have consulted with the Foreign and Commonwealth Office before they did anything of this kind," Mike Gapes, the chairman of the foreign affairs committee, told BBC Radio 4's *The World at One*. "I wonder what promises have been given to the Bermudians, potentially about going a bit soft on the tax haven status or something else as a quid pro quo."

The Chinese government demanded the men, who had been cleared of terrorism allegations, be returned to China. The U.S. termed the four "moderately dangerous."

Privately, FCO representative Hugo Frost wrote: "The Governor's Office continues to keep us well informed about the level of public concern raised by the Government of Bermuda's decision to accept the transfer to Bermuda of the four former detainees from Guantanamo Bay.

"As you know, the Government's actions were contrary to the Bermuda Constitution, which reserves to the Governor special responsibility with respect to internal security and external affairs. In addition, by not informing the Governor, the Government did not act in accordance with the spirit of the General Entrustment which delegated, subject to certain conditions, the authority to negotiate and conclude agreements in certain specific areas.

"The UK Government has announced a review of the operation of the General Entrustment; this is a significant step, but a necessary consequence of the Government of Bermuda's action," Frost wrote.

Britain's shadow foreign secretary William Hague demanded an explanation from Foreign Secretary David Miliband, saying the British government appeared to have "lost grip of running the country...It is astonishing that an agreement of such significance between the U.S. and Bermuda...could have taken place without a ripple reaching Whitehall.... The UK is responsible for Bermuda's external relations, defense, and security, and for appointing its governor. Yet the FCO appears to have had no idea that these discussions were taking place."

Again, the premier explained that he had to mislead--this time both the UK Government and Bermudian voters. Brown expressed surprise at "the (public's) reaction" to the Guantanamo four.

Britain's Foreign Secretary David Miliband made a formal complaint to U.S. Secretary of State Hillary Clinton, reminding that Brown was not prime minister, a job that didn't exist on a territory—he was premier, and he had acted out of line.

Clinton, who vacationed in Bermuda with her husband two months later, sent Brown a letter of appreciation. A hurricane threat cut their visit short.

TO ABOUT A THOUSAND PROTESTORS gathered outside Sessions House in 2009, demanding his resignation, Premier Dr. Ewart F. Brown told demonstrators that he had grown up in days of protest and had seen many that were "longer and louder" than this one, which he and his colleagues blamed on racism--whites who were dissatisfied by their perceived lack of privilege.

A few days later Brown survived a UBP-led no confidence vote, with the full support of his PLP counterparts.

Meanwhile, a few suggested, the incident might have been intended to annoy those colonial masters, making a potential Parliamentary vote for independence, instead of Bermudian voter referendum, which was likely to fail, quite palatable.

However, by 2010, when he realized Bermuda likely wouldn't be leaving its place beneath Britain's wing in the near future, he reminded a group of young students that youth of his generation had stood up for autonomy, and he was surprised they seemed not to do the same. But most Bermudians seemed to be expressing their satisfaction, seemingly lying quietly in the tide, while crime and financial questions swirled. Brown resigned in October, 2010.

WHILE BRITAIN WAS RECEIVING Cindy Bennett's letters asking for help in achieving justice in her daughter's murder, the leaders of Bermuda's Voters Rights Association (VRA) called for England to confirm that the UN Covenant on Civil and Political Rights applies to Bermuda.

Bermudians Geoffrey Parker Sr. and Stuart Hayward joined more than a few who perceived Premier Dr. Ewart F. Brown's raised left fist, snapped by a *Royal Gazette* photographer during a 2006 PLP election rally, as the 1960s black power salute.

The VRA complained about national, "racial or religious hatred that constitutes incitement to discrimination, hostility or violence."

MARSHA JONES, MOTHER of murdered Shaundae Jones, led a "Stop the Violence March" through Hamilton in November, 2007. Police had called in Scotland Yard to find out who leaked a dossier detailing a police investigation involving the premier and others, but didn't do so for murder cases, she charged. "Who released the murderers? Who killed our children?"

Jones' friend Shirley Raines, a mother of two who helped organize the walk, told reporters, "As a human being, it really touched me that all these murders are going on. That could be anyone's child…the family lives on with the sorrow and all this hurt in their hearts."

Even when tourists have been involved, police refuse to identify the location of assaults, drink spiking, or robberies. A spokesman for the Women's Resource Center said the organization wouldn't encourage Bermuda's night clubs supply drink testers to spot Rohypnol or other drugs.

People in Bermuda didn't want to use them, or, she reasoned, the testers might give an "inappropriate sense of safety."

THE BODY OF FRENCHMAN Mehdi Yahi, who disappeared in spring, 2009, has never been found. An avid Heather Nova fan, Yahi travelled to

Bermuda to see the Bermudian born singer perform at the Southampton Princess, placing flowers on stage during her performance. He was escorted away, never seen again. Some of his belongings were found stacked neatly on a south shore beach.

A search of the shoreline turned up nothing.

The body of an Englishman, who disappeared a year later, washed up on shore.

Police could explain neither death.

AFTER THE KELLON HILL case collapse, former Attorney General Philip Perinchief publicly called for Bermuda to change the appeals code law.

In a 2007 caucus, not open to the public, Attorney General Kim Wilson had opposed the change. Ministers were split and the measure defeated.

Perinchief continued vociferously maintaining that one person alone never should have the right to decide whether a murder will be prosecuted.

In 2010, the PLP relented, but Wilson said that unlike the law in Britain, any change in law would not be retroactive, citing a section in Bermuda's constitution that she said prevented making the law retroactive.

Perinchief, however, argued that Wilson had misinterpreted the law. "Double jeopardy has nothing to do with this section, and neither does retroactivity."

Instead, Perinchief, among many black Bermudians who were appalled by fact that no one faced a jury in Becky's murder, explained to the *Royal Gazette* his own view of government's unwillingness to make the law retroactive: "Quite frankly, I think they are making it up only to buttress an untenable political position. They don't want to be seen to be pandering to a lot of the white people who are pressing to have the Rebecca Middleton case reopened. It's as simple as that. It's a political thing rather than ...constitutional. They really have to fess up and come forward and say so," reporter Tim Smith quoted the former attorney general. "Justice does not go from this day forward...Justice is for all time."

IN FEBRUARY, 2006, BERMUDIANS Walter and Mary Middleton Cook donated a plot of their own land in Becky's memory. The half-acre garden lies in picturesque Paget on the historic Railway Trail and bears her name: *The Rebecca Middleton Nature Reserve.*

Children from Bermuda's schools tend to the land which is held by the Bermuda Trust, a foundation dedicated to the preservation of Bermuda. Mrs. Cook, no relation to Becky, told children during the reserve's dedication how on a trip to Barbados, she very nearly fell victim to violence.

"Words are inadequate at such a time as one can only imagine the depth of your sorrow," she wrote to Dave Middleton. "When Rebecca was murdered, I remembered that when I was a young girl (with the same last name, Middleton) on a trip to Barbados I went for a ride with a man I had only just met, and it is only by God's mercy that I was not raped or worse. The young have a feeling that they are invincible, no matter what their parents have taught them to the contrary."

Said Mary Middleton Cook, "in two hundred years and more, when children ask who Becky was, she and her story will not be forgotten."

THE BERMUDA NATIONAL GALLERY in 2008 displayed Bermudian John Gardner's abstract, *The Rape and Murder of Rebecca Middleton*. Gardner, an architect and artist resident in Bermuda, and father of two teenage daughters, found himself profoundly haunted by the tragedy.

"After many years of sketching I have finally found a painting style and format, a ten-foot high watercolor, to express my profound sadness, respect and feelings," Gardner said. The gallery held a forum on the twelfth anniversary of Becky's death, *Art as an Agent of Change*.

BETH HOLLOWAY, MOTHER of Natalee Holloway who disappeared in May, 2005, during a school trip to Aruba, visited Bermuda in 2009, during the local Physical Abuse Centre's thirtieth anniversary commemoration. Holloway made no public mention of the murder of Rebecca Middleton. A spokesman declined to say whether Holloway had been made aware of Becky's case.

While the man who allegedly last saw Natalee languished in a prison in Peru, charged with murdering a young woman there, and with the U.S. FBI continuing its investigation into Natalee's disappearance, charging Van der Sloot with extortion, Canada remained with Bermuda and Britain in their continued silence about the murder of Rebecca Middleton.

BERMUDA'S THREE DECADES OF independence threats and the diplomatic row over the Uyghurs, on the surface, seemed to be forgotten matters in late November, 2009, when Queen Elizabeth II, accompanied by her husband, Prince Philip and Foreign Secretary David Miliband, landed in Bermuda to observe Bermuda's four hundredth anniversary of colonization.

Premier Dr. Ewart F. Brown presents wood carvings of Bermuda's Gombey dancers to Queen Elizabeth II during her 2009 visit to commemorate the island's 400th anniversary of colonization.
Photo Courtesy of the Royal Gazette

TWO MONTHS AFTER BECKY'S death, her family set up a trust fund at the four Belleville high schools for students with the qualities of "compassion, a cheerful zest for life, and a genuine concern for others--the characteristics that Becky exemplified." Belleville's high schools have distributed scholarships in Becky's name each year since 1997.

Cindy Bennett traveled to Bermuda in 1997 to present the first Bermuda College scholarship. However, to the family's shock in 2005, they learned that the college failed to award scholarships for three years, from 2002 to 2004. Queried by Becky's parents and Dr. Ian Campbell, Bermuda College officials, holding nearly forty thousand dollars, said the program in which Becky's scholarship fell had ended.

It took the school three years to correct the problem.

MATTHEW AND LEANNA MIDDLETON welcomed Emma Margaret Rebecca Middleton in September, 2002. Emma's sister, Mary Cynthia, was born in 2004. Mark and Patti Middleton welcomed Samantha Jane early in 2005.

JASMINE MEENS, now married to Todd and mother of two little boys and a baby girl, Abagail Rebecca, still grieves for her murdered friend. Jasmine remembered their laughter and the beauty of Bermuda, along with their happy moments in Belleville. Becky is still her best friend, Jasmine says.

BECKY? Her family and friends say she's never far away in the hearts of those who love her—especially when they look for the moon.

ADDENDUM

SIX WEEKS AFTER BERMUDA'S VISIT BY QUEEN ELIZABETH II, on January 6, 2010, when Bermuda and the United Kingdom seemingly believed that the Rebecca Middleton matter had come to its end, Rick Meens made application to the European Court of Human Rights, asking the court to uphold the accountability of the United Kingdom to assure good governance of its territory, Bermuda.

"We hold that the matter of Britain's responsibilities for its territories should be examined by the court," Meens wrote.

Meens also asked the court to uphold that:

--Becky and her family, as well as Meens, as "loco parentis," have been victims of "multiple violations of the rights and guarantees set out in the Convention... both during her murder and afterward in the judicial management..."

--Article 2: (right to life) has been violated as a result of Rebecca's murder and failure to conduct an effective investigation: "Although Bermuda recently announced a policy of reviewing open murders, two Commissioners of Police have pointedly noted that evidence in the murder of Rebecca Middleton will not be reinvestigated using current technique, expected of modern jurisdictions."

--Article 3: prohibiting torture, ignored by prosecutors, was violated: "No one ever has been asked to answer for the horrific suffering of this child and her family."

--Article 5: no one has been held responsible for her kidnapping.

--Article 13: (right to an effective remedy): acts of rape, sodomy, kidnapping and torture—against international law, and of lesser penalty than murder (making it possible to charge despite the murder case failures), none ever charged.

--Article 13: (right to an effective remedy). Bermuda, with silence from the United Kingdom, has refused to address the "repugnant" appeals law upon which courts have depended for their explanation of failures to charge in Rebecca's murder, a law that makes one person able to decide a murder case and against the general principle of law recognized by civilized nations.*

--Article 14: (prohibition of discrimination): Both Bermuda and the United Kingdom have denied my requests for a full judicial enquiry, presided over by a United Kingdom High Court judge, with appropriate advisors to examine the entire management of the Rebecca Middleton murder, subsequent failed investigation, and the botched judicial handling of the prosecution and trials, specifically to investigate alleged racist/sexist statements said to have been made in reference to the handling of Rebecca Middleton's murder.

--Article 41: (just satisfaction). The case should be reviewed, with fresh forensic examination. Moreover, the costs of these proceedings should not be the responsibility of the family, rather, "the court should order reimbursement of costs and expenses to the applicant's legal representatives" in all matters relevant to Rebecca Middleton's murder.

On February first, 2010, Rick Meens received the ECHR's acknowledgement that it would consider his application.

A sign in Meens' office quotes American author and lecturer, Marilyn Vos Savant:

"Being defeated is often a temporary condition. Giving up is what makes it permanent."

The ECHR has been notified that Bermuda has changed this law, but has refused, unlike Britain, to consider retroactivity; thus, government's refusal to address Becky's and other mismanaged cases remains in place.

APPENDIX A

The following individuals have provided interviews, documents and/or inquiry testimony:

Police

    Colin Coxall, Bermuda police commissioner when Becky was murdered

    Lionel Grundy, London Foreign and Commonwealth Office (FCO) officer

    Jonathan Smith, director of training and later Bermuda police commissioner

    Kevin Leask, Bermuda government analyst

    Howard Cutts, Scenes of Crime lead inspector

    Sergeant Terry Maxwell, assistant to Bill Pearce

    Carlton "Socky" Adams, investigator, assistant commissioner

    Harold Moniz, assistant commissioner Vic Richmond, detective superintendent, lead investigator of the Rebecca Middleton murder

    Inspectors Cal Smith, Christopher Graham Ward, Maurice Pett, Stuart Crockwell, Norrell Hull, Peter Clarke, Eustace (Lee Gay) Farley

    Police Constables Stephen Symons and Frank Vasquez

    Police photographer Rodney Trott

Attorney General's Office

Attorney General Dame Lois Browne Evans

Attorney General Elliott Mottley, QC,

Crown Counsel, Director of Public Prosecutions Khamisi Tokunbo

Senior Crown Counsel Brian Calhoun

Solicitor General Bill Pierce, chief prosecutor, Justis Smith trial

Attorney General Larry Mussendon

Director of Public Prosecutions Vinette Graham-Allen

Director of Public Prosecutions Rory Field

Crown Counsel Sandra Bacchus

Attorney General Philip Perinchief

Pathologists

Dr. Michael Baden, former chief medical examiner of New York City and presently chief forensic pathologist for the New York State Police

Dr. Henry Lee, chief emeritus of the Connecticut State Police, founder and professor of the forensic science program at the University of New Haven

Drs. James Johnston and Keith Cunningham, King Edward VII Memorial Hospital of Bermuda

Dr. Valerie Rao, Miami-Dade forensic pathologist

Dr. Henry Pearse, Bermuda police/prisons physician

Defense Attorneys

Richard Hector, QC, attorney for Mundy, head of Bermuda Bar Association; Serious Crimes Commission marshal

Mark Pettingill, attorney for Mundy

Saul Froomkin, QC, attorney for Mundy, former Bermuda attorney general, former honorary Canadian consul John Perry, QC, attorney for Justis Smith

Elizabeth Christopher, attorney for Justis Smith

Charles Richardson, attorney for Kirk Mundy

Serious Crimes Commission

Richard Hector, marshal

Colin Coxall, former police commissioner

Elliott Mottley, former attorney general

Bill Pearce, former solicitor general, lead prosecutor, Justis Smith

Khamisi Tokunbo, Kirk Mundy prosecutor; DPP Saul Froomkin, former attorney general and honorary Canadian consulate, Mundy lawyer

Mark Pettingill, Mundy defense attorney

Stanley Moore, SCC chairman

Don Dovaston and Shirley Simmons, SCC commissioners

Dennis Bean, local citizen

LeYoni Junos, Bermuda activist and former director of Amnesty International

Dame Lois Browne Evans, Attorney General

Judicial Review

Supreme Court Chief Justice Richard Ground

Cherie Booth, QC, Middleton family representative

John Riihiluoma and Kelvin Hastings-Smith, Appleby Global

James Guthrie, QC, attorney for DPP Vinette Graham-Allen and Government of Bermuda

Affidavits: Dave Middleton, Cherie Booth, QC, Former Bermuda Police Commissioner Colin Coxall, Dr. Carol Shuman (including LeYoni Junos and Women's Resource Center Director Penny Dill) and Appleby Global, James Guthrie, QC, Charles Richardson—judicial review of the Rebecca Middleton murder

Foreign and Commonweath Officials

Acting Governor Ian Kinnear, following murder of Richard Sharples (1973)

FCO officials (1973) in response to murder, Governor Richard Sharples

FCO Territories Minister Meg Munn (2008), letters to Rebecca's mother, Cindy Bennett

Hugo Frost, FCO officer (personal communications, 2004-2009).

FCO Territories Minister Gillian Merron, letter to Rick Meens, 2009.

Foreign Secretary David Miliband, UN report on human rights, 2007.

Foreign Affairs MPs Andrew MacKinlay, John Horam and Malcolm Moss, tasked with examining standards of governance, the role of governors, transparency, financial regulation, treaties, constitutions, and human rights, territories review, 2008.

A.M. (Tony) Bates, Overseas Territories Directorate, Caribbean and Bermuda Section, 2009 response to Rick Meens.

Judicial Decisions

Supreme Court of Bermuda--Queen vs. Kirk Mundy (1996); Queen vs. Justis Smith (1998).

Appeals Court: Judgments, Kirk Mundy (1997); Justis Smith (1999).

United Kingdom's Privy Council: Kirk Mundy (1998); Justis Smith (2000).

Director of Public Prosecutions Vinette Graham-Allen case review (2006).

Chief Justice Bermuda Supreme Court Richard Ground judicial review (2007).

Human Rights Claims

Appeal for Accountability, to Governor, Bermuda, Foreign and Commonwealth Office, 2001, LeYoni Junos.

Application, European Court of Human Rights, Frederick P. (Rick) Meens, 2010.

APPENDIX B

Timelines

The Political Murders

1959	"Tempest in a Teapot." Bermuda's theater boycott results in desegregation of island's six cinemas.
1963	The Progressive Labor Party (PLP) forms in response to decades of island control by "Front Street" merchants and other wealthy white businessmen, sometimes called "The Forty Thieves."
1964	House independents establish the United Bermuda Party (UBP) in response to the PLP, gaining an automatic House majority.
1965	Bermuda Electric and Light Company (BELCO) workers strike leads to violence, with hundreds jailed. The *New York Times* comments: "Beneath the surface of Bermuda's wave of labor disputes, racial currents are sweeping the oldest British Crown Colony from Victorian serenity toward the anxieties of the present."

1968	April rioting leaves Hamilton skies "blood red" from flames, and the Bermuda Regiment joins local and British police to quell violence. The governor imposes a curfew and "state of emergency." The first election under Bermuda's new Constitution postponed two months. A riot commission makes recommendations to prevent future unrest
1969	John Hilton (Dionne) Basset forms the Black Beret Cadre (BBC), adopting as the group's motto, "Peace if possible, compromise never, freedom by any means necessary," citing Cuba as a role model for revolutionary action.
1970	April again brings riots and flames. The PLP boycotts the visit of Charles, Prince of Wales, who calls upon the island to solve its problems.
1972	Police Commissioner George Duckett lured outside to change a light bulb, shot to death.
1973	Governor Richard Sharples, ADC Hugh Sayers, and governor's dog Horsa shot to death.
1973	Shopkeepers Mark Doe and Victor Rego bound and shot to death.
1976	Ernest (Buck) Burrows and Larry Tacklyn convicted of murders.
1977	Burrows and Tacklyn hang, setting off island-wide riots and a fire at the majestic Southampton Princess, killing two tourists and a hotel employee.

The Murder of Rebecca Middleton

June 20, 1996	Rebecca Middleton and Jasmine Meens arrive in Bermuda.
June 24, 1996	Russell McCann and Ben Turtle in Bermuda with Jonathan Cassidy.
June 27, 1996	Becky celebrates her seventeenth birthday in Bermuda.
July 3, 1996	Becky is murdered.
July 3, 1996	Jasmine Meens tells police two men took off with Becky; Dean Lottimore, who drove Jasmine home safely, denies he knows the identity of the men who took Becky.
July 6, 1996	Becky's parents, Dave and Cindy Middleton, returning to Canada with Becky's body, meet Senior Crown Counsel Brian Calhoun in the Bermuda airport, who assures them Becky's murderers will be found and prosecuted.
July 9, 1996	Dean Lottimore identifies Kirk Mundy, Justis Smith as men who left with Becky. Sean Smith and Tajmal Webb identify Mundy and Smith as having passed their broken down car moments after the time Becky disappeared.
July 10, 1996	Kirk Mundy and Justis Smith arrested.

July 12, 1996	Fatal charging decisions during AG/police meeting.
July 13, 1996	Justis Smith formally charged with premeditated murder, Kirk Mundy as "accomplice."
October 16, 1996	Kirk Mundy pleads guilty, accomplice after the fact to murder.
October 18, 1996	RCMP confirms in writing that DNA identifies Mundy, not Smith.
October 21, 1996	17-year-old Smith indicted, premeditated murder.
March, 1997	Coxall and Mottley: first of three meetings to deal with case's failures.
July 7, 1997	Police Commissioner Colin Coxall's drug bust leads to Coxall's firing.
January 9, 1998	Indictment and committal for murder: Kirk Mundy and Justis Smith.
February 6, 1998	Dismissal of application to dismiss murder charge by Kirk Mundy.
March 16, 1998	Court of Appeal rules in favor of Mundy, dismisses murder charge.
July 6, 1998	Privy Council dismisses Crown's request to appeal Mundy ruling.
November 23, 1998	Justis Smith murder trial begins.

December 15, 1998	Meerabux ruling.
Spring, 1999	Justice Richard Ground rules new trial for Smith, Appeals Court agrees.
February, 2000	Privy Council finds judge's decision to halt the Smith case "astonishing" but cites double jeopardy.
May, 2000	Success of tourist boycott distresses Bermuda, inquiry ordered.
August 7-31, 2000	Serious Crimes Commission (SCC).
Summer, 2001	LeYoni Junos gathers petition for independent inquiry. Three thousand sign.
September, 2001	Deputy Governor meets with LeYoni Junos regarding her *Appeal for Accountability*. Junos hears nothing more from officials.
February, 2002	Smith stabs again.
March, 2003	Smith found guilty in Dockyard violence, sentenced to "time served."
August, 2003	Crown appeals "manifestly inadequate" sentence. Smith gets 18 months, and with time in remand, serves only two more weeks.
March, 2004	Director of Public Prosecutions Vinette Graham-Allen agrees to review the handling of Becky's murder.
January 31, 2006	Group forms to finance Middleton appeal and assist violence victims.

March 1, 2006	Cherie Booth, QC, agrees to represent Rebecca Middleton case.
March 30, 2006	Allen announces she will not bring new charges or review evidence using current technique.
October, 2006	Lawyers file request for judicial review of the DPP's decision. Justice Ground approves process.
April 16-17, 2007	UK and Canadian media swarm Bermuda. Cherie Booth, QC, argues that Bermuda has ECHR obligations to assure justice in Rebecca's murder.
May 6, 2007	Justice Ground rules against Middletons.
September, 2007	Fund raising group withdraws its financial support.
November, 2007	Dave Middleton withdraws family's appeal.
April, 2008	DPP Vinette Graham-Allen fulfils her contract and returns to Jamaica. Cindy Bennett writes to new DPP Rory Field.
May, 2008	With silence from the new DPP, Cindy Bennett writes to Foreign Minister David Miliband, three members of a committee tasked with inspecting Bermuda, and FCO Territories Minister Meg Munn.

July, 2008	Territories Minister Meg Munn refuses Rebecca Middleton's mother's request for assistance, saying she also speaks for Foreign Secretary David Miliband. Bermuda DPP Rory Field agrees that nothing further will be done.
August, 2008	Violence and murder reach record highs in Bermuda. The UK-appointed governor offers "strong support, silent support."
February 2, 2009	Rick Meens writes to FCO, requesting formal review.
April 1, 2009:	Territories Minister Gillian Merron responds to Rick Meens.
July 22, 2009	FCO repeats "no action" decision, letter to Rick Meens.
January 6, 2010	Rick Meens appeals to European Court of Human Rights (ECHR).
February 1, 2010	ECHR acknowledges receipt: assigns case number.

Index

A

Adams, Carlton 70, 178, 180, 181
Allen, David 148
Amnesty International 60, 62, 64, 232, 243, 274, 300
Appeal for Accountability 227, 229, 232, 262, 274, 284, 302, 307
Appleby Global xv, 242, 250, 265, 301
Arretta's 25
autopsy 31, 33, 37, 38, 41, 84, 115, 120, 123, 124, 178, 206
Ayton, Mel 55

B

Bacchus, Sandra 105, 106, 108, 109, 123, 126, 142, 193, 283, 299
'back of town' 13, 23, 24, 55, 58, 103, 147
Baden, Dr. Michael 95, 112, 116, 118, 121, 124, 127, 187, 193, 241
Bean, Dennis xiv, 166, 167, 168, 300
Belleville Intelligencer 41
Belleville, Ontario 7, 30
Bermuda Regiment 3, 68, 304
Bermuda Sun xiv, 76, 92, 104, 146, 164, 255, 285
Bermuda Triangle 13, 61
Bermudiana 62
Birmingham Post 7, 23, 47
Black Beret Cadre (BBC) 49, 54, 58, 165, 166, 304
Black Power 54, 83, 185
Black Watch Pass 23
Blair, Tony 149, 242, 269
blood alcohol content 117
blood spatter 95, 132, 242
Bloomberg, Michael 49
Blue Hole 63, 64, 72, 272
Booth, Cherie xiii, 149, 233, 242, 245, 248, 250, 255, 257, 258, 262, 270, 273, 283, 301, 308
Brown, Dr. Ewart F. 50, 52, 155, 267, 272, 278, 280, 286, 287, 288, 289, 290, 291, 294
Burrows, Erskine 'Buck' 227, 245, 249, 274
Burrows, Freedom 25
Burrows, Jean 54
Bush, George H.W. 48
Bush, George W. 49, 51, 52

C

Caines, James 37, 38
Calhoun, Brian xiii, 32, 76, 77, 80, 84, 85, 87, 90, 96, 98, 169, 178, 190, 192, 198, 225, 263, 279, 299, 305
Campbell, Dr. Ian xv, 42, 294
Casemates Prison xvii, 57
Casling, Diana 87
Cassidy, Jonathan 14, 17, 18, 19, 125, 305
Castro, Fidel 47
Christopher, Elizabeth 70, 115, 231, 236, 237, 247, 281, 300
City Confidential 145
Clarke, Peter 69, 70, 215, 216, 298
cocaine 54
Coleman, Denis 49, 51
colonialism 58, 91
Connelly vs. The Queen 253
Court of Appeals 97, 160, 237, 265, 270
Court Street xvii, 13, 24, 68, 103, 166, 222, 247, 257, 286
Coxall, Colin xiii, 35, 79, 85, 86, 88, 89, 90, 91, 92, 93, 155, 168, 170, 241, 263, 264, 266, 281

282, 298, 300, 301, 306
Cox, Paula 94, 146
Creech-Jones, Arthur 56
Crockwell, Stuart 71, 75, 178, 182, 217, 236, 298
Cuba 47, 49, 304
culture of impunity 248, 253
Cunningham, Dr. Keith 37, 69, 128, 129, 152, 220
Cutts, Howard xiii, 35, 36, 83, 84, 126, 151, 172, 175, 298

D

Daily Express 83, 185, 225, 235, 245
Dangling cloth 37, 108
Darby, Bryan 191, 241
Dead Man Walking 73
Death on the Rock 145
Deepdale Road 69
defense wounds 33, 85, 194
'Devil's Island' 25, 64
DNA evidence 71, 84, 151
Dodwell, David 32
Doe, Mark 55, 304
Douglas, Michael 48
Dovaston, Don 163, 164, 166, 172, 175, 179, 180, 198, 300
Duckett, George 53, 55, 88, 90, 304

E

Edness, Quinton 89, 92
Emancipation 54
European Convention on Human Rights 207
European Court of Human Rights 207, 265, 296, 302, 309
Evans, Lois Browne xvii, 57, 59, 60, 70, 76, 143, 161, 163, 165, 166, 168, 172, 204, 205, 231, 242, 272, 279, 299, 300

F

Ferguson, John 30, 202
Ferry Reach 3, 22, 26, 35, 36, 63, 67, 68, 70, 71, 72, 87, 105, 106, 109, 137, 190, 194, 206, 214, 217, 222, 223
Field, Rory 270, 271, 273, 299, 308, 309
Flatts 21, 25, 26, 70, 194, 218
'Fly' 219
Foreign and Commonwealth Office xiii, 24, 94, 262, 289, 298, 302
forensic evidence 84, 96, 118, 187, 192, 206, 266
'Forty Thieves' 58, 274, 303
Four Ways Inn 48
Fox, Coy 3, 4, 5, 68
freedom of information xiii, 152, 213, 221
'Front Street Boys' xiii, 58, 152, 213, 221
Froomkin, Saul 96, 181, 279, 300
Frost, David 48
Frost, Hugo xiv, 255, 274, 289, 301
Fundamental right 249
Furbert, Laverne 154
Fyke, Mark 47

G

gang warfare 4, 286
Gibbons, Sir David 56, 57
Globe and Mail 148, 154, 261
Glover, Catherine 147
Gordon, Pamela 87, 89, 92, 146
Government House 23, 54, 55, 111, 121, 165, 187, 240, 273, 284, 289
Gozney, Sir Richard 272, 284
Graham-Allen, Vinette xiv, 239, 240, 241, 242, 246, 247, 249, 256, 262, 270, 283, 301, 302, 307, 308
Greene, Bobby 166
Greenfield, Tim 153
Ground, Richard 97, 159, 239, 246, 247, 252, 259, 261, 264, 270, 273, 301, 302, 307

Grundy, Lionel 90, 95, 298
Guardian 240
Gurney, Tim 146, 168, 284
Guthrie, James 243, 247, 256, 257, 301
Guyana 24, 105, 162, 169

H

Hainey, Raymond xiv, 154
Hall, Julian xvii, 272, 274, 278
Hamilton, Bermuda xvii, 13, 14, 18, 23, 26, 55, 57, 58, 62, 68, 70, 87, 93, 142, 150, 193, 226, 227, 278, 286, 291, 304
hangman xvii, xviii, 24, 56
Harbour Nights 227
Harrington Sound 22
Hart, Robert 127
Hastings-Smith xv, 242, 247, 250, 259, 265, 266, 301
Hayward, Stuart 61, 291
Hector, Richard xiii, 24, 71, 77, 105, 162, 163, 164, 166, 171, 172, 175, 177, 178, 181, 185, 186, 187, 189, 194, 199, 202, 204, 208, 230, 283, 300
Heritage Night 64
Herkommer, Antje 236
Hewey, Marjorie 221, 222
Hill, Kellon 272, 273
Holloway, Beth 293
Holloway, Natalee 149, 293
Hooley, Frank 56
House of Lords 160, 258, 262
Hull, Norrell 95, 112, 131
Hurricane Fabian 284

I

independence 54, 55, 58, 185, 247, 269, 278, 287, 288, 290, 293
international business 275, 286
'Isle of Rest' 64
'Isle of Rest' 64

J

Jamaica 51, 54, 104, 221, 240, 243, 246, 308
Jericevic, Diana 87
'Jewel in the Atlantic' xviii, 145
Jewelry 18, 37, 71, 105, 126, 139, 218, 220
Johnston, Dr. James 37, 84, 124, 152, 220
Jones, Jim 162
Jones, Leon 60, 280
Jones, Marsha 291
Jones, Shaundae 246, 291
Junos, LeYoni xiii, xviii, 60, 63, 64, 72, 73, 162, 164, 166, 172, 177, 181, 183, 187, 189, 191, 197, 204, 206, 208, 213, 215, 220, 221, 223, 225, 226, 227, 229, 230, 232, 233, 235, 239, 242, 255, 257, 262, 274, 284, 300, 301, 307

K

Kelly, Michael 128
Klenavic, David 147

L

Lawrence, Stephen 266
Layton, Larry 162
Leask, Kevin xiii, 84, 298
Lee, Dr. Henry 95, 105, 116, 129, 242, 263, 299
Legal Status of British Dependent Territories 207
Lemay, Jean Jacques 94
Lewis, Peter and Margaret 18
London Times 29
'Long tails' 20
Lottimore, Dean 21, 22, 32, 67, 68, 105, 106, 178, 193, 222, 223, 305

M

Mandela, Nelson 41
Masefield, Thorold 90, 93, 94, 146, 151, 161, 162, 168, 202, 229, 232, 262
Maxwell, Terry 105, 106, 149, 256, 298
McCann, Russell 14, 17, 19, 305
Mc Millen, Lois 164
Meade, Barry 178, 198, 279
Meens, Jasmine xv, 7, 9, 20, 22, 26, 32, 47, 51, 53, 72, 106, 125, 193, 223, 305
Meens, Jordan 9, 26, 27, 41
Meens, Rick xiv, xv, 9, 13, 22, 26, 27, 30, 31, 32, 41, 42, 61, 69, 78, 79, 108, 109, 142, 143, 144, 146, 148, 152, 160, 162, 164, 172, 173, 177, 181, 187, 189, 191, 196, 197, 199, 203, 204, 213, 220, 233, 236, 237, 239, 240, 241, 242, 245, 266, 273, 283, 284, 296, 297, 301, 302, 309
Meerabux, Vincent 104, 105, 111, 121, 125, 129, 134, 136, 141, 142, 150, 151, 159, 160, 162, 169, 202, 247, 249, 254
Merron, Gillian 274, 301, 309
Mid Ocean News 94, 227, 275, 286, 288
Miliband, David 270, 271, 290, 294, 301, 308, 309
Miller, Norma Wade 247
Moniz, Harold 36, 38, 40, 298
Moonglow 25, 70, 71, 72, 214, 221, 222
Moore, Rhianna 272, 273
Moore, Stanley 162, 163, 164, 166, 167, 168, 169, 171, 172, 174, 175, 180, 181, 185, 189, 190, 192, 193, 194, 197, 198, 204, 205, 208, 300
morgue attendant 41

Mottley, Elliott 32, 75, 77, 79, 84, 85, 86, 90, 91, 92, 142, 143, 147, 151, 162, 168, 178, 185, 186, 189, 191, 192, 193, 194, 196, 203, 205, 206, 207, 232, 299, 300
Mullet Bay Road 109
Mundy, Kirk Orlando 23, 24, 25, 65, 67, 69, 72, 75, 76, 77, 78, 80, 83, 84, 87, 95, 96, 97, 98, 127, 141, 143, 144, 145, 150, 151, 152, 159, 160, 161, 181, 186, 189, 193, 194, 195, 197, 198, 202, 203, 205, 206, 209, 213, 217, 219, 220, 221, 222, 230, 243, 245, 247, 249, 257, 263, 264, 281, 284, 300, 302, 305, 306
Mundy, Sharon 217, 221, 222
Munn, Meg 271, 274, 287, 288, 301, 308, 309
'Murder Mile' 59
Mylod, Michael 35, 39, 90, 94

N

Net shirt 71
Nike symbol 68
'Nothing like this....' 29

O

Oakes, Sir Harry 54
off shore industry 49
'Old Town' 14, 25, 53
Operation Cleansweep 89, 94, 282
Owen, David 56

P

Panama 54, 55
Parker, Doug 147
Paul, Robert 152
Pearce, Bill 98, 105, 106, 107, 108, 111, 112, 115, 124, 128, 129, 130, 135, 136, 140, 141, 143, 148, 149, 151, 190, 191, 193,

194, 195, 197, 198, 199, 203, 207, 279, 298, 300
Pearman, John Irving 91, 92
People's Parliament 57
Perry, John 104, 106, 108, 109, 111, 118, 121, 124, 126, 127, 128, 130, 135, 136, 140, 141, 142, 143, 147, 160, 247
Pettingill, Mark 71, 75, 76, 84, 96, 150, 164, 177, 181, 195, 216, 236, 272, 300
Physical evidence 37, 195, 203
Playboy Magazine 51
Point Finger Road 208
political murders xvii, 54, 55, 56, 57, 105, 144, 146, 166, 274, 278
Prerogative of Mercy Committee 56, 257
Prince Charles 48
Princess Anne 48
Princess Louise 48
Princess Margaret 48
Progressive Labor Party (PLP) 58, 303

Q

Quasar, Gian J 61
Queen Elizabeth II xiii, 23, 294
Queen Victoria 48
'Quo fata ferunt' 52

R

Railway Trail 109, 292
Ramsbotham, Sir Peter 239
Rao, Dr. Valerie 86, 95, 187
Rape kit 37
Ratneser, Kulandra xiv, 239, 240, 284
Rawlinson, Dorothy 54
Rayney, Lloyd 237
Rego, Victor 55, 304
Richardson, Charles 247, 257, 284, 300, 301
Richards, Sir Edward 54
Richmond, Vic 30, 31, 32, 36, 38, 75, 78, 79, 85, 171, 172, 178, 181,

182, 187
Riihiluoma, John xv, 242, 301
Rioting 54, 57, 75, 201, 278, 304
Roberts, Liz xiv, 257
Royal Canadian Mounted Police (RCMP) 43
Royal Gazette xiv, 32, 38, 39, 40, 41, 42, 49, 52, 77, 78, 86, 87, 91, 92, 93, 94, 97, 98, 99, 115, 116, 143, 146, 147, 152, 153, 154, 170, 172, 204, 208, 227, 230, 241, 250, 251, 252, 257, 266, 272, 277, 278, 279, 282, 286, 288, 291, 292, 294
Ryan, Leo 162

S

Sargasso Sea 61, 62, 104
'Saturday Night Special' 4
Saul, Dr. David 32, 94
Sayers, Captain Hugh 53
Schonfield, Dr. Hugh 63
Scotland Yard 24, 31, 35, 43, 55, 67, 90, 173, 288, 291
Scott, Alex 41, 49, 51, 247, 278, 286
Secrecy 31
Serious Crimes Commission (SCC) 165
Sharples, Sir Richard 53, 54
Shopping Centre 55, 111
Simmons, Charles Etta 236
Simmons, Shirley 163, 166, 197, 300
Slavery in Bermuda 280
Slayton, Gregory 51
Smith, Barbara 72
Smith, George 149
Smith, Jennifer 50, 59, 87, 146, 148
Smith, Jonathan xiv, 36, 232, 239, 298
Smith, Justis Raham 24, 25, 59, 68, 69, 70, 71, 72, 75, 76, 77, 78, 79, 80, 83, 84, 85, 87, 95, 96, 98, 101, 103, 104, 105, 106, 107, 109, 114, 115, 118, 120, 128, 129, 135, 136, 137, 139, 141,

142, 143, 144, 145, 147, 149, 150, 151, 159, 160, 161, 177, 178, 186, 189, 190, 191, 193, 202, 203, 205, 209, 214, 217, 219, 220, 221, 222, 231, 235, 236, 237, 243, 245, 246, 249, 252, 256, 258, 273, 281, 299, 300, 302, 305, 306
Smith, Keasha 71, 219
Smith, Richard 24, 143, 202, 203
Smith, Sean 26, 68, 69, 106, 139, 223, 305
Somers, Admiral George 53
Southampton Princess Hotel xviii, 56, 292, 304
'Special circumstances' 253, 259, 262, 263
Steyne, Lord Johan 160
St. George, Bermuda 13, 14, 18, 20, 22, 25, 26, 32, 41, 53, 64, 68, 69, 70, 71, 72, 108, 137, 179, 193, 214, 215, 219, 222, 223, 274, 285
Strangeways, Sam xiv
Swing bridge 71, 72, 84, 109, 127, 139, 144
Swinging Doors 68, 222, 286

T

Tacklyn, Larry Winfield 55, 278
taxi controversy 285
Taylor, Matthew xiv, 277, 278
'Tempest in a Teapot' 58
Thatcher, Margaret 90
'The Forty Thieves' 303
Thompson, Vikki 281, 282
Thorpe, Jeremy 56
Tokunbo, Khamisi 76, 79, 85, 161, 177, 178, 192, 193, 198, 202, 203, 205, 206, 284, 299, 300
Toronto Sun 145, 147
Tourism 32, 148, 257, 280
Trace evidence 33, 36, 123
Turf wars 38

Twain, Mark 48
Twiggy 48
Two-man theory 113, 115, 119, 120, 141

U

United Bermuda Party (UBP) 54, 58, 303
United Nations (UN) 243, 249

V

Van Susteren, Greta 241
Vasquez, Frank 25, 298
Vereker, Sir John 240, 247, 269
Victoria Park 57
Victoria Street 55
Vigodda, Michael 148, 154
Vos Savant, Marilyn 297

W

Waddington, Lord David 39, 79, 85, 90, 247
'Wall of Silence' 67
Ward, Austin 79, 87, 151, 247
Warner, Archie 70, 80, 106, 108, 136, 246
Webb, Tajmal 68, 218, 223, 305
Westgate Prison 90, 247
Whale Bone Bay 3, 109
White Horse Tavern 14, 25
'White walls' 24
Williams, Randolf 58
Willis, Peter 93
Women's Resource Center (WRC) 149
Wooding Commission 103

Z

Zeta Jones, Catherine 48
Zuill, Bill 154

About the Author

Dr. Carolyn (Carol) Shuman, who holds a Ph.D. in psychology, has long held an advocacy platform, beginning with her ten-year career as a newspaper reporter and editor in the U.S., cited by the Georgia Associated Press for enterprise reporting. She also holds a Ph.D. in behavioral medicine psychology from Texas A&M University-Commerce, with military and private clinical practice in Bermuda before becoming a fulltime writer in 2003.

Born in Canada three months after her English war bride mother arrived in there—raised some sixty miles from Becky's home in Belleville, Ontario--Shuman left Canada with her parents as a child, then spent most of her adulthood in the U.S., moving to Bermuda in 1990. There she has worked with the U.S. Navy, practiced clinical psychology, writes, researches, and advocates for human rights, investigating cross cultural and other psycho-social issues.

Along with her professional writing that has encompassed more than forty years, Shuman has published a book for children to deal with the events of September eleventh and other catastrophes: Jenny Is Scared: When Sad Things Happen in the World, Magination Press (2003). Used by professionals and parents internationally, this work also has been published in Japanese and Korean.

Kill Me Once...Kill Me Twice: Murder on the Queen's Playground is her first adult non-fiction book.